RAISING A HEALTHY, HAPPY CHILD

RAISING A HEALTHY, HAPPY CHILD

A. Frederick North, M.D.
Richard H. Granger, M.D.
Catherine S. Chilman, PH.D.
and
U.S. Department of Health, Education,
and Welfare—Children's Bureau

David McKay Company, Inc.
NEW YORK

Acknowledgments

We wish to gratefully acknowledge the contributions of Dr. Elsa Stone; Drs. Albert J. Solnit, Donald J. Cohen, and Julian B. Ferholt of the Yale University Child Study Center; Dr. Richard W. Olmsted of the American Academy of Pediatrics; Dr. Woodruff L. Crawford, from the American Medical Association; Dr. Stewart A. Clifford, from the American Academy of Pediatrics; Dr. Mitchell I. Rubin, from American Pediatric Research; and Dr. Myron E. Wegman, from the Society for Pediatric Research.

Published by
David McKay Company, Inc.
2 Park Avenue
New York, N.Y. 10016

No portion of this edition may be mechanically reproduced by any means without approval in writing from the publisher.

Library of Congress Cataloging in Publication Data
North, A Frederick, 1931-
Raising a healthy, happy child.

Includes index.
1. Children—Care and hygiene. I. Granger, Richard H., joint author. II. Chilman, Catherine S., joint author. III. United States. Children's Bureau.
IV. Title.
RJ61.N67   649'.1   80-17995
ISBN 0-679-51327-2
ISBN 0-679-51328-0 (pbk.)

Illustrations by Sandra Garelik

2 3 4 5 6 7 8 9 10
MANUFACTURED IN THE UNITED STATES OF AMERICA

Contents

Introduction   vii

Infancy

1. The First Weeks   3
2. After the First Weeks   18
3. Development and Health   34

One to Six Years

4. Patterns of Development   53
5. Everyday Life   61
6. Special Problems   93
7. Health Care   104

Six to Twelve Years

8. Personality and Physical Development   115
9. Family Life   132
10. In the Outside World   154
11. Health Care   180

When Your Child Needs Help

12. Handicaps and Emotional Problems   201
13. Illnesses and Other Disorders   210
14. Emergencies and First Aid   232

Index   245

Introduction

A cookbook will not make a great cook. And no book on child care will make you the great parent that you want to be. But every cook does start out with a few basic recipes and techniques and then adds new ideas from his own experience and that of others to develop his own style. And all parents must start out with some basic skills and knowledge on which they can develop their own style of caring for their children.

Raising a Healthy, Happy Child has been compiled to help you as a parent develop the kind of skills you will want to have to care for your child and to help him develop into a healthy and able adult. It should answer many of your questions about what to expect during the important years from birth to age twelve, and it gives simple instructions about solving problems that most parents will face during this time.

In the pages that follow, we have tried to bring together, in a practical, easy-to-read way, the chief results of the research and observations of a large body of scientists who specialize in studying children and their families. These scientists represent many fields, such as: a number of medical specialties, education, psychology, sociology, home economics, and social work.

There is a general scheme of growth and development which almost all children follow, and which we will attempt to outline. Nevertheless, each child follows an individual timetable that is different from all others. Children will let you know when they are ready for new activities, experiences, or skills. If you are alert to the signals you can help them work out their own schedules satisfactorily.

This book covers the high points of development from the standpoint of the child and the major problems or stumbling blocks as they are usually expressed by parents. As an individual with your own way of doing things you will have to take any of the advice that makes sense to you and adapt it to your own way of working.

You and your children live in a large and complex world which will influence both of you—sometimes for the better and sometimes very much not. But remember that for the early years you are the most important part of that world as far as your children are concerned. What they become will in large part reflect your influence and that of the small world you create around them and actively help them to create for themselves. Within that framework there are two overall bits of advice you should keep in mind:

• Your goal should be to help your child become more independent and self-reliant.

• Your child is different from every other child just as you are different from every other parent.

No book can deal with every possible occurrence in the first twelve years of a child's life. You will be faced with many situations for which you will not find specific explanations here. But we have attempted to provide simple, direct, and valid answers to the most usual and frequent questions parents face. *Raising a Healthy, Happy Child* presents the basic knowledge for a sensible approach to child raising, and also a framework within which you can use that knowledge to make your own decisions in new situations. It is to be hoped that such an approach will contribute to a healthier and happier family life for both you and your children.

For simplicity, this book refers to all children as "he." Don't be offended if your child is a girl! Similarly, the care-giving person is sometimes referred to as the "mother" or "she" even though the parenting tasks might be performed by a father, a grandparent or another person. Also, the medically trained person from whom you seek health advice is referred to as "your doctor" even though it might be a series of doctors in a clinic, a nurse, or a specially trained physician's assistant.

Infancy

1
The First Weeks

YOU AND YOUR NEW BABY

Babies are really quite sturdy; they can take a good deal of handling, and usually they enjoy it. If you are unsure about how to pick up, hold, dress, or undress your baby, ask someone—a nurse or an experienced mother—to show you. Then do it yourself until you are comfortable. There is almost nothing you can do that is wrong except actually drop him. He will let you know by crying or struggling if he is unhappy. If you and he are both comfortable, you are doing fine, despite what critical neighbors, grandparents, or even nurses or doctors might say.

Get the feel and the fun of handling and playing with your baby right from the start. If you are in the hospital, insist on having him with you more than just for feedings, no matter what the hospital "rules." Both you and the baby will learn about each other from these contacts, and it will make it much easier to care for him when you are alone with him at home.

Ask Questions

If you have questions, don't keep them to yourself! Doctors and nurses may think you know more than you really do, or may think you understand something they have tried to explain when you don't. Keep asking questions until you understand. The kind of care and advice you get will depend as much on how you use the doctors and nurses as on how much they know. When they use medical or other words you don't understand, ask them to explain. When they give advice that sounds hard to follow, find out whether they really mean what you think they mean.

For example, you might be told to bathe your baby each time you have to change a soiled diaper. You could wind up giving a lot of unnecessary baths if you did not ask and find out that what they mean by "bathe" is to wipe him gently with a clean washcloth or diaper that has been moistened with a little water!

Take Care of Yourself

Your health as a mother is almost as important to your baby as is his own health. Giving birth to a baby is exhausting, and the changes that take place in a mother's body after she has had a baby are also tiring. Don't be surprised if you don't feel like yourself for several weeks. Ask the hospital doctors and nurses about yourself as well as about your baby.

You will be tired when you get home from the hospital. You will probably have plenty of strength and energy to take care of yourself and the baby, but housework, the care of other children and meal preparation for the whole family may be more of a strain than you think. If you can possibly get someone to help, the first few days home are the time to get it. Help with the housework and the other children is usually more necessary than help with the new baby, but if you have other young children at home you may want some help with the baby so you can spend time with the other children, who have missed you while you were in the hospital. Postpone visitors for several weeks; you and the baby will feel and look better, and you won't tire yourself playing hostess.

You will need at least one medical checkup about six weeks after the birth.

FEEDING YOUR BABY

Breast Feeding. This is the most natural way of feeding your baby, and many women find it simpler and far more satisfying than

bottle feeding. However, it must be learned by doing, a book or printed page can help in only a few ways.
 • Should you breast feed? Yes, if you think it will be comfortable and convenient for you. No, if you have any strong objections to the idea. Modern infant formulas and bottle feeding are convenient and safe as a substitute for breast feeding. Human milk is probably a little better, especially if members of the family have been allergic to cow's milk. Otherwise there is really no strong medical, psychological, or economic reason for choosing either breast feeding or bottle feeding, so the choice can be made according to your own preferences.
 • Find someone who is experienced and sympathetic to teach you about breast feeding. Most hospital nurses are good helpers, but some may be so strongly prejudiced for or against breast feeding that they are of less help. Other mothers who have breast fed their babies and enjoyed it can give you excellent help. In some communities such mothers have organized into groups to help new mothers with breast feeding. The hospital or public health nurse, your doctor, or other mothers may know of such groups.
 • Don't blame yourself, or let others blame your milk, for all the ups and downs of your breast fed infant. Babies fuss, spit up, cry, and have unusual bowel movements no matter how they are fed. Just go right ahead with your breast feeding and chances are that such minor "problems" will disappear.
 • The following practical points may help:
 Most women find that a good nursing bra, one that provides good uplift and that opens easily for nursing, makes nursing easier and more comfortable. Many wear such a bra day and night during the months they are nursing.
 Use the first few days, when there is little milk in the breast, to get your nipples used to your baby's nursing. Let him suck for only two minutes at each breast at each feeding the first day, three minutes the second day, and five minutes the third day. If your nipples get sore at any time later, you can limit nursing time to five minutes at each breast. Even a slow nursing infant gets at least four-fifths of the milk in his first five minutes at breast.
 Find a position that is comfortable for you and your baby; a foot stool, a pillow, and a chair with arms are often helpful.
 Touch the baby's cheek with the nipple to start. He will turn his

head to grasp the nipple. (If you try to push him to the nipple with a finger touching his other cheek or chin he will turn away from the nipple toward the finger.)

Allow him to grasp the entire darkly colored part of the breast in his mouth. He gets the milk by squeezing it from the nipple, not by actually sucking. His grasp on your nipple may hurt for the first few seconds, but the pain should disappear once he is nursing in a good rhythm. When you want to remove his mouth from your breast, first break the suction by inserting your finger in the corner of his mouth. This will save sore nipples. If your entire breast becomes sore, you may be able to relieve the painfulness simply by lifting and supporting the breast with one hand during nursing.

A small amount of milk may come out of your nipples between feedings. A small nursing pad or piece of sanitary napkin inserted in the bra over the nipple will absorb this milk, keeping the bra clean and preventing irritation of the nipple.

Wash your nipples with mild soap and water at least once a day, and rinse off any messiness with clean water before or after most feedings.

If you notice a spot of tenderness or redness on your breast or nipple that persists for more than two feedings be sure to seek medical advice promptly.

Bottle Feeding. Hold the baby in your arms or on your lap. Be sure that milk is in the nipple. Touch the nipple with his mouth.

Hold the bottle so that it sticks straight out at a right angle to his mouth.

The nipple holes should be large enough so that milk drops slowly from the bottle when it is held with the nipple down.

The cap should be loose enough so that air bubbles can enter the bottle as the milk is sucked out of it.

Halfway through the bottle, stop feeding and "burp" the baby. Hold him on your shoulder and pat him gently on his back until he burps. Or hold him over your hand and pat his back and gently rub his stomach. He will usually burp up some air, and often a little of his formula. (Be sure to protect your clothing with a diaper or other covering.)

How Often to Feed. Feed the baby when he seems hungry. If he takes less than six feedings a day and still takes a normal amount each day, you are lucky. (A "day" means twenty-four hours, not just the daylight hours.) Most babies will fall into a pattern of 6 or 7 feedings about 3 to 5 hours apart. If your baby is more irregular than this, you can get him on a more regular schedule by waking him a little early or by letting him be hungry a little longer. It is easier and better to develop a regular routine by working from the baby's own schedule than by just deciding he will be fed at certain times whether he is hungry or not.

After the first several weeks, most babies will begin to sleep through one of their feedings. Most parents prefer the baby to skip the night feeding rather than a daytime feeding. If your baby chooses to give up the wrong feeding, don't hesitate to wake him and feed him at the usual time so that he will, hopefully, give up one of the night feedings.

How Much to Feed. If you are breast feeding, you don't have to worry about how much to feed—your baby decides. Most mothers who are breast feeding worry at some time about whether they have enough milk. Actually, too little milk is extremely rare. The best reassurance is your baby's normal activity and growth. Another way to reassure yourself if you are really worried is to offer him a bottle of formula just after he has finished nursing. If he is still hungry, he will take several ounces and take them in a hurry. If he doesn't you can be sure that your milk is satisfying him.

Most babies, after the first few days, take two to three ounces of milk per day for each pound of body weight. Most babies want to have six or seven feedings each day. For a 7 lb. baby, this would mean 14 to 21 ounces of formula a day, or 2½ to 3½ ounces in each of 6 or 7 feedings. You might begin by offering three ounces in each bottle. When your baby begins to empty the bottle completely at two or three feedings each day, add one-half ounce to the bottle at each feeding. Stay a little ahead of the baby, and let him decide how fast he wants to increase his intake of formula. If your baby takes much more or less than two to three ounces per pound per day, discuss his feeding with a nurse or doctor. Don't worry about how much he has taken at a single feeding, most babies will have times when they just aren't hungry and other times when they take more than you expect.

Spitting Up. Most babies spit up some of the milk after many of their feedings. The milk seems to overflow from the baby's mouth. It is often curdled from the normal action of the stomach. The problem is more of worry and messiness than of health. Babies who spit up a great deal grow as fast and as strong as those who do not.

There are several tricks to reduce the amount of spitting up. But none of them works all the time, and most babies will continue some spitting up even when all the tricks are used.

• Burp the baby carefully mid-way through the feeding, at the end of the feeding, and a few minutes after the feeding.

• Prop him in an infant seat or cradle with his head a few inches above his stomach for 10 or 15 minutes after each feeding.

• Try feeding a cold formula directly from the refrigerator.

WHAT EQUIPMENT AND SUPPLIES YOU NEED

Babies don't need more than a few things:

- A PLACE TO SLEEP
- CLOTHING
- EQUIPMENT FOR FEEDING
- EQUIPMENT FOR BATHING

A Place to Sleep

• All you need is something with sides to keep him from rolling out and a soft but firm bed or mattress for him to lie on. A basket or cardboard box will serve just as well as the fanciest crib or bassinet. The pad or mattress should be waterproof or have a waterproof casing. Watch out for sharp protruding edges on cribs or bassinets, and be sure that the spaces between the rails of the crib are too small for the baby's head to be caught. No pillow is desirable or necessary. A pillow usually makes too soft a mattress for a baby; you're better off using a pad made from 4 or 5 thicknesses of blanket, or a thin plastic foam pad.

For bedclothes you will need:
- *2 or 3 pieces of flannelette-covered waterproof sheeting.* This sheeting should be large enough to cover the mattress or pad;
- *3 or 4 sheets.* Sheets that are fitted or contoured to the shape of the crib mattress or pad are much easier to use;
- *4 to 6 18-inch squares of waterproof flannelette sheeting.* Placed under the baby, these will protect the sheets from overflow from the diaper or from spitting up, and will save many changes of sheets;
- *3 or 4 cotton flannel "receiving blankets."* These blankets are for use in warm weather, for bundling before and after baths, and for use as towels;
- *A blanket bag, sleeping bag or coverall.* These are usually much easier to use than individual blankets for cold weather sleeping. Get one that is machine washable and that is easy to get on and off and to open for diaper changes. With such a sleeping bag you don't have to worry about blankets coming off.

Clothing

- *3 or 4 cotton knit nightgowns.* The long ones don't get kicked off as much. They provide plenty of cover for sleeping in most climates.
- *3 or 4 cotton knit shirts.* The kind that slip over the head without buttons, snaps, or tapes are the easiest to use. They usually have short sleeves, and large arm and head openings. Taping or pinning shirts to the diapers just means they will get wet with the diaper. Leaving an inch or two of bare midriff will save a lot of shirt laundering.
- *2 or 3 sweaters or sacks.* Nylon or orlon washes well. A few easy-to-open buttons in front are more manageable than bows or ties or many small buttons.
- *A cap.* Knit nylon, orlon, or dacron, for going out or sleeping in colder weather.
- *3 to 6 dozen diapers.* Pre-folded diapers save a lot of time and

don't cost much more. A diaper service will cost about 10 times as much as buying and laundering your own diapers. Disposable diapers will cost about the same as diaper service. Either one is a real time and work saver if you can afford it.

• *2 or 3 plastic pants.* Use them to protect outer clothing. Some babies can wear them nearly all the time, but many will get a diaper rash. If the diaper area gets red and irritated, leave off the plastic pants except for outings and other times when soiling will be particularly difficult.

Equipment for Feeding (Using Formula)

There are dozens of formulas and almost as many recommended methods of preparation. Here is one method that is easy to use in most homes. It is quite inexpensive and very convenient. To use it you must have a refrigerator that works and pure water from a good public water supply. You will need:

• *Nursing bottles with caps.* 6 to 8 8-oz. bottles, or fewer if you wash them more than once a day. Get the boilable, plastic ones. They cost a little more, but they will save you from the breaking and spilling that can occur with glass bottles.

• *Nipples.* 1 for each bottle with a few spares. The ones made of silicone last best.

• *A bottle and nipple brush.*

Procedure:

• Use a concentrated prepared infant formula containing vitamins and iron. There are many brand names. These formulas come in 13-oz. cans and are sold at drug stores and supermarkets. They usually cost a little less than a quart of milk.

• Use bottles, caps, and nipples that have been washed in clean water and dishwashing soap or detergent (wash them first when you do the family dishes). Use a bottle brush. Squeeze water through the nipple holes to be sure they are open. Rinse them well so that all soap or detergent is gone, and let them stand in a rack to dry.

• When you wish to prepare a feeding, clean the top of the formula can with soap and water. Rinse it.

Open the formula can with a clean punch-type (beer can) opener. When you have poured out the necessary amount, cover the can with fresh foil or plastic wrap and put it in the refrigerator.

• Pour formula from the can directly into the feeding bottle. Use

The First Weeks

the markings on the bottle to measure just one-half as much formula concentrate as the total amount of formula you want in the bottle (if you want 4 ounces of formula to feed, use 2 ounces of formula concentrate).

• Add to the bottle an equal amount of fresh water directly from the tap, then put on the nipple and cap. No warming is necessary—babies take cold formula as well as warm.

• Feed the bottle within 30 minutes of the time it is made. If it is not used up within an hour, throw out the formula and start again with a fresh, clean bottle.

Special Instructions—If you use water from a well or pump or from a water supply that is not regularly inspected, boil each day's supply of water for 20 minutes, pour the boiling water into a clean jar and keep it covered in the refrigerator for use in making formula. Wash and clean the water jar daily.

If you do not have a reliable refrigerator use powdered formula containing vitamins and iron. This formula is prepared by pouring safe tap water or boiled water into the nursing bottle and adding one level tablespoon of powdered formula for each two ounces of water. (The measure that comes in the formula can is one tablespoon.) One tablespoon or measure of powder makes two ounces of formula, two measures make four ounces, four measures make eight ounces, etc. Put on the cap and nipple, then shake the bottle well until the powder is dissolved. Feed the formula within 30 to 60 minutes. Throw out any formula that is not fed within 60 minutes. The can of powdered formula should be covered, but need not be refrigerated.

If you are breast feeding and need only an occasional formula feeding, the above method using powdered formula is especially convenient and inexpensive.

What Not to Do—However you prepare formula, by one of the methods above or by one of the many other methods which may be recommended by your doctor, nurse, or clinic:

• Don't feed formula that has been left standing at room temperature in a nursing bottle or open can for more than 30 or 40 minutes. Germs grow rapidly in warm milk and can become a problem whenever milk from open cans stands for more than an hour at room temperature or stays in the refrigerator for more than three days.

• Don't feed any formula unless you have read the instructions on the can or bottle. Some formulas are sold ready to feed and should not have water added to them. Powdered formulas are mixed one tablespoon of formula for each 2 oz. of water. Most concentrated liquid formulas are mixed half and half.

- Don't give added vitamins or iron if you are using a prepared infant formula unless these are specifically prescribed by a physician who knows that you are feeding a vitamin- and iron-containing formula.
- Don't expect much change in bowel habits, spitting up, or other symptoms by changing from one brand or type of formula to another.

Bathing

During the first week, before the cord has fallen off and healed, you can bathe the baby by washing him lightly with a cloth wrung out in warm water. His face and diaper area require frequent washing, since food, urine, and bowel movements can irritate his skin. The rest of his body may need washing only several times a week.

After the first week or two, you may find it more convenient to give him his bath in a tub or dishpan. You will need the following:

- A warm room
- A table or counter top of convenient height
- A tub or dishpan containing an inch or two of warm water
- A cake of mild soap
- A wash cloth or other soft cloth
- A full size towel or "receiving blanket" to dry the baby
- You may want to put a small towel or diaper in the bottom of the tub to keep him from skidding on the slippery surface

Wash his head and face first, while the water and wash cloth are clean. You won't need soap for his face. After you wash and dry his face, use your hand to lather the rest of his body with soap. Wash the girl's labia and the boy's penis just as you would any other part of the body. You may find it easiest to wash him on the table on a towel, and use the tub only for rinsing. Rinse the baby thoroughly with the wash cloth—at least two rinsings—pick him up, wrap him in a towel, and pat him dry.

Wash his hair with a non-irritating baby shampoo about once a week, more frequently if he has the scaly, waxy rash of cradle cap. Don't worry about the soft spot on his head, it's tough!

The First Weeks

Don't worry if you can't bathe him every day. Two or three baths a week are plenty for many babies. Some babies quickly learn to enjoy their baths and it becomes a daily pleasure for both mother and baby. Others strongly object to the bath the first 8 or 10 times it is tried. They will gradually learn to tolerate the bath and perhaps even to enjoy it.

Use a nail clipper to keep his fingernails and toenails short. Cut straight across, and try to clip them when he is relaxed or asleep. At other times his playful sudden motions may make clipping difficult and you might accidentally clip the skin.

NEVER LEAVE THE BABY ALONE IN THE WATER FOR ANY REASON WHATSOEVER! If the telephone or doorbell rings, or your two-year-old hollers, wrap the baby (soap and all) in a towel and put him under your arm. The bath is *never* safe, no matter how little water you may use, until well into the second or third year of life. If there is a real crisis or emergency, put the baby on the floor; he can't fall or drown there.

Always check the water temperature. Hot water causes scalds and burns! Don't leave him in the tub with the water running.

Don't try to clean the ears, nose, navel, vulva, or anus with cotton-tipped sticks. Anything you can't clean with a corner of a wash cloth isn't worth cleaning.

Don't use special disinfectant soap for every bath and cleansing. Plain soap is best. Too much soap can be almost as irritating to his skin as is dirt, food, or soiled diapers.

SLEEPING

Everybody will get more rest if the baby does not sleep in the parents' room. Especially in the first weeks, his frequent snorts, gurgles, sneezes, coughs, and irregular breathing are bound to keep you awake wondering what he'll do next. If he really needs you, he'll cry loud enough to be heard from nearly everywhere in the house! Even in the smallest apartment, a crib or makeshift crib can be moved to the living room, kitchen, or bathroom when the parents retire for the night.

Don't put him in bed with you, either. There is always a danger of smothering him or hurting him by rolling over on him in your sleep, and it is most certain he will want to become your constant bedfellow. Neither you nor your spouse will want to put up with a wiggling, wet baby for very long.

He shouldn't sleep in a strong draft or breeze. Your baby does not need open windows where he sleeps. Air that is fresh enough for him to breathe during the day is fresh enough for him to sleep in.

He will decide for himself how long he wants to sleep—anywhere from 12 to 20 hours during the 24-hour day. You won't be able to make him sleep any more or less, but certainly you can arrange to keep him awake during the times of the day that are most convenient for you, so that he will sleep during the night and during morning or afternoon naps.

CRYING

A baby's cry is his way of telling you that he is in some way dissatisfied or uncomfortable. Your job is to find out why and if possible, to do something about it. Hunger is the most common cause, loneliness is probably the next most common cause, especially after the first few months. Actual pain from an open diaper pin or colic (see below) is much less common. The baby's own temperament makes a big difference; some will let out a roaring cry at the first sign of hunger or discomfort, others will become quietly restless and not actually cry for some time. Some will cry whenever the diaper is wet or soiled, others will ignore the diaper until it creates enough irritation to cause actual pain. Some will object to baths, to being placed in bed, to having the lights put out, or to other sudden changes. Excessive clothing or clothing that is not warm enough will cause discomfort and crying.

But there is always a cause, and you should usually be able to figure out what the cause is and to do something about it. This does not mean that you can't let a hungry or wet child wait for several minutes while you finish what you are doing. But it does mean that no child should be left to cry for any prolonged period of time without serious attempts to find out what is wrong and to correct it.

Many babies do have a time each day when they are just fussy or crying without any reason that you can discover. After you have checked for a cause of crying, you can safely ignore these fussy periods.

Most children want attention and handling. If a baby becomes quiet and content when picked up, he was probably just lonely. A few minutes of fondling and play, and then perhaps leaving him in the room with you where he can see you, is all that he needs. If he is actually hungry or in pain he will soon cry again, even if you are holding him or playing with him. Don't worry about "spoiling" him! Giving him the attention he needs during his first year will help him build the trust he will need to learn more "grownup" behavior later on.

Many infants rest better if they are snugly wrapped, or swaddled, in a blanket or wrapper.

COLIC

Some babies have attacks of crying nearly every evening, usually between 6 and 10 P.M. During an attack, his face suddenly becomes red, he frowns, draws his legs up and screams loudly, a cry quite different from his cry of hunger or loneliness. The crying continues from 2 to 20 minutes, even though he is picked up and comforted. The attack may end suddenly or soft crying may last a few minutes after the hard crying stops. Just as he is about to fall asleep, another attack may occur. Gas may rumble in his stomach and he may pass gas out of his rectum.

No one knows what causes such attacks. They often come at the same time every day. At other times of the day he is happy, alert, eats well, and gains weight. During an attack, holding him across your knees on his stomach often will give some comfort. There is little you can do except comfort the baby until the attack stops. Be sure he isn't just hungry, wet, or lonely, or that some part of his clothing is not uncomfortable. Most importantly, remember that colic does not interfere with his general health and growth and that he will grow out of it by the time he is 12 to 16 weeks old. Colicky babies *do* annoy their mothers and fathers and anybody living in the household. Remind everyone that it is not the baby's fault, it is not your fault, and he'll get over it. If the colic becomes a real problem for him or the family, it is worth a special trip or call to the doctor, who may be able to prescribe a medicine to make the baby rest more comfortably.

BOWEL MOVEMENTS

The baby's first bowel movements are a sticky green-black material. After a week or two, they become lighter and less sticky, the way they will be for the next year. The baby may have anywhere from one movement every three or four days to five or six movements a day. Movements may be as firm as those of a normal adult or as soft as watery scrambled eggs. The baby may turn red in the face and cry with each bowel movement, or he may seem totally unaware of them. The color of the bowel movements may be yellow, green, or brown. All of these are normal. (For a discussion of possible problems, see Chapter 13 under *Bowel Movements.)*

A WORD ABOUT SIBLINGS

Older brothers and sisters are often jealous of the time that you spend with a new baby. Try to find some time to give each of them special attention. Don't be surprised if a child between age 2 and 5 starts sucking his thumb, wetting his pants, or asking for bottles or diapers in imitation of a new baby. He is simply seeking attention. Give him as much as you can of the attention he wants, but don't encourage him to return to baby-like habits. A child older than 3½ or 4 years can usually understand the arrival of the new baby and can help you take care of him.

Children between age 1 and 3½ years should never be left alone with the baby. They are too young to understand the baby. They may pick him up, drop him, squeeze him too hard, sit on him, put dangerous things in his mouth or crib, or hurt him with tools, utensils, or furniture! This is not because they are "bad" but because they are naturally jealous of the new arrival. Give them the individual attention they need, let them help you and the baby in whatever way they can when you are alone with the baby, and never leave them alone with the baby.

GETTING ADVICE

Especially with your first baby, you will have more questions in the first few weeks than at any time in his life. If your question isn't

The First Weeks

answered in this book, get an answer from another source. Try asking experienced mothers and grandmothers, but don't necessarily accept all the advice you get. If what you hear is simple and makes sense, give it a try. If not, get other advice.

You might call a doctor, a well-baby clinic, or the hospital where your child was born. Write down all your questions before you make the phone call so you will be sure they are all answered. As we said at the beginning of this chapter, if you don't understand the advice you are given, keep on asking until you do understand. Many doctors and nurses use medical terms which few mothers can understand. If that happens, tell them so. Ask them to say it in plain language. Don't give up until you understand what they mean. Just because advice is given by a doctor or nurse doesn't mean that it is right. If it doesn't make sense to you, or if it sounds extremely complicated or difficult, even after you have had a full explanation, don't hesitate to ask someone else.

The more you can tell your doctor about what is bothering you or your child, the better he will be able to help you. For example, if your child is crying more than you think he should, your doctor will want to know at what time of day he cries, how long it lasts, whether he seems to be in pain, whether there is anything you do that makes it better or worse, for how many days he has been crying, and whether he seems sick or uncomfortable in any other way. The more you can tell about your baby, the better advice you will get.

2
After the First Weeks

FEEDING

Your baby doesn't really *need* any food except your breast milk or his formula until he is at least 6 months old. But you may want to get him used to different tastes, textures, and temperatures of food before he is that old. Whenever you decide to start "solids" or spoon-foods, there are a few rules that will help you.

Start slowly. A few spoonfuls once or twice a day is plenty. His main nutrition still comes from milk, and the spoon-foods, water, and juice are really just ways that you and he play with each other and teach each other.

Try just one new food at a time, and feed it every day for several days. Start with simple, pure foods. Use lamb, not meat dinner; rice cereal, not mixed cereal; applesauce, not fruit dessert. New foods will sometimes cause vomiting, diarrhea, or a skin rash. By starting only one new food every 4 or 5 days and by using simple foods you will know which one is to blame. Once he has eaten a food for 3 or 4 days and it hasn't disagreed with him, you can use it any time in the future without worrying. Choose new foods from each of the food groups listed below.

Don't spend much money on expensive baby foods. There is nothing special about the foods that are sold as baby foods except that they are finely strained. Regular adult applesauce, mashed potatoes, ground meat, etc., are just as good and often much less expensive, as are the "junior foods."

The ready-cooked infant cereals are much easier to prepare and they contain iron and vitamins that are not found in adult cereals.

Up to about 6 months, all your baby's needs may have been met by your nursing or by his formula. After 6 months, he should get part of his nourishment from other foods. Don't give him more than 25-30 ounces of formula a day. Let him fill up on other foods. You can cut his milk down to 16 ounces a day if more seems to spoil his appetite for other foods or if he seems to prefer other foods.

The best way to be sure that his diet is nutritious is to be sure it contains a wide variety of foods. In any two-day period he should have several servings from each of the following food groups:

- Milk, cheese, cottage cheese, ice cream
- Fruits and vegetables—at least 1 serving of dark green vegetable
- Meat, fish, poultry, eggs
- Bread, crackers, cereal, rice, spaghetti
- Butter, margarine, cream (or whole or condensed milk)

Candy, cookies, sugar, sweet desserts, and soft drinks are all right on occasion, but they have little food value, they are bad for his teeth, and they spoil his appetite for more nutritious foods. Use them only occasionally or, better yet, forget about them altogether. You can tell if a food is not being digested properly if it comes through in your baby's bowel movements. If it does, chop it finer or use other foods.

When you feed him table foods—foods that you prepare for the entire family—be sure they don't contain chunks or stringy material he can choke on (no peanuts or raisins; watch out for strings in celery and green beans).

Encourage him to feed himself "finger foods" such as crackers, bits of bread or toast, or bits of cheese or meat. He will enjoy using his fingers and you will be able to let him feed himself.

Let him try drinking from a cup by the time he is 5 or 6 months old. Pour just a little bit of liquid into the bottom of the cup at first, then increase the amount as he learns to drink more skillfully. Encourage him to hold the cup and the bottle as you feed him; the sooner he learns, the less you will have to help him later on.

Let him help you handle the spoon when you are feeding him. If you sit behind him as you feed him, he can hold onto the spoon or your hand and learn the movements he will use to feed himself. It may slow you down and make some mess, but he will learn to feed himself sooner.

By the time he is 9 or 10 months old, he will be able to eat most of the things you cook for the rest of the family. You will still have to mash up some of the vegetables and cut the meat fine.

CLOTHING

Your baby doesn't need much more than a diaper and a shirt in a comfortably heated house. During hot weather he may be happier without a shirt. After the first weeks you can judge what he needs to keep him warm by what you need to keep yourself comfortable. If you need a sweater while resting quietly, so will he. If a sweater or extra shirt makes you too warm while exercising, he will probably feel the same way. He doesn't need a cap or hat if you don't.

There is no magic in outdoor air. It is neither particularly good nor particularly bad for a baby as long as he is properly clothed. Again, your own comfort is the best guide. Bright sunlight won't hurt his eyes, but he can get sunburned just like anyone else, and probably a little easier.

Shoes

Shoes protect the baby's feet from rough surfaces and sharp objects. They do not change the shape of his feet (unless they do not fit properly) or help him walk or stand. Until he starts walking on rough surfaces or in places where there may be dangerous or sharp objects, he doesn't really need any shoes. Socks, booties, or clothing with feet sewn in offer plenty of protection, and bare feet are usually fine. When you get shoes either for "dress up" or because they are needed for protection, be sure that they are well fitted. Most shoes made for babies are well designed, and expensive shoes are not necessary. When your baby is first wearing shoes, his feet will be growing so fast that shoes will have to be replaced every 6 to 8 weeks. You should pay much more attention to keeping him in shoes that fit than in getting shoes early or getting expensive shoes. Sock sizes also must be changed! High topped shoes are harder for your baby to remove, but they have no other advantage.

Laundering

You can launder clothing and diapers together. Wipe or rinse the bowel movement off soiled diapers and clothing and rinse them before adding to the diaper pail. Place dirty diapers, bed clothes, and clothing in a covered plastic pail or washbasket between washings.

Use a mild low sudsing detergent, and rinse everything three or four times after the washing. If you use an automatic washer, run it through an extra "rinse" cycle. Adding a cup of vinegar to the final rinse may help prevent diaper rash.

If possible, use a clothes dryer; it leaves the laundry much softer than drying on a clothes line.

TEMPERAMENT

Babies differ from each other in many ways. They may be big or small, fast growing or slow growing, early developers or late developers, brown-eyed or blue-eyed. One of the most important ways in which babies differ is in their temperament—the usual way they react to you, to other people, and to things around them. You will find it much easier to understand your baby, to take care of him, to teach him and to enjoy him if you pay attention to his temperament.

There are at least nine ways in which young babies differ from each other in "temperamental characteristics." No one knows whether these characteristics or differences are inherited, whether they are formed when the baby is growing during your pregnancy, or whether they develop in the first weeks of life. In any case, they are present in the first months of life, and you will want to understand how they affect your child.

Activity Level. How much does your baby move around? When you put him in bed, does he wiggle all over the crib or does he stay in one place? When you change a diaper or put a shirt on him, do you have trouble because he is constantly wiggling about or does he lie quietly and let you change him?

Normal babies may be very active or very inactive. The job of caring for a very active baby will be quite different from that of caring for a very inactive one. If you believe that all babies should be active, you may be disappointed or frustrated by an inactive baby. If you think that all babies should stay still and lie quietly while being dressed or bathed, you may think that an active baby is bad or that he is active because you are not caring for him properly. Don't blame yourself or the baby. He is just made that way.

If your baby is super-active, you may just want to enjoy him, or you may want to behave in a more soothing and gentle way so as to encourage him to slow down a little. With a very inactive baby, you may want to take more initiative in playing with him, moving him about, and rewarding him for the activities which he does start on his own.

Regularity. How regular are your baby's habits? Does he always awaken at the same time, get hungry at the same time, take his nap at the same time, have his bottle at the same time? Does he vary by a small amount each day? Or is he completely unpredictable? Does he eat and drink about the same amount at his morning feeding each day?

If he is very regular, your job is usually quite easy. If he is very irregular, you will have to be prepared for daily changes. Or you may have to do more scheduling for him rather than sitting back and waiting for him to find a comfortable schedule of his own. Of course, you can't feed him if he isn't hungry, or make him sleep if he isn't really tired. But you can feed him before he really cries in hunger and you can put him down for a quiet time or for sleep even though he isn't especially tired.

Adaptability. How long does it take him to get used to new situations or to changes? When you changed from sponge bathing to a bath, did he accept it immediately, or did it take six or seven tries before he really accepted it? If you offer him a new food or toy, does he take it promptly or does it take many trials before he will really eat it or play with it? If he objects the first time you put a cap on his head, does he object every time you try it, or does he get used to it very quickly?

High or low "adaptability" is neither good nor bad. The child who resists change may take longer to teach. But, once taught, he won't change every time a slightly different situation comes along.

Approach or Withdrawal. How does your baby usually react the first time to new people, new foods, new toys and new activities? Does he reach out for them and seem pleased, or does he shy away and fuss? Approach and withdrawal differs from adaptability in that it describes the baby's *first reaction* to something new rather than the length of time or number of tries it takes him to get used to it.

The baby who immediately reaches out for something seems easier to deal with at first. But the baby who withdraws slightly from a new situation may be much easier to keep out of trouble and danger when he is a little older. Again, neither characteristic is good or bad, but they do require different handling.

Threshold Level or Sensitivity. Is your baby very aware of slight noises, slight differences in temperature, slight differences in tastes or in different types of clothing? Will he wake up at the slightest noise, or can he sleep through anything? Do bright lights or sunlight make him blink or cry? If he doesn't like new food, does he notice the difference when you mix a little of it with an old food that he does like? Does he let you know every time his diapers are wet or does he ignore it?

Very high sensitivity may make your job more difficult at first, but the child who notices small differences may learn some things faster or more easily at a later age.

Extreme insensitivity to sounds may be caused by deafness, not temperament. You should certainly mention it to your doctor.

Intensity of Reaction. How strong or violent are his reactions when he is pleased or displeased? Does he laugh and wriggle all over or just smile when he is pleased? Does he frown and fuss quietly or does he scream loudly when he is upset? If he doesn't like a new food does he quietly turn his face away, or does he hit the spoon away, spit out the food, and cry?

If your baby reacts very strongly and intensely, you will want to teach him that he can get what he wants without being quite so loud and active. Don't let him learn that you only pay attention to him when he reacts very strongly. Of course, his active way of showing pleasure will make up for some of his loud crying when he is disappointed.

Distractibility. How likely is your baby to turn his attention from what he is doing to something new? If you are feeding him, will he keep on sucking no matter what happens? Or will he stop and pay attention when a door opens or someone else comes into the room? If he is hungry, will a toy keep him quiet for a few minutes while you are getting the bottle, or will he just keep on demanding his bottle? If he is playing with his rattle, will he quickly turn his attention to a new sound or sight?

You may want to feed him in a quiet place if he is very distractible, and to give him just one or two toys at any one time. If he is not at all distractible, you will have to be very firm when you want him to change from one thing to another.

Positive or Negative Mood. How much of the time does your baby show friendly, pleasant, joyful behavior as compared to unpleasant crying, fussy, or unfriendly behavior? This means not just his first reaction to new situations, or to the times when he is actually hungry or uncomfortable; it means the way he seems to be during most of the day. His mood may be expressed quietly with a frown or a whimper, or with a smile and a twinkling eye. Or it may be loud screaming or a deep laugh.

A baby with a negative mood is much harder for anyone to deal with. You will have to realize that the few bright spots in his day mean you are doing a lot of things the right way. You must remember that his general unpleasantness does not necessarily mean that you are doing something wrong. He will wear you out much more quickly. You may need more recreation and more time away from him. You will have to learn to ignore some of his crying and fussing once you have made sure he really doesn't need anything at the moment and has no reason to be uncomfortable.

Attention Span and Persistence. How long will he stick with something he is doing? Will he continue to try even if it is difficult for him? Even if you try to stop him? If he reaches for something out of reach, will he keep trying? Or give up quickly? Will he keep watching something above his crib for 10 or 15 minutes; or will he turn to something else after a few minutes? Attention span and persistence mean how long he sticks with something on his own, not how easy it is to distract him with something new or different.

You will be pleased when he persists in things you like, but not pleased when he persists in making trouble! You will want to be firm and patient, and use distraction in getting a persistent child to change activities. You will want to encourage and praise a non-persistent child for sticking with a useful activity.

If you pay attention to how your child measures up in each of these traits, you will be able to help him in the ways he needs help. And you will be much more certain that what you are doing is right for him. An awareness of the different temperamental characteristics should make you much less likely to think that he is a "bad" baby or that you are a "bad" parent.

"Difficult" Babies

While no single trait of temperament makes a baby much more difficult, babies with certain combinations of traits are certainly much harder to care for. If you have such a child it may be a great comfort to know that you really have a much harder job than do most other parents.

A baby with a combination of irregularity, withdrawal from new situations, slow adaptability, negative mood, and intense reactions will be very hard to care for indeed. You will need a great deal of patience. You will have to be firm, and willing to be firm not just once, but many times, one after another. You will need more time away from him and more help from your spouse and from others. Such a baby will especially need your signs of approval and affection at those times when he is comfortable and "cooperative." But even such a difficult baby will learn to be less difficult, and as he does, you will have the satisfaction of knowing that you have performed a very difficult job in a skillful way. And you will have saved your baby from a lot of trouble in later life!

DISCIPLINE AND TEACHING

The word "discipline" means teaching. It does not mean punishment, as many people think. Your child will be well "disciplined" when he learns to do those things which please you and which help him to grow and develop, and when he learns not to do those things which displease you and the people around him, and which keep him from growing and developing.

The key to learning and discipline is not punishment, but reward. When your baby first smiles, you pay attention to him and smile back. When he smiles again, you smile back and pay attention to him again, and you may talk to him and cuddle him. He soon learns that when he smiles good things happen to him, and he learns to do a lot of smiling when you are around. In just the same way, when you pay attention to his first cooing and gurgling sounds, your smile, your voice and your fondling reward him. He coos and gurgles more and more frequently. When he is five or six months old, he begins to notice that you "reward" him more when he repeats sounds you make than when he makes just any old sound. Pretty soon he imitates everything you say, and begins to learn to talk.

The same thing holds true for almost all other kinds of behavior. When you respond to something your child does by giving your attention, a smile, a kind word, or by fondling or joy, your baby will do that thing more and more frequently. If you ignore it, it will be done less and less frequently. With these two methods, rewarding and ignoring, you will teach your child almost everything he learns.

What about punishment? Will a baby stop doing something if he is constantly punished for it? It should work that way, but actually punishment doesn't work well in the first years of life. The baby usually can't figure out just what behavior is being punished. If you slap him when he throws a spoonful of food on the floor, he may not know whether he is being punished for eating, for trying to feed himself, or for something else. He may stop eating or trying to feed himself rather than start to become a neat eater. Then too, punishment is a form of attention. Some babies may enjoy attention more than they dislike the punishment. If the child who threw a spoonful of food on the floor saw just a slight frown on his mother's face and was rewarded with a smile for many of the times he got the spoon in his mouth, he would soon give up any purposeful spilling.

Of course, the baby sooner or later must learn that some of the things he does make people around him irritated or angry. You don't have to be always calm, smile or hold your temper. But, the fact that his behavior is sometimes irritating and that you show your irritation in natural ways at times is quite different from trying to teach him how to behave through punishment.

There are some things your baby will do which are just plain dangerous. During the first year of life, if he gets hold of something sharp or something he can swallow, you must take it away from him promptly. At the end of the first year, you can begin to teach him the meaning of "no" by rewarding him when he stops doing something dangerous when you say the word. Soon you will be able to use the word "no" to keep him out of dangerous situations. Save most of your harsh words and punishments for teaching him about things that are really dangerous. Don't waste your "no-no's" on things that really don't matter.

PLAY AND EXERCISE

You and your baby get to know and understand one another as you play together. He learns about his own body and about the world around him as he plays by himself. He reaches out and examines things, first with his eyes, then with his hands, and then with his whole body. He listens, then responds, then imitates you as you talk to him in play.

In the first months, baths, feeding times, and diaper changes give you and your baby the opportunity to handle each other, to listen to each other, and to watch each other. You can stretch him out, pull him up into a sitting or standing position, and get to know the real strength he has in his grip and his muscles.

At first, he will play mostly with his eyes, looking at objects and following them as they move. A few objects dangled on a string from his crib will give him something to watch, and so will the view out the window or the sight of you carrying on your usual household tasks.

By the time he is two to three months old, he will spend a great deal of time watching his hands as he reaches out and brings them back in front of his face. He will begin to laugh and squeal so you will know when he really enjoys his own games and the games you play with him.

Toys

A toy is anything the baby plays with. He doesn't care whether it was purchased in the most expensive children's shop or is a cardboard tube from a roll of toilet paper. Spoons, boxes, pie tins, pieces of cloth, or clothespins will give him just as much to explore and just as much pleasure as expensive silver rattles.

To be safe, any toy you give your baby should:

- Be sturdy enough that it will not splinter or break;
- Be large enough so that he can't swallow it;
- Have no sharp points or edges;
- Have no parts that can come loose and be swallowed, such as whistles on rubber toys, or buttons or eyes on stuffed animals and dolls;
- Be painted with a safe paint (see Safety Checklist, p. 46).

The child needs only a few things to play with at any one time—his crib shouldn't be stuffed with a great number of toys and household objects. However, the more different things he can look at, handle, bite, squeeze, scratch, bang, rattle, and throw, the more he will learn about what things are like. So change his toys frequently. Any household contains plenty of safe objects for even the most curious baby.

Out of the Crib

By three to four months, your baby will probably demand a little more excitement than he gets in his crib and in his usual daily care. He may let you know by screaming and crying from boredom or he may just be a little fussy.

He will be happier spending a few hours a day sitting in an inclined infant seat watching you do your housework or cooking. He will also want to spend some time on the floor where he can roll, kick, and begin to learn to crawl. Keep a close eye on him when he is on the floor; he has enough strength to pull down a lamp or a small table and he can move amazingly far and fast even before he learns to crawl or creep. A playpen can be useful because you can leave him there out of your sight for a few minutes while you carry on your household tasks. Later on he can use the bars or net of the playpen to pull himself up. And a playpen can make a handy crib for naps or even for all-night sleeping. When he is quite small, you can make a playpen by blocking off a corner of a room with furniture or boxes. As he gets stronger, you will need something stronger that he can't move. As he grows older, he should be given some time each day when he is free to move about on the floor outside of the playpen. The older he gets, the more carefully you will have to watch him to keep him out of trouble.

GOING OUT

Babies can go anyplace their parents go, and they often do. Whenever possible, it is wise to avoid taking him into crowded public places where people whose health is unknown to you may poke at him, handle him, or sneeze in his face! When necessary, he can certainly sit with you in church or on the bus and go with you to the supermarket. Most babies seem to love trips in cars. If you take him in the car with you, get a suitable infant restraining device, which can be fastened to the seat by seat belts. Automobiles are always dangerous to everyone, and they are especially dangerous if a parent must worry about the movements of a baby while driving.

A canvas "baby tote" or back pack is easier to use than a carriage or stroller. It is much more convenient for traveling. You may even find yourself using it at home when your baby wants to be near you while you are busy.

LEAVING THE BABY

You need some rest from the baby, and he has to learn that others can care for him. Plan to get out without him for at least several hours a week after the first month.

Baby Sitters. Select the person with care. Relatives, neighbors, friends all can be great—or terrible. You want someone who really cares about your baby and whom you can trust. You will want her to be healthy. If you don't know the sitter well, have her come for a brief stay while you are home. Show her where things are, how you care for the baby and tell her what you expect. Watch her feed and diaper the baby and see whether she seems to know and care about what she is doing.

Whoever is left to care for your baby, even for a brief time, should know:

- Where you can be reached
- Telephone numbers of your doctor, fire department, and police
- The name and telephone number of a responsible relative or friend who can be called if you can't be reached
- Details about your house—how to regulate heat, how to lock and open doors, etc.
- What and when to feed the baby
- When you will return

Crying When You Leave. Up to the age of 5 to 7 months your baby will probably accept care from anyone. After that, he may take some time to get used to a stranger, and he may scream when you try to leave him. Do give him some time with the baby sitter before you leave him, and use the same one or two baby sitters as much as possible. But don't be fooled by his screams; he will probably be happy within 5 minutes. He needs to learn that he can trust you to come back, and he can only learn it if you leave him and do come back.

Full-Time Baby Sitting and Child Care. Many mothers return to full-time or part-time work after the baby is born. Most mothers will want to wait at least 3 months before returning to full-time work, many will want to wait longer. (See also Working Parents, p. 151.) There are many ways to arrange baby sitting or child care:

- Someone may care for your child in your own home, such as a relative, maid, or housekeeper;
- Someone may care for your child in her home—foster day care or home day care;
- Your child may be cared for in a center designed and staffed especially for the care of children—a day care center.

A trusted friend or relative is often the best baby sitter. Housekeepers and maids are expensive, but they may provide the least expensive form of child care if you have several children requiring care. You have complete control and responsibility for the kind of care your child receives. Supervising and training such a maid or housekeeper will require a good amount of your time and effort.

After the First Weeks

Leaving your child in another person's home is often the least expensive form of child care. However, you have very little to say about how such a person takes care of your child, so you must choose very carefully and visit frequently to be sure that your baby is getting the kind of care you want him to get. If at all possible, choose a home that is licensed by a health or welfare department and which is part of a day care association which trains the day care "mother" and which supervises her and makes sure her home is safe.

Day care centers for infants are available in many cities, towns, and armed forces bases. A few are very good, most of them are, at the present time, very bad. Good centers are costly. Sometimes part of this cost is covered by a church, industry, or other sponsor, so the actual charges to parents can be less.

CHECKLIST FOR JUDGING A DAY CARE HOME OR CENTER:

☐ Does the person caring for the children really care about your child as an individual?
☐ Is there at least one person to care for each 4 to 5 children (including the day care "mother's" own children)?
☐ Does the care-giver treat each child as her own, talking to him while she is bathing or changing him, holding him when he is fed, "teaching" him and paying attention to his temperament and development?
☐ Is the home or center safe and healthful, with room for children's play and care, fresh air, reasonable cleanliness and free of safety and accident hazards? (See the Safety Checklist pp. 46-49.)
☐ Are your suggestions for the care of your child welcome and listened to?
☐ Do the care-givers and children seem to be happy, alert, and enjoying themselves?
☐ Are you welcome to visit at any time, with or without telling them in advance that you are coming?
☐ Has the care-giver had a medical examination to prove that she has no disease that your child could catch and that she is strong, and healthy enough to care for children?

☐ Is there a telephone which the care-giver can use to reach you or to call for help in an emergency?

PENNY PINCHING

There are several ways that you can safely cut the cost of caring for your baby, and some costs that you should not try to cut.

Furniture. Any box, basket or drawer will make a fine cradle for a newborn baby. Don't buy a small cradle.

A playpen narrow enough to push through a door can also be used as a crib. The thin pad is just as good as a mattress. You will have to do a lot more bending.

Food. Powdered infant formula costs less than liquid concentrate, and much less than ready-to-feed formula or whole milk. It takes only a few extra seconds to measure it and shake it up in the bottle. After age 1 year, when the extra iron and vitamins in an infant formula are no longer necessary, use evaporated milk mixed half and half (4 oz. water and 4 oz. evaporated milk) with water. It is much less expensive than fresh milk and probably a little safer.

Baby foods in small jars are usually much more expensive than the same foods in larger cans or jars. Don't start food other than cereals before age 4 months. Don't use much baby meat at any age; one jar a week is plenty until he is eating table foods. Use regular juices, applesauce, etc., instead of those specially prepared for babies.

The special infant cereals are very convenient and contain added iron and vitamins; they are well worth the slightly higher cost.

Don't use vitamin or mineral drops if you are using a powdered or liquid infant formula. The formula contains all the vitamins and iron the baby needs.

Miscellaneous. Launder your own diapers. You can probably buy a washing machine for the $300 you save by not using diaper service or disposables! Even if you must use a coin laundry, you will save a few dollars every week.

Fancy clothing may be fun for you, but it doesn't help your baby. Save the money for well-fitted shoes and sturdy play clothes.

A bassinet is no better or more useful for bathing and changing a baby than is a sturdy table or kitchen-type cabinet, and you can use the table or cabinet later for other things.

Public well-baby clinics are often free, and usually give very good advice and shots. However, if you can't get telephone advice, and if you must go to a private doctor or pay clinic for any illness, you may find that a private doctor costs little more. This is especially so if you must lose time from work to use the free clinic. Don't be afraid to ask a doctor how much he charges for visits and shots when you call him for an appointment.

A canvas "baby tote" or back pack is much less expensive than a stroller or baby carriage, and much easier to use when shopping or riding a bus.

3
Development and Health

While temperamental characteristics or traits tend to remain quite constant over a long period of time, many other kinds of behavior change rapidly—and many of these changes can be predicted by your baby's age. Some of these "developmental" characteristics and behaviors are listed in the chart on pp. 35-37, along with the ages at which your baby is first likely to show them.

Don't spend much time trying to teach him something that most babies don't learn until they are older; he will learn it easier and faster later on.

Knowing what your child will be doing next helps you plan to protect him. When he begins to crawl, you have to keep him away from stairways and things he can pull over.

When he begins to grasp things, you will have to keep dangerous (or valuable) things out of his reach. When he can pick up small objects, you must be sure he doesn't reach and swallow anything that isn't food.

A child who sits early will probably stand early, but he won't necessarily talk early. The things that are grouped together in the chart usually go together in a child.

If your baby is slower to do something than the expected times

DEVELOPMENTAL CHART

Characteristic	Most Babies First Do This Between
How he handles his whole body:	
Holds head off of bed for a few moments while lying on stomach	Birth and 4 wks
Holds head upright lying on stomach	5 wks and 3 mos
Holds head steady when you hold him in sitting position	6 wks and 4 mos
Rolls over from front to back, or from back to front	2 mos and 5 mos
Sits without support when placed in a sitting position	5 mos and 8 mos
Gets himself into sitting position in crib or on floor	6 mos and 11 mos
Takes part of his weight on his own legs when held steady	3 mos and 8 mos
Stands holding-on	5 mos and 10 mos
Stands for a moment alone	9 mos and 13 mos
Stands alone well	10 mos and 14 mos
Walks holding onto furniture	7½ mos and 13 mos
Walks alone across a room	11 mos and 15 mos

Characteristic	Most Babies First Do This Between
How he uses his hands and eyes:	
Follows an object with his eyes for a short distance	Birth and 6 wks
Follows with his eyes from one side all the way to the other side of his head	2 mos and 4 mos
Brings his hands together in front of him	6 wks and 3½ mos
Grasps a rattle placed in his fingers	2½ mos and 4½ mos
Passes a toy from one hand to the other	5 mos and 7½ mos
Grasps a small object (like a raisin) off a flat surface	5 mos and 8 mos
Picks up a small object using thumb and finger	7 mos and 10 mos
Brings together two toys held in his hands	7 mos and 12 mos
Scribbles with a pencil or crayon	12 mos and 24 mos
How he uses his ears and voice:	
Pays attention to sounds	Birth and 6 wks
Makes vocal sounds other than crying	Birth and 6 wks
Laughs	6 wks and 3½ mos
Squeals	6 wks and 4½ mos
Turns toward your voice	4 mos and 8 mos
Says "Dada" or "Mama"	6 mos and 10 mos
Uses Dada or Mama to mean one specific person	10 mos and 14 mos
Imitates the speech sounds you make	6 mos and 11 mos

Characteristic	Most Babies First Do This Between
How he behaves with other people:	
Looks at your face	Birth and 1 mo
Smiles when you smile or play with him	Birth and 2 mos
Smiles on his own	6 wks and 5 mos
Pulls back when you pull a toy in his hand	4 mos and 10 mos
Tries to get a toy that is out of reach	5 mos and 9 mos
Feeds himself crackers	5 mos and 8 mos
Drinks from a cup by himself	10 mos and 16 mos
Uses a spoon, spills little	13 mos and 24 mos
Plays Peek-a-boo	6 mos and 10 mos
Plays Pat-a-cake	7 mos and 13 mos
Plays with a ball on the floor	10 mos and 16 mos

NOTE: A baby who was born before he was expected—who was "premature,"—will normally be later in development. If your baby was early by a month, add one month to the above ages to find out when to expect him to do things. If he was two months early, add two months, etc.

shown in the chart, you should think about why this might be. If he is slow in just one or two items, and average or quick in the others, it may be just his style of doing things. But if he is slow in all items in any category it is cause for some concern. Have you been giving him an opportunity to learn, and have you been praising him for his efforts? Is he physically ill? Was he premature? If you can't find any reason, and if he doesn't learn when you try to teach him, have your doctor check his health and development. If you are told "he'll grow out of it" and you don't see him doing so, check again—or even get another doctor's opinion. If your baby is much slower than the expected times in several areas of development either there is something wrong with him, or there is something wrong with the opportunities he has to learn and develop. In either case, you will want to know about it.

PHYSICAL GROWTH

A baby's steady growth in height and weight is one of the best signs that he is healthy and is getting the kind of care he needs. It is the steadiness of the growth that counts, not how much it is or how fast it is. Most babies gain about ½ lb. per week during the first few months of life and about one pound per month from age 5 to 12 months. Smaller babies usually gain less and larger babies may gain more. You don't need a scale to tell. Your judgment and his regular checkups are plenty. The Growth Charts below show the average length and weight of large, small and average-size babies, and indicate about how much they will gain from month to month during the first year of life. The most common cause for a young baby not to grow as well as these average babies is that he is being fed too little or too infrequently. Try offering your baby more frequent bottles or more milk in each bottle, and he will usually catch up very quickly. If he doesn't check with your doctor.

GROWTH CHARTS

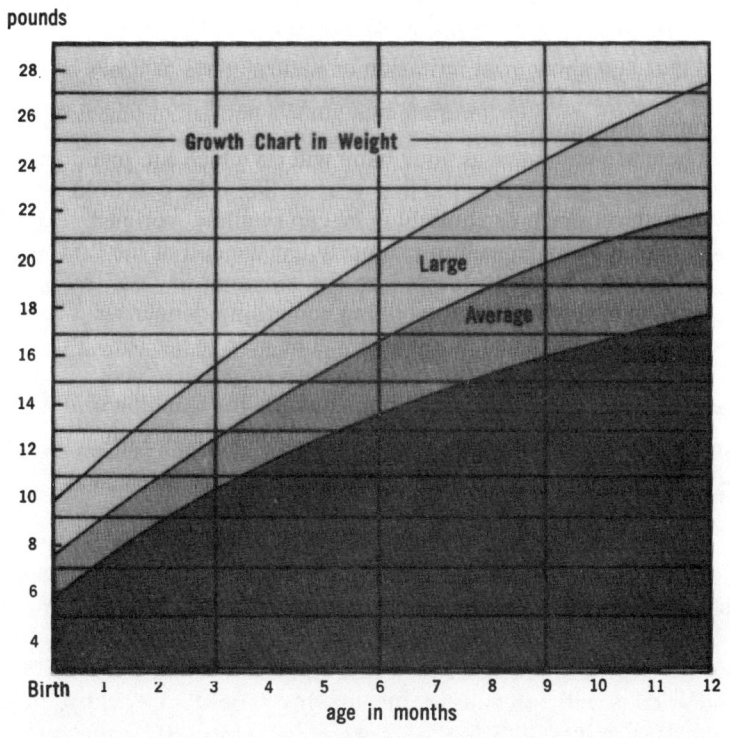

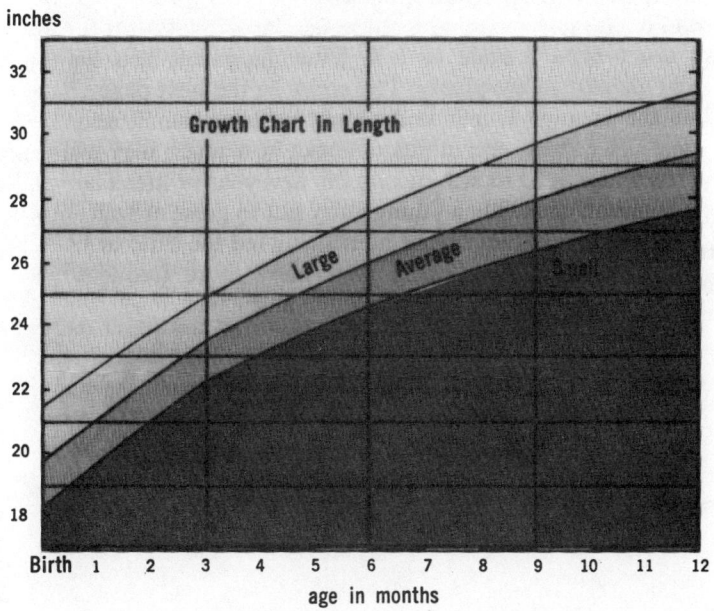

Growth Chart in Weight

Large / Average / Small

age in months: Birth to 12

pounds: 4 to 28

Growth Chart in Length

Large / Average / Small

age in months: Birth to 12

inches: 18 to 32

HEALTH SUPERVISION

You will have many questions about your baby that can best be answered by a medically trained person. Your baby should be checked from time to time to discover whether he is growing and developing normally and whether he has any problems which you may not notice, but which a doctor can notice in his examination. There are certain tests that should be performed for every child, and your baby needs specific "shots" or immunizations to keep him from having certain illnesses. For these reasons your baby should be seen by a doctor (or a suitably trained doctor substitute) several times during his first year of life. (See Recommended Immunization Schedule on page 106.)

Choosing a Doctor or Clinic

You will want to choose a doctor or clinic whose office is convenient, whom you trust, who is likely to be available by telephone when you want advice, and preferably one who can take care of your child, both when he is well and when he is sick. Neighbors and friends will often have suggestions. The doctor who delivers your baby and the hospital nurses can be helpful. If you have other children, you will certainly want to use the same doctor for all your children.

Using the Doctor

If possible, choose your baby's doctor before the baby is born. Call him, tell him when you expect the baby and that you would like him to visit you and the baby in the hospital and care for him after he is born. Some doctors will suggest a visit before the baby is born to get to know you and to discuss your plans for caring for the new baby.

Be sure to talk with the doctor who examines your baby in the hospital to find out if all is well. Ask questions and get answers!

Most doctors and clinics will schedule the baby's first checkup when he is about one month old, and then plan further visits every 4 to 6 weeks for 3 or 4 visits and somewhat less frequently in the last 6 months of the first year.

Your conversation with the doctor is the most important part of each visit. The doctor may actually examine the child only 3 or 4 times during the first year, but he will always want to know how your baby is growing, how he is learning and developing, and whether you have noticed any problems. Write down your questions and observations so you can be sure to remember them.

Keeping Your Own Records

You may have to change doctors, or you may have to get medical care when your doctor is not available. A busy clinic or doctor may lose your child's records. If you keep your own record and take it with you whenever you visit a doctor or a clinic, you will probably save time and trouble. The form at the back of this book is one way of keeping such a record.

When Doctors Disagree

Don't be surprised if one doctor doesn't give you the same advice as another, or even if they actually disagree with each other or with what you read in this book.

For many problems, there are many successful treatments, and this book may only mention one. For some other problems, such as colds, each doctor may have his own favorite medicine, none of which makes much difference. For still other problems (whether boys should be circumcised, for example) there are real differences of opinion. When two doctors give you directly conflicting advice you should ask for an explanation. If the explanation is convincing, fine. If not, you will have to get a third opinion or make up your own mind.

COMMON PROBLEMS AND WORRIES

Care of a Sick Child. Don't worry if a sick child doesn't want to eat, but be sure he gets plenty to drink. If he has a fever or diarrhea, he may be particularly thirsty. Give him only his usual amount of milk, and offer him water, juice, or sweet soft drinks in between.

Let him decide how much exercise and sleep he wants. If he wants to be up playing, let him up to play. If he is sick enough to need extra rest, he will soon lie down and fall asleep. Better a happy child playing quietly than a child screaming in his crib because someone said, "He's sick, keep him in bed."

Try to keep him comfortable. This often means fewer blankets and clothes rather than more, especially for a child with a fever. There is nothing wrong with outdoor air or with automobile trips provided he is comfortably dressed and allowed to rest when he wants to.

Colds. Many babies have a slightly stuffy, rattly noise in their noses nearly all the time. This is not a cold, it just seems to be the way they are made. It will become less and less noisy and noticeable as he gets older, the air passages of the nose get larger, and he learns to clear his nose by sniffling. Don't use a lot of cold remedies with such a baby. You may be able to reduce the noise by sucking out his nose several times a day with a small rubber bulb called a nasal syringe.

Most babies will have 2 or 3 real colds in the first year. Your perfectly normal baby may have 8 or 9. (For cold symptoms and treatment, see Chapter 13.)

Eyes. When he comes home from the hospital, the baby's eyes may have some white or yellow *discharge* caused by irritation from the medicine that was put in at birth. This should clear up within 5 or 6 days and should not get much worse at any time. If it does get worse or lasts more than a week, get medical advice promptly.

Your baby's eyes should not *cross*, but should look straight at you when he is awake and alert. One may turn in or out slightly when he is particularly tired, but both eyes should work together almost all of the time. If not, seek medical advice at your baby's next checkup. Don't be fooled by a wide nose which may make the eyes look as if they are turning in.

Genitals. The boy's penis and scrotum and girl's clitoris and labia are usually rather large at birth. They get slightly smaller over the next few weeks.

A girl may have a slight white creamy discharge from her vagina in the first few weeks, which is normal. It should become less and less and should not irritate the skin. Get medical advice if it becomes worse or if she develops a discharge after the first week or two. Any bulge or lump in a girl's genitals should be checked by a doctor.

One or both of a boy's testicles may seem particularly large, and be surrounded by a water sac or "hydrocele." These are painless and cause no harm. They go away by themselves, usually within a few months. Seek medical care for any swelling in the groin, and seek medical care immediately for any painful swelling in the groin or testicles.

A circumcision should heal completely within a week to 10 days. The tip of a circumcised boy's penis may become irritated by the diaper. Put a little Vaseline or zinc oxide paste on the irritated area each time you change the diaper.

If you want your boy circumcised, have it done while you are still in the hospital. It is not necessary, and it should almost never be done as a special operation once you and he have left the hospital (except for religious circumcisions).

If your boy is not circumcised, don't try to pull the skin back over the tip of the penis. It will hurt and irritate. As he grows the skin will gradually loosen until it will pull back with ease (it sometimes takes as long as 3 or 4 years).

Head Shape. In passing through the birth canal, his head may become molded into a peculiar shape. It will become more normal in the first several weeks of life.

Body fluid may accumulate under part of the skin of the scalp causing a firm, spongy lump or *caput*. This will disappear in a few weeks. Blood may accumulate on the surface of one of the bones of the skull, causing a soft squashy *cephalohematoma*. This kind of lump may take several months to disappear completely. A child who always lies on one side of his head may show flattening and loss of hair on that part of his head. This, too, will disappear as he grows older. None of these "abnormalities" will cause any problems later in the child's life.

Legs and Feet. Most babies' legs and feet don't look "normal" until the child has been walking for several years. The feet seem to turn in or out in the first year of life. The legs look bowed by the time he is 12 or 18 months old.

Almost all of these funny-looking feet and legs are perfectly normal and will gradually straighten out as he runs, plays, and climbs. If you can move the foot easily into a "normal" looking position, and if the foot moves freely when he kicks and struggles, it is almost certainly a normal foot that developed a bend or twist while he was sitting on it during your pregnancy.

You won't cause bowed legs by pulling your baby into a standing position or letting him walk or stand "too early." Also, he won't learn to walk any sooner by being placed in a walker—which usually isn't much fun for him anyway.

Skin. Baby's skin just isn't as smooth and clear as the advertisements say it is. Almost every baby develops a fine pink or red rash whenever his skin is irritated by rubbing on bedclothes, by spitting up, by very hot weather. Almost all of these fine pink rashes will go away promptly if the skin is bathed with clean water whenever it is dirty, and washed with mild soap once a day.

Many babies develop waxy scabs on the scalp and forehead, called *cradle cap* or *seborrhea*. Daily scrubbing with mild soap and a washcloth will usually keep this under control.

Small, red, blotchy "birthmarks" on the eyelids and back of the neck are so common that they are called "stork bites." They usually show up when the baby is between one and four weeks old. They go away by themselves after a year or so, and cause no trouble of any kind. There is nothing to do but wait.

Bright red raised "strawberry marks" are also quite frequent. They appear after one or two months, grow rapidly for a few months, stop growing and gradually disappear. Unless your baby has one that is particularly large or in a spot where it is constantly being irritated, it is best to let it go away by itself.

Large areas of pale blue discoloration, called *mongolian spots* are common, especially on the trunk of dark skinned infants. They become less obvious as the child grows older and have no importance.

Diaper Rash. Urine and bowel movements are irritating to the skin, especially when they stay in contact with the skin for a long time.

Prevent diaper rash by changing diapers frequently, by rinsing the diaper area with clean water at each diaper change, by rinsing diapers thoroughly after washing, and by applying a layer of zinc oxide paste (you can buy it at any drug store) whenever the diaper area appears irritated.

If your baby gets a diaper rash in spite of this, you should:

- Leave off the plastic pants (or plastic covered disposable diapers) except when absolutely necessary. Using 2 or more diapers at nap time and at night will make this less messy.

- Leave the diaper area completely uncovered for a few hours each day (nap time or early evening is most convenient), put a couple of diapers under him to soak up any "accidents."
- Apply a thin layer of zinc oxide paste after cleansing at each diaper change.

When to worry. Any pimple or rash that gets bright red and enlarges, or that develops blisters or pus, may be the beginning of an infection that will need medical care. You can soak such a rash with a washcloth or towel wrung out in hot water, and keep it clean by washing with mild soap and water twice a day. If it gets worse, or if it doesn't get better in 24 to 48 hours you should get medical advice.

Any rash that looks like bleeding or bruising in the skin should be seen by a doctor promptly (unless you know it really is a group of bruises).

Sucking. Most babies get their thumbs and fingers in their mouths and suck on them. Many seem to find it especially enjoyable and do it often. It causes no harm and can be ignored.

Some mothers don't like the looks of thumb and finger sucking and substitute a pacifier for the thumb. This also is fine, and the pacifier can be thrown away toward the end of the first year. But don't substitute the pacifier for the attention, food, or diaper changes that your baby wants and needs when he is crying!

Teeth. The first teeth usually appear at about 6 months of age and the average one-year-old has about 6 teeth. But don't worry if they come by 3 or 4 months, or not until 12 or 13 months. Early or late teeth don't seem to make any difference to the baby. He can chew most foods with his gums.

When a tooth is coming through the gum, the gum may become red and sore, and the baby may seem irritable for a day or so. Sucking on something cold may help. Half of a baby aspirin every 3 to 4 hours may relieve the pain. Don't use teething lotions or paragoric to rub the gums; they are often dangerous. And don't blame fever, vomiting, or other signs of illness (other than mild fussiness, some spitting up, and slight change in bowels) on teething. If your child really seems sick, it is not his teething that is causing it.

The Umbilical Cord and the Navel or Belly Button. The stump of the umbilical cord, which is cut at birth, usually falls off by the 5th to 9th day. The navel then often shows a *slight oozing* or *bleeding* for a few days. If it doesn't, clean it once or twice a day with soap and water or with alcohol. Bleeding or oozing that lasts more than two or three days after the cord falls off should be brought to the attention of a doctor.

About ¼ of all babies develop a *swelling* at the navel (umbilical hernia). This usually grows rapidly for several months, then grows with the baby for several months, then gets smaller and disappears. Large hernias may not go away until the child is 4–6 years old. The bulge often gets tight or tense when the baby cries or coughs.

Since these hernias almost always go away if they are left alone for long enough, there is no reason to have them repaired by surgery. They almost never cause any kind of trouble or pain. Occasionally a 4–6 year old child may be embarrassed by a particularly large hernia, and it can be repaired at that time. By waiting, you will almost certainly save your baby an unpleasant and unnecessary operation.

Very Frequent Urination. Most babies urinate nearly every hour until they are two or three months old, every two or three hours for the rest of the first year, and will sometimes urinate two or three times in a very short period. But if your young baby never seems to go more than ½ hour without urinating or your older baby seldom goes more than an hour, if he strains hard to urinate, or if he always urinates in a weak trickle or very fine tight stream, you should tell the doctor about it at the next checkup.

SAFETY

If your baby was born healthy, he is more likely to die or be injured by an accident than by any illness. You can prevent almost all accidents by knowing what your baby is able to do and making sure he can do it in a safe way. Use the following checklist to be sure your home is safe.

BIRTH TO 4 MONTHS
What the baby can do:
1. Eat, sleep, cry
2. Roll off a flat surface, wiggle a lot

SAFETY CHECKLIST: BABY NEEDS FULL-TIME, COMPLETE PROTECTION

Bath

- ☐ Check bath water temperature to avoid scalds.
- ☐ Keep one hand on baby at all times in bath.

Falls

- ☐ Never turn your back on baby who is on a table, bed, or chair.
- ☐ Always keep crib sides up.
- ☐ If interrupted, put him in crib, tuck him under your arm, or place him on the floor.

Burns

- ☐ Put screens around hot radiators, floor furnaces, or stoves.
- ☐ Don't smoke when you are caring for him.

In Crib, Bassinet, Carriage, and Playpen

- ☐ Be sure bars are close enough so that his head can't get stuck. (3 to 3½ inches at most.)
- ☐ Don't use a pillow.
- ☐ Select toys that are too large to swallow, too tough to break, with no small breakable parts, no sharp points or edges.
- ☐ Keep pins, buttons, coins, filmy plastics out of his reach.
- ☐ Never put anything but that which a baby can eat or drink in a baby bottle, baby food jar, or baby's dish. Someone might feed it to him.
- ☐ Don't use a harness or straps in the crib.

In Automobile

- ☐ Have a safe infant restraining device (see p. 29 "going out").
- ☐ Keep him in a place where he cannot touch or otherwise disturb the driver.

Supervision

- ☐ Don't leave him alone with a 1 to 3½-year-old brother or sister.

☐ Have the telephone numbers of physician, rescue squad, and poison control center posted near your telephone.

4 TO 7 MONTHS
What the baby can do:
Move around quickly
Put things in his mouth
Grasp and pull things
Needs more time out of the crib

SAFETY CHECKLIST

☐ Recheck all *Birth to 4 Months* list (preceding).
☐ Never leave him on the floor, bed, or in the yard without watching him constantly.
☐ Fence all stairways, top and bottom.
☐ Don't tie toys to crib or playpen rails, the child can strangle in the tapes or string.
☐ Baby-proof all rooms where he will play by removing matches, cigarette butts, and any other small objects, breakable objects, sharp objects, tables or lamps that can be pulled over.
☐ Cover all unused electric outlets with safety caps or tape.
☐ Keep high chairs, playpens, and infant seats away from stove, work counters, radiators, furnaces.
☐ Keep all electric cords out of his reach.
☐ Keep cans, bottles, spray cans, and boxes of all cleansers, detergents, pesticides, bleaches, liquor, and cosmetics out of his reach.
☐ Never put a poisonous household product into a food jar or soft drink can. Someone may eat it or feed it to the baby.
☐ Don't use paint that contains lead on any toy, crib, furniture, or woodwork, or other object he might chew. Look for a label on the paint which says, "Conforms to American Standard 266.1–1955 for use on surfaces which might be chewed by children." If a toy or crib is old and repainted, better remove the old paint completely and refinish it with safe paint.
☐ If your house was originally built before 1940 and has any chipping paint or plaster, repair it completely and cover it with wall paper or safe paint. If there is chipped paint or plaster in halls or other places you can't repair yourself, have it tested for lead by the health department and be sure to have it repaired.

8 TO 12 MONTHS
What the baby can do:
Move fast
Climb on chairs, stairs
Open drawers and cupboards
Open bottles and packages
Needs more opportunity to explore *while you are watching*

SAFETY CHECKLIST: BABY STILL NEEDS CLOSE SUPERVISION

- ☐ Recheck the *Birth to 4 Month* list.
- ☐ Recheck the *4 to 7 Month* list.
- ☐ Baby-proof all cupboards and drawers that he can possibly reach and open. Remove all small objects and sharp objects, breakable things, household products that might poison, plastic bags, food that might cause choking (such as nuts or popcorn).
- ☐ Keep coffee, hot foods, and hot pots and pans out of reach of his high chair.
- ☐ Don't use a dangling table cloth; he can pull it and everything on the table onto the floor and onto himself.
- ☐ Keep medicines and household products that might poison in a *locked* cabinet.
- ☐ Be especially careful when you or someone else in the family is sick. Medicines are likely to be out of their usual safe place, and the baby may want to imitate you by eating them.
- ☐ Keep medicines separate from household products and household products separate from food.
- ☐ Never give a medicine in the dark. Turn on the light and read the label, every time.
- ☐ Never leave your baby alone in the bathtub or wading pool. He can drown in only a few inches of water. He can also turn on a faucet and scald himself.
- ☐ Avoid sunburn.
- ☐ Get 1 oz. of Ipecac syrup from the druggist and keep it on the medicine shelf to treat certain kinds of poisoning.

One to Six Years

4
Patterns of Development

PHYSICAL GROWTH AND DEVELOPMENT

Babies grow very rapidly in the first few months of life, but as the year goes on their rate of growth becomes slower. This growth slowdown becomes even more obvious in the next five years. The child who gained, on the average, 15 pounds or so in the first year will gain only 4–6 pounds a year in this period. Children differ; some will gain more and some will gain less, but that is the average. The height gain is also slow.

The overall shape of the child will change in this period. Infants seem to be all head and trunk. However, between the ages of 1 and 6 different parts of the body grow at different speeds so that gradually the legs become proportionally longer and the body and head proportionally smaller. The 6-year-old looks much more like a small adult than the 1-year-old does.

All children are in a hurry to grow bigger, but the important thing to the child in this period is not so much the increase in size but the increasing control over the use of all parts of the body. The large muscles which control big movements of the arms and legs and the body as a whole are the ones the child learns how to use first. The small muscles which move the hands and fingers take longer to learn. At a year most children can sit up, pull themselves to stand, and crawl or walk, but they cannot yet perform complicated movements with their hands.

The same pattern persists in the second and third years. Children perfect their walking, learn to climb, to run, to jump, and to go up and down stairs. All these skills make it possible for them to go more and more places and explore more and more of their surroundings. (It also makes it possible for them to get into more trouble. See Safety, p. 107.) The urge to learn more about everything is tremendous in this period. The child wants to see, touch, and even taste everything. This urge, as well as your encouragement and approval, makes children push themselves to the limit, constantly trying out their new skills and abilities until they have perfected them.

Much of this activity may seem like a nuisance to parents. It's hard to believe that children need to keep repeating experiences so many times in order to learn. The on-off button on the TV for instance. Toddlers don't keep pulling and pushing it because they're bad, or want to annoy you, but because they don't really understand until they've done it a hundred times or more that pulling and pushing that button really does make the patterns and sounds come and go. Also, they enjoy making exciting changes in the world.

By about the age of 3 most children will have had enough of repeatedly exploring the house, if you have given them the chance to do so. They are ready to move on to the outside world. Fortunately, it is just about this time that they develop enough coordination to ride a tricycle, use playground equipment like swings and see-saws, and even play games with adults or other children. For the first time they become able to catch and throw a ball—a fairly large one is easier than a small one—or play tag and hide-and-seek. But they can only begin those games. They don't yet understand rules or being fair. They want to enjoy a game, not win one.

Actually, by this age they have pretty much learned control of all the large muscles. Balance and coordination aren't perfect, they can't yet ride a two-wheeler, for example, but the patterns are all there. From this time on, they will increasingly build on bodily skills which already exist.

Meanwhile, children have been learning how to manage finer and more delicate movements with their hands and fingers. These movements are more complex than you might think. In this respect look at the way children learn to handle buttons. At 12-15 months they learn to unbutton buttons, but only large ones which they can get a grip on. Somewhere between 2 and 3 they finally learn how to unbutton buttons of any size, but it is not until 5 years of age that most children learn to perform the other task of buttoning buttons. Parents who watch their children undoing buttons for years might easily get irritated when the child refuses to button them again. But this would be unfair because the two tasks are clearly not the same and one is obviously much more complicated than the other. The same thing is true of many other such tasks.

A lot of fuss has been made about educational toys for children in the second year of life. These are generally objects or collections of things which can be put into each other, or stacked, or taken apart and put together. These are all things children like to do in this age group, but almost every house is already well-equipped with educational toys. Children very much enjoy working with ordinary kitchen utensils like pots and pans, coffee pots, jars with lids, different-sized measuring cups, and so forth. These are just as much fun as store-bought toys and much cheaper for parents to provide.

Gradually in the second and third years children learn to turn the pages of books and magazines, which makes it possible for them to look at pictures. Then they learn how to do puzzles and how to use pencil, paper, and crayons. These activities are all important because they begin to provide the basis for those skills which children need when they are in school. If children have access to books and magazines, pencils and paper, etc., they can learn with their parents' active help to develop the important skills in which the eyes and the hands learn to work together. This gives them a head start in these areas.

By the age of 2, most children have learned to use a spoon and a cup to feed themselves. The process is messy along the way and if parents interfere because of the mess then the skills don't get learned so early or so easily. By 3, children can do a pretty fair job of cleaning their teeth if they have been shown how and allowed to practice on their own. And between 3 and 4 they can wash their faces and hands well enough for most sanitary purposes, if you will let them do so. In short, by 4, or 5 at the latest, children can assume most of the responsibility for their own feeding and hygiene. An occasional super cleanup by you will catch the corners that get missed in the daily routine.

Crayons and pencils and paper are important not only in the development of hand skills but also in helping children to learn to express themselves. Many parents hesitate to let their children have crayons and pencils because they are concerned that they will mark up the walls or the furniture. If you provide a good place for your child to draw and lots of paper to draw on you can teach him that pencils and crayons are to be used only on paper.

The earliest pictures or writings will look just like scribbles to you, but they are an important part of the learning process for your child. They help him find out which movements of the hand and arm produce what kinds of lines on the paper. If you are enthusiastic about them, regardless of what they look like to you, your child is encouraged to continue trying and in time will become more skillful. Children do better if they are allowed to draw what they want to, rather than if they try to draw something they are told to draw. Although you will often be curious about what the drawings are, it is better not to ask directly, "What is it?," but rather to say to the child, "Tell me about it." The answers are often interesting and sometimes surprising. You may learn a lot about what is actually going on inside your child's head. But if the child doesn't want to tell you, don't push.

LANGUAGE DEVELOPMENT

You and your baby learned to communicate with each other in the first year of life with a number of different signals including gestures, facial expressions, crying, other non-specific sounds and body movements. The thoughts communicated in these ways were basic and simple. "I'm hungry," "I'm happy to see you," "Something hurts" on the part of the baby. "I'll feed you," "I love you," "Don't cry" on the part of the parents. In order for you to begin to share more complicated thoughts and ideas the child must begin to develop language, speech at first and then writing.

Actually, by a year or so, your child should already have begun to develop speech that is specific and meaningful. Most children at a year can say two or three words like "mama," "dada," and "bye-bye." If your child hasn't tried to make sounds much at all or to respond to your talking, it would probably be a good idea to have his hearing and other speech related areas tested by your doctor.

If your child has begun to develop normal speech, more words will come in the next few months and then, in the second half to the second year, he will begin to put two or three words together in short phrases or sentences. These won't be regular sentences with all the right parts and grammar, but they will have more meaning than just single words can manage. By 2½, children can do something that makes both them and their parents very proud—they can tell their whole name, thereby proclaiming to the world exactly who they are and where they belong. Finally, by 3 or so most children can begin to put together whole sentences which do have all, or almost all, of the right parts and structure. From that point on the development of language is merely polishing up grammar and style and adding words.

How much and in what way children will talk depends, to a great extent, on you. Children hear their first speech from their parents and for the first few years most of the speech they continue to hear is from you. If a lot of talking goes on in the home, particularly directed to them, they will assume speech is important and they will work harder at it and will talk sooner and more. If very little talking is directed at them, children will not talk so much or so early. A lot of speech learning is by imitation. Children will tend to imitate the way of talking—loud or soft, fast or slow, clear or unclear, and so on—they hear from the people they are around the most and respect the most. They will also pick up words in the same way. Parents who don't want their children to use baby talk will not themselves use baby talk when they talk to the children. The same goes for shouting, or bad language, or what have you.

The development of language is very complicated. It depends on the child's having normal hearing, normal tongue and mouth muscles, normal speech centers in the brain, and the proper connections among them all. Difficulty in any of these areas may delay or distort the way speech develops. Also, difficulties between parents and child may interfere with normal speech. Developmental problems may show up in the speech area sooner than in any other way.

If your child is developing normal speech patterns at the right time it tells you that a lot of things are going right with both of you.

There are, incidentally, a number of minor speech impediments such as lisping, stammering, reversing syllables or sounds, ignoring certain sounds, and the like, which may occur in the course of normal speech development in almost any child. If they begin to show up in your child's speech the best thing for you to do is just watch and wait a while without making him self-conscious and tense by pointing out these errors. Most of the time these minor problems will go away in a few weeks just as quickly and mysteriously as they appeared. If they last several months or more it is then worth doing something about them. Even then, talk to your doctor first before drawing the child's attention to the problem.

SOCIAL DEVELOPMENT

One to six might be called the civilizing years. The 1-year-old is still self-centered and unreasonable, making demands and expecting these demands to be met right away. He has no patience and little or no consideration of others. But by 5 or 6 the child is going to have to enter school, get along with the other children and the teachers, and learn. In these 4 or 5 years children have to go from thinking only of themselves to being considerate of the needs and priorities of other individuals and the group.

In order to make this miraculous transformation children must know people who demonstrate the qualities of patience, tolerance, and consideration and they must want to imitate those people. The people young children most want to imitate are the people who are closest to them and take care of them—generally their parents and older brothers and sisters. For the first two years the identification with this small group is so close that children can really learn only from them and do not need a larger social group. In fact, too large a group is probably upsetting to many children of this age and interferes with their social learning. Children can tolerate a few other adults as regular care-givers but only one or two at a time. If you work and have to leave your young child with others, it is better if you can use the same caretaker most of the time. Home day care, with one or two adults and only a few children, is better for 1- or 2-year-olds than large groups in center-based day care.

Between 2 and 3 years of age children become better able to learn from other adults. By the end of that year they really need the opportunity to widen their social experiences so that they can compare different adult styles against each other. But it is not until children are 3 years or older that they are able to begin to play cooperatively with other children of the same age. Up to this time they do not understand how to take turns and share toys or equipment. Therefore, it is not sensible for parents to punish children under 3 for not sharing or taking turns or playing together. Even after 3, children can tire easily or get quite frustrated in playing with children their own age. So short play periods are better than long ones.

Having learned what they can from the real people they know, children between 3 and 4 often go ahead and invent for themselves a best friend—an imaginary person or animal who has all the qualities they admire and would like to have themselves. Some children will make up all kinds of play situations with these imaginary playmates, and some will want them included in all the normal activities of the day. Sometimes they have trouble sorting out the real from the make-believe. You may have to be careful to set a place at the table for the friend or be careful not to sit on him or her in an apparently empty chair. It is rather like having the invisible man living in your house. Sometimes the friend is a bad friend who is constantly stirring up trouble and getting your child into it. Other times the friend is quite good and only occasionally spills things or otherwise messes up.

Some parents have a difficult time dealing with these imaginary playmates and this world of make-believe. They don't understand that this is a normal stage for all children to go through, even those who don't talk about it. The parents thinks their child is lying, and they worry that he will become a chronic liar. They often punish him for continuing to tell stories about the make-believe playmates or friends. This frightens and confuses children. Because they do not feel they have done anything wrong, they do not understand what the punishment is for. Thus the difference between right and wrong becomes harder for them to figure out.

Other parents, not frightened by the child's adventures in the world of make-believe, tolerate and even take pleasure in his fantasy life and encourage it. They do their best to keep the real part of the child's life safe and sensible and find that the child needs to spend less time in make-believe as time goes by. These children learn how to use imagination as a part of their real world work in a helpful and creative way.

Actually, children do not really understand the difference between truth and lying in the real world until they are almost 5. Punishment for lying before that age is just not appropriate.

5
Everyday Life

SLEEP

In the first year of life the two major activities of the infant were eating and sleeping. This is still true for sleeping at least at the end of the first year but less so than it was. Studies indicate that 9 out of 10 children are sleeping through the night by their first birthday. But they don't all sleep soundly through the entire night. Many children have periods of wakefulness when you will see or hear them talking or playing quietly in their cribs. Usually they go back to sleep by themselves without any attention from you. It is a good idea to let them do so. There really is no good reason whatsoever for parents to interrupt children's sleep during the night.

Much is written about how much sleep children need. In the second year the range runs anywhere from 8 to 17 hours. This enormously wide range indicates once again how very different children are from each other. Children who need only 8 hours sleep a night cannot be kept in bed for 15 hours without driving themselves and their parents crazy. On the other hand, trying to set a schedule for children who need 12 hours, without making full allowance for that time, can also set up a real disturbance in the household.

Obviously it is essential to treat each child's sleep needs individually. How do you tell when your child has had enough sleep? One good way is by setting regular bedtimes from the beginning and noting when he wants to get up. The child who always gets up very early in the morning may be one of those short sleepers and may need to go in a little later at night to keep peace in the family.

Another way of telling whether children get enough sleep is by watching how they act in the daytime. If they are alert and active, and eat and play well, their sleep needs are probably being well met. If, on the other hand, they are cranky, irritable, fall asleep in the wrong places at the wrong times, or are under- or overactive in most situations, then they may not be getting enough sleep at night. Of course, days which are more exciting, more active, or on which the child is ill, will change sleep needs and patterns.

Young children don't like surprises very much. They prefer to do the same things in the same way day after day. Other than mealtimes the most important routines in the day revolve around sleeping. Most parents find that it is useful to have a standard bedtime for each child, although as already noted this does not mean having the same bedtime for each child. Parents will set different bedtimes for their children revolving around their own needs. Things like the parents' work schedules, mealtimes, and social needs all are taken into account in deciding how the children's schedule should be set. Both parents and children are happier when family patterns are set with regard to everyone's needs. In general, though, once set they are better kept the same from day to day except when some special occasion comes up, or when the needs for sleep change as children mature.

Children in the second and third years don't actually want to go to bed most of the time. In order to avoid doing so, children begin to develop all sorts of elaborate excuses to stall off the "evil" hour. Often these excuses and requests develop a pattern—one more drink, one more story, one more look out the window and so forth. In turn, parents often develop a regular way of reacting to the child's stalling and the whole going-to-bed period develops a regular ritual.

These rituals are important and can be quite helpful in settling children down at the end of an active day. But to work the rituals have to be pleasant and relaxed and quieting rather than exciting and stimulating. Wrestling, running around, and watching scary TV, for instance, are not relaxing. Quiet listening to music or stories, or talking about the activities of the day can be good ways for the child to unwind and get ready to accept sleep. Even the nightly bath can be stimulating, and it is better to allow some time to elapse between the bath and going to bed.

For many children an important part of the bedtime ritual is not only familiar people but also familiar things. In particular, children may become very attached to a special doll, stuffed animal, or blanket which has to go to bed with them as part of the ritual. The doll or blanket may become important to them beyond all common sense or reason, and they want it to go everywhere with them, especially if they have to sleep away from home. Parents will do well to guard such toys carefully against loss or destruction. Children will eventually outgrow them, but until they do their loss is often a disaster and may cause everyone sleepless nights.

Many parents are themselves uncomfortable about going to sleep or remember their own feelings as children about bedtimes. Children are very sensitive to their parents' feelings. If you are saying "go to bed" but remembering "sleep is scary" your child is likely to feel the mixed message and get quite confused as to which message you really mean.

A big issue in many homes is where children should sleep. The answer is simple. Whenever possible children should sleep in their own bed, in their own room with the door closed. If this is not possible then they should sleep in their own bed in a room with other children in the family. Preferably children should not sleep in the same room with their parents and they should never sleep in the same bed with the parents.

There is no question that children sleep better and have fewer fears and fantasies if they sleep in their own beds. Parents, on the other hand, often bring children into their beds for convenience, to deal with their own feelings of loneliness or other parent-centered reasons. It is not a good idea to do this even now and then. The first time sets a precedent that is difficult to break and, for the child at least, it is a bad precedent. If there are not enough bedrooms in the home it is preferable for the parents to sleep in some other room and to allow the children to have a closed bedroom.

Although we have been discussing only nighttime sleeping it is important to remember that children in this age group still sleep in the daytime as well. Most children nap twice a day until almost the age of 3 when the morning nap usually drops out. A year later the afternoon nap has shortened to a half hour or less. By 5 or 6 years children are in school and can no longer take afternoon naps, although many of them will still want a rest period when they come home from school. If the nap is really to be helpful it should be taken, like other sleep, in the child's own room and bed. Some special areas can best be discussed in brief form:

How Long Can Children Sleep In A Crib? Until they outgrow it, until they climb out of it regularly, or until it is needed for another child in the family are some answers. However, if you take children out of the crib at the same time you bring a new baby home they will be much more upset than if you do it well before or sometime after that event.

Do Children Need A Night Light? No, many children are more comfortable in a completely dark room than in one where a small light throws big and often scary shadows. But if the child does ask for a night light it is perfectly all right to put one in.

What Covers Should Children Have? Most children won't stay under a blanket and are better off in pajamas with feet in them in cold weather.

Most children will sleep better and more healthfully without pillows.

Why Do Children Have Nightmares? An especially tiring or overactive day, or a day in which some upsetting event happens may be the cause of nightmares. But sometimes they just happen and we don't know why. If parents can stay calm and be reassuring children will usually quiet down and go back to sleep. Children up to 5 or so have trouble knowing the difference between real and make-believe, so for them nightmares may be even more frightening. If nightmares become frequent or seem especially severe they are worth talking to your doctor about.

What About The Children Who Wake Up At Night, Cry, And Won't Stay In Their Own Room Or Bed? The answer to this is patience and firmness. First make sure the child doesn't seem sick, doesn't need diapers changed and has had a drink of water. Then put the child back to bed—the child's own bed—and leave the room. (Don't put the child in your bed. Don't lie down with the child in the child's bed.) You may have to repeat the process 20 times or so the first night this happens. However, if you are firm and stick to it over and over again you will have to do it fewer times each night. Try not to give in and not to become upset. The child really needs to know you mean business all the way and giving in once can undo a week of patience. Almost always, in a week or two the child will go back to sleep without trouble or will stop waking at night altogether.

A last word. Sleeping is a very important activity for children, and parents should do nothing to make children fear it or view it as punishment. Putting children to bed as a punishment does not really fit any discipline problem, and is only likely to make the children feel that even the regular sleep period is some form of punishment. They will then fight sleep even more than usual. As children reach the age of 4 or 5 they begin to enjoy sleep and look forward to it as adults do. From that time on sleep problems, except in rare instances, are seldom seen.

EATING

Eating is still fun for the 1-year-old, but it is no longer the main interest in the child's life. Children's need for food is determined mostly by their activity and by the rate at which they are growing in height and weight. Because this rate slows down greatly in the second year of life, many children are actually eating less at 15-18 months than they were at 8-10 months. Not unexpectedly this concerns a great many parents who feel it is obvious that the bigger and older children are, the more they should eat. That concern often leads parents to try to force children to eat more. When parents force and children resist a chronic battle is set up which may become more important to all concerned than the question of food which started it all in the first place. If this happens everybody loses. The parents lose because they never get over their frustration at the way their children eat. The children lose because they really do become finicky, difficult eaters or else chronic over-stuffers.

The truth is that normal children will never get into trouble from not eating enough *if an adequate supply of the right foods is presented to them.* Children won't eat everything all the time, and their diet may balance out only over a period of weeks or months, but it will meet all their growth and activity requirements. In fact, for the child over 1 year *if a proper supply of foods is presented* there is rarely need for the child to receive vitamins or other supplements with the possible exception of fluoride for their teeth. Children do need protein in order to grow well and some special diets are not good enough for them unless some thought is given to protein content or supplementation.

All this, of course, assumes that the child has been weaned from the bottle or breast. Children are capable of taking fluids from a cup or glass before they are a year old, and some are fully weaned by that age. In the second year, milk and other liquids should be offered from the cup more and more often and in larger quantities, so that children will not continue to think they must have a bottle in order to drink.

Many parents continue to allow children to take most of their milk from the bottle through the second and even the third year. Children seldom object because they find it easier to suck from the bottle than to drink from a glass, and they can carry their food supply around with them most of the time. Although this pattern seems convenient to both parents and children there are reasons why it is better not to allow it to continue.

First, milk is a good food but not a perfect one. A good many children as they get into the second and third year have more difficulty digesting milk well. Also, children who get most of their nutrition from milk primarily will become short of iron and some vitamins. They will not grow as well as other children.

Second, when children can carry a constantly filled bottle around with them and drink whenever they want to, they begin to refuse to sit at the table to eat. So they lose the chance to take in solid foods and to enjoy eating with the family at an age when they would most naturally begin to do so. They are likely to become lazy, limited and fussy eaters and to develop chronic constipation because of the lack of roughage in their diets.

Third, milk contains sugar. When children carry a bottle around and suck on it constantly they have sugar left in their mouths most of the time. This is very bad for teeth; it causes cavities and decay. For all these reasons it is important that parents wean their children from the bottle in the second year (except, perhaps, for a bedtime bottle), introduce them to solid foods at regular mealtimes, and, above all, prevent them from carrying the bottle around all day.

Solid foods should be pureed at first so that they are mashed up and made runny. In the second year children begin to eat more regular table foods like those you eat. They particularly like things they can pick up with their own hands and chew on. Incidentally, even young children tend to like foods with some flavor to them better than very bland foods. Foods which are reasonably spicy or otherwise tasty are just as safe and healthy for young children as for adults. They do not cause stomachaches or interfere with growth and development. Of course, children cannot actually eat all foods until they have some bicuspids, the large flat teeth in the back, with which to grind food. The sharp teeth in front only serve to bite off pieces. Some foods like nuts, fruits with pits, bones, popcorn and others are unsafe for small children because small pieces may break off and get caught in the windpipe.

Whatever you feed your child it is better not to heap the plate too full. The sight of a too-big helping often seems to make children less eager to eat. They do better if they are offered small portions and are allowed to ask for more if they want it. How much the child eats varies from day to day and week to week depending on a number of things like the child's health, activity, and even the weather. Their interest in kinds of foods will also vary from time to time. Sometimes they may go on jags when they only want one thing—peanut butter sandwiches or mashed potatoes, for example—at every meal every day. Parents will do best if they just ride along with the likes and dislikes as they occur. Tomorrow or next week they will change again.

Surprisingly, children do not necessarily like sweet foods better than other foods. Left on their own children develop a taste for, and learn to like, an amazingly wide selection of foods. They come to prefer sweets because we teach them to do so. Sometimes this is just because adults like sweets better and children imitate them. More often though it is because parents use sweets as a bribe to get children to eat other foods, or they hold back sweets as a punishment for some kind of misbehavior, whether related to eating or not. This makes children think sweets are really something special and begins to interfere with children's natural willingness to try out different foods. It seems reasonable to suggest that food should never be used as either a reward or a punishment.

Mealtime can be a lot more than just a chance to get nourishment into the child. Family mealtimes are one of the few times in most houses that the whole family gets together to do the same thing at the same time. If these family meals are fun for the child they can also be times when the child learns a good many things besides eating. Children learn manners, new words for their vocabularies, new experiences, how to talk both to adults and other children, and many other social skills.

But all this will happen only if mealtimes are fun. Young children are messy eaters. If parents find that the children's messiness interferes with their own eating pleasure, then they should eat separately from the children until such time as the children are able to eat with reasonable manners and neatness. Whichever, though, parents should encourage children to begin with spoons and other utensils as early as possible. This may increase the messiness for a time, but children encouraged in this way will learn to feed themselves earlier and will enjoy eating more in the long run.

A question which has received a lot of attention in recent years is that of allergies to foods. The idea of food allergies has been greatly overstated, and most children can safely eat most foods without trouble. Even such serious problems as asthma and eczema are seldom related to food allergies. In any case, the only way to find out for sure would be to consult your doctor.

CLOTHING

Not too many years ago parents often dressed children up in rather fussy and fancy clothes as though they were dolls on display. Now that rarely happens. Parents have learned that clothes for children should fit comfortably, be easily cleaned and made of materials that will wear well. A number of new materials have made all these things possible and less expensive at the same time. Children at play should be dressed in clothes that you don't have to worry about, that won't interfere with free movement and that will clean up easily afterwards. Even for the occasional dress up time clothes can now be made of materials which will hold up if they get rougher use than intended.

A lot of parents don't know how to decide how warmly to dress their children for going outside. A good rule is for you to dress the young child in the same number of items you would wear for the day—with perhaps one extra coat, sweater or blanket in cold weather. This is to allow for the fact that the very young child will be less active than you are. As children get older and more active they begin to want to have some say about what they should wear. Often they can predict what they need to wear better than you can. No child chooses to freeze to death. Children will almost always choose clothes warm enough for the weather. In general, parents tend to dress children at a level that seems comfortable for them, the parents, rather than for the children. Active children who spend a good deal of their outdoor time running, jumping, and climbing need less clothing than the slower moving adult.

As children get to 3 years of age or so they may begin to be able to select and put on their own clothes each day. Shortly after that they may want to go along and look at clothes in stores and make some of their own choices if you will let them do so. It is fine if you can let them make some of their own choices within limits you have set—even though some of them will look less attractive to you. They need to begin to accept responsibility for the choices they make. Often they will do well. In selecting clothes it is worth remembering that short sleeves can be worn all year with other things over them, and therefore they are probably more useful in the long run than long-sleeved clothing which is too warm for summer.

Shoes are worn for two reasons—protection and warmth. They are not really needed for arch or foot support unless your child has a special foot or leg problem for which your doctor prescribes a special kind of shoe. Shoes don't have to be expensive but they should fit well and be shaped like the child's foot, broad and quite square across the toes and with relatively flat soles. High heels are not good for young children. Parents used to feel their children needed high shoes but they really don't add any extra support and are neither helpful nor needed. Modern sneakers are actually quite fine for everyday wear and play. It is also acceptable for children to go around barefoot if the floors or ground is free of splinters or broken glass. Running around in stocking feet is likely to be dangerous because they are too slippery on most surfaces.

Unless the child is to be outside in very cold weather or for long periods of time, hats are unnecessary. Hats do help keep the body warm, but it is not true that hats protect against colds, earaches, or anything else. Hoods on coats or sweaters are easier for children than hats. But when needed, soft knitted caps are best because they are easily pulled on and kept on.

DISCIPLINE

There is probably more misunderstanding and disagreement about this subject than almost any other in the care of children. As we stated in Chapter 2, the word "discipline" means teaching or training, but a lot of people think of it as meaning punishment. One reason for the confusion is the belief, inherited from less informed times, that children are born with badness in them that has to be driven out. Nowadays, we know that children are born neither good nor bad. How they turn out depends on the strengths and weaknesses they inherit and how they get along with us and we with them.

The goal of discipline is to help children gain self-control, learn to respect the rights of others, and learn the rules by which the adult world operates. The best way to help children to achieve these goals is to set them a good example and reward them for doing the right things. Young children have a powerful need to have their parents like them and approve of them. They will try very hard to do the right things if they know what those are.

Young children need and want only simple rewards—your attention, your approval, your smile and some kind words. They do not want material rewards like toys or candy. They want you to like them so that they can feel good about themselves. As children get older their parents' approval is still the most important reward they can have. However, they do get old enough eventually to recognize that the world values material things and they may then begin to include some requests for tangible rewards when the subject comes up.

A major part of the disciplinary process is talking about it. Parents and children have a great deal to talk about in relation to discipline even when the children are so young that the parents have to do most of the talking. First of all, parents have to explain to children what is expected of them in terms of behavior and what limits the parents will tolerate. This is crucial. Children do not automatically know what is right or wrong. Conscience is not built in, it is developed. So you have to tell your children in each kind of activity and in each kind of setting what they may and may not do. Not only that, you have to tell it to them over and over again.

Children don't learn rules the first time they hear them any more than they learn anything else the first time. Every parent knows how many times you have to say "nose" to children before they finally learn to point to their noses and then, finally, actually repeat the word themselves. But those same parents will take those same children and say "no" to them once about something and expect that the child has learned the lesson and will remember it forever. Those parents will get angry and even punish the child the second or third time.

Parents also need to tell children their feelings about the children's behavior. Even when they are still too young to understand the meaning of the words being spoken, children understand a great deal from the tone of voice in which they are spoken and from the facial expressions which accompany them. Therefore, telling the child how you feel about some behavior is an important way of indicating approval or disapproval. This is so simple it probably seems perfectly obvious to you, but it is amazing how many parents seem to feel that the only way of communicating with young children is through physical, rather than verbal, means—hitting rather than talking. Clearly, as children get older it is possible to tell them a lot more about your feelings and to indicate more shades of approval and disapproval. As the meaning of words becomes understandable to children you can tell them more specifically what part of their behavior was good or not-so-good, that the action was all right but the spirit in which it was done was wrong, and so forth. Many different aspects of behavior can be talked about if you are willing to take the time to do so.

Finally, children get old enough to assume some responsibility for planning their own actions and helping set their own limits. At that point parents face the very hard job of beginning to share with the children decisions such as what will be considered acceptable behavior, what limits will be tolerated, and what sort of discipline will be brought about if the child fails to live up to the agreed upon behavior or limits. Parents who have begun early to discuss these things with their children, as suggested above, are not surprised to find that children of 5 or 6 are quite capable of helping set their own limits and quite willing to face the consequences if they goof.

This must seem like a great deal of talking, particularly if you are not naturally a very talkative person. But the need to talk things out means you have to do some thinking as well, and that can be very helpful. For instance, if you are going to have to tell children in advance what things are all right for them to do and what things are not all right, then you have to think out in advance what you are going to say. That means you will decide about those actions and limits at a time when you are being calm and reasonable instead of at a time when you are angry, or upset, or have a headache. It means you can think about and set those limits at a time when you like your children instead of wishing they had never been born. It means you are more likely to make sense to both yourself and the children.

Rules and threats parents make when they are angry usually prove very hard for either the parents or the children to live with. Parents tend to shoot from the hip and say things like: "Just for that you can't go out and play for a month"; or "Do that again and I will spank you within an inch of your life"; or "That does it. I'm never going to talk to you again." As soon as things like that are said both parents and children know they don't make sense. Children are often confused and parents are sorry they said them. And the whole process ends up doing nothing to improve or change the child's behavior. All of this can be avoided by thinking things out in advance and discussing them in advance.

None of this means that parents can't ever get angry. Even the best parents get angry at times and say and do hasty things at those times. Children can often be irritating, and they sometimes seem to be provoking their parents deliberately. Such behavior would try the patience of a saint. But it is best if the parent's anger can be aimed at the particular act or behavior of the moment rather than at the child as a whole. That will make it clearer to the child, especially the young one, exactly what it is that has made the parents angry and disapproving.

It is also much better if the anger is expressed in words rather than by hitting. Although parents may occasionally feel like hitting their children they must realize that spanking is not a good way of helping children to learn what is right and wrong. It is seldom the right punishment for the crime. It may relieve the parent's anger, but it doesn't really tell the child what the actual complaint is. When parents hit children at a time when they are out of control and don't know their own strength, or when they hit the child somewhere other than on the hand or bottom, then they are in danger of inflicting real harm on the child. Besides, an important way of helping children learn is to set an example for them. Acting out of control is no way for parents to help children learn to control themselves. What is really needed at such times is a cooling off period. Sending children to their rooms until they can come out and discuss matters reasonably may be a good way of doing this. Sometimes the parent, too, needs to withdraw to a quiet place and think things over before acting.

We need to talk more about hitting children, because it is a serious problem in our country. A lot of people still think it is the only way to deal with children's problems—spare the rod and spoil the child. But a lot of other people are equally sure that hitting is the cause of a lot of problems, of both children and adults. Child abuse, the doing of serious, often permanent, violent damage to children by their parents or other care-givers is being increasingly recognized as a major concern. The problem is that much of the damage is done by parents who get in a terrible rage and convince themselves that all they are doing is helping to discipline their children to make them better children. Deliberately whaling the tar out of children, hitting them with straps, beating them until they bleed or bruise, burning them with stoves or cigarettes, tying them up, closing them in dark rooms or closets, or starving them are *not* ways of making children better people.

Parents who get violent with their children were often themselves beaten as children. Many of the adults who carry out violent crimes were abused as children. It is imperative, then, if we hope to cut down on the amount of violence in future generations, that we reduce the amount of physical punishment inflicted on children now. In fact, if we were to make a rule about it, it would be safer and better *never* to hit children at all, rather than take the chance of hitting them too much.

There is another good reason for parents to remain cool about discipline. The less often you really get hot and bothered, the more impression it will make when you do. The main reason for discipline in the second and third years is to safeguard the child against accident or harm. It is precisely at moments of danger that you want to be heard and obeyed promptly. If you have been fairly reasonable and calm most of the time, your yell of distress at the moment of danger is most likely to be heard loud and clear and obeyed.

One word of warning is worthwhile here. The limits and rules set at a calm time when parents are feeling well, may seem far too liberal on a day when parents are busy, overtired, or sick. Remember, children cannot be expected to know all by themselves that such a day is happening. If, therefore, you are going to change the rules on a given day it is a good idea to come right out and say so. You can point out that normally it is all right to do *this* much, but today, because of whatever reason, it is only all right to do *that* much. Children, except the very youngest, will be able to understand and go along with this kind of change from time to time provided it doesn't happen too often. They will even feel good about trying to be especially well behaved to help their parents out.

Sometimes, though, parents change the rules every time other adults are around, and only because of that. These parents are unsure of the way they handle their children and are afraid of being embarrassed by their children's behavior or criticized for it. That kind of change will not make much sense to children and will be hard for parents to explain, even to themselves. It is better for parents who feel that way to remove themselves and the child from such a situation rather than to deal with it by being unexpectedly harsh with the child at such times.

Often children act up because that is the only way they can get attention from their parents. Children who never get attention from their parents when things are going well will look for some way to get it. They quickly learn that getting in trouble wins them attention, even though the attention is punishment. These children come to prefer punishment to being ignored. They will be in hot water a lot of the time because that is the only way they can stir up some interaction between themselves and their parents. Other children, whose parents normally do pay attention to them, may act up at times or days when the parents are preoccupied with other things and are paying less than normal attention. The message ought to be clear. The more time and attention you can spend on your child when things are going well, the less time you are likely to have to spend responding to things going badly. Being ignored by the parents is the worst punishment any child can imagine.

In discussing the needs of children at such length we cannot ignore the fact that parents have needs and rights, too. It is important to both parents and children that those needs and rights be asserted. The easiest way for children to learn to respect the rights of others is by learning to respect those of their parents. Parents' rights to quiet, to privacy, to set rules and limits, and to do their own work should be set forth just as definitely as are other limits about the child's behavior. As children get older they can learn to help clean up their own belongings and to conform to patterns of neatness, eating, sleeping, and the like in which the whole family or household are involved. Children can and will learn that individuals have quirks and that all of us have to learn somewhat to conform to each other. In the same way they will also learn to become more comfortable about expressing their own likes and dislikes.

Temper Tantrums. These are events which parents have great difficulty handling because they are panicked by them. The tantrum usually begins with the child wanting something and not getting it. In order to influence the situation he starts to cry deliberately and gradually works up into uncontrolled crying, screaming, kicking, hitting, and falling to the floor. At this point the tantrum, which was started on purpose, has gotten out of the child's control. He then becomes quite frightened about what is happening and things get further out of control. By this time the child is totally beyond reach of talking or other reasonable communication. The best solution for parents is to wait calmly for the tantrum to subside if they can. Often the presence of the parent is important to help the child calm down. Isolating or punishing the child during the tantrum is not helpful.

What parents seem to fear most is that if they don't step in and actively stop the tantrum immediately, the out-of-control child will grow up to be an out-of-control adult. What parents need to understand is that all children have temper tantrums at some time or other. An occasional tantrum, particularly in a young child, is not the sign of a life-long pattern. Actually, trying to order the child to stop immediately or starting punishment may be the worst approach. If parents act frightened by the tantrum, if they punish the tantrum, or if they give in to it they reinforce the child's tendency to repeat the performance. As noted above, the best thing parents can do is to stay calm, wait for the tantrum to subside, and then deal, not with the tantrum, but with the original issue on its merits.

Punishment. Rewarding children for good behavior teaches them more than does punishing them for bad behavior. But sometimes the child's behavior requires correction and just a frown hasn't been enough. Some more impressive kind of punishment is needed. What should you do?

There is no one punishment you can use all the time. Quite the opposite. Punishment should be specific; it should always help children remember exactly what action they are being punished for. That is, of course, another reason why hitting is not a good punishment—it is always the same for any offense and is specific for none. A complete list of possible punishments would not fit in this book but some examples may give you an idea.

Example: A child who has been warned not to ride a bicycle in the street does so anyhow.
Punishment: Child is not allowed to ride bicycle at all for a full day or longer.

Example: A child who has been asked to clean up toys scattered all over has not done so.
Punishment: Child is not allowed to play with any toys or to go outside to play until job is done.

Example: A child who has been asked to quiet down or stop shouting has become even louder and more rambunctious.
Punishment: Child is sent to some other room, preferably his or her own, and told not to come back until quiet can be maintained.

These are merely examples, and they may not even be the ones you would use for those specific situations. Nevertheless they do give some ideas of the kinds of punishments which parents can use to help children learn about good behavior. Many times, with older children, the punishment for a specific offense can be discussed with the child either before or after it happens. This may seem like discussing the sentence with the criminal. But it has the advantage, with children, of letting them understand exactly what part of the behavior is upsetting the parents.

TOILET TRAINING

Toilet training is a learning process, not a disciplinary process. It should not become a struggle between the parents and child as to which of them will control what the child will do. Such a struggle doesn't make much sense because it is clear that neither side wins. Parents lose because only the children, themselves, can control their own going to the bathroom. But the children lose too, because the fighting about training often leads to serious difficulties with the parents which may permanently affect behavior.

The purpose of toilet training is to help the child get control over certain body functions in a way that is comfortable for, and makes sense to, the child. The age at which a child becomes ready for such training is highly individual. NOBODY can give you a specific month or other time to tell you exactly when your child will be ready. You must, instead, look for certain landmarks which will tell you your child has developed the basic skills necessary to accomplish the more complicated skill of controlling bowel and bladder function.

There are three important areas to watch for:

Muscle Control. There are special muscles, like small valves, which control the opening and closing of the outlets of the bladder and bowel. Children must be able to work those muscles deliberately when they want to. They also must be able to squeeze with the larger muscles of the abdomen at the same time. This is a level of control which no child has until well into the second year of life. It is acquired a short time after children begin to walk alone. Once children have been walking well for several months they will almost certainly have the muscle control needed for toilet training.

Communication. Children have to be able to tell you in some way or other that they want to go to the bathroom at that time. They cannot undress themselves or get up on a toilet alone, so they must be able to ask your help when they need it. If they cannot yet talk clearly or well they must at least be able to tell you with gestures or in some other manner.

Desire. The child must want to become trained. Getting rid of messy diapers seems very desirable to parents, but not necessarily to toddlers. But the natural desire of young children to please their parents can be a powerful help in the training process. Another help is the desire of children to imitate slightly older brothers and sisters or other children who are already trained. In using these aids it is important to remember that children must want to be trained for their own reasons and their own benefit, not only to please you.

In short, in order to be ready for toilet training children must have the proper muscle control, must be able to tell you when they have to go, and must want to do both of these things. Often parents want to start training long before the child has reached this state of readiness. Starting too early is a waste of time. It asks children to do things they are incapable of doing. Some parents are clever enough to train themselves to catch the child at just the right moment, but their luck doesn't usually last too long. Then the whole process has to be repeated, anyhow, when the child is old enough.

What kind of training seat you use will depend on personal preference. Some parents prefer a potty chair which sits on the floor, others prefer a seat which fits on top of the regular toilet. The potty is convenient because the child can sit on it without assistance and will not be afraid of falling. However, it must be emptied and cleaned after each use. The toilet-top seat is more convenient but the child must be helped on to it. If such a seat is used, parents should be sure to choose one which has arms and a back rest so that the child will feel secure and comfortable, and a foot rest so that the child will have something to push against.

Parents should explain to the child, in terms he can understand, exactly what the equipment is for and what it is expected he will eventually do with it. The parents should express confidence at the child's capability for such accomplishment and point out that they, the parents, are there merely to help, not to force. If parents never did anything at all, most children would eventually train themselves without any effort on the parents' part.

The child at 2½ or 3 will begin to become uncomfortable when soiled or wet, will want to be changed promptly and will also want to begin wearing underwear like older children, instead of diapers like babies. For parents who can wait until then, this becomes another potent force in helping the child become trained. Even then, parents should limit their role to pointing out that if the child used the toilet regularly diapers would not be necessary, and the child would not experience the discomforts of wetness or soiling.

Parents who cannot wait can try to begin putting the child on the seat at times when they think he is most likely to perform. The key times will vary from child to child, but often include the periods right after meals, before or after naps, bedtimes, and so forth. It is a good idea to watch the child for a while to see if a pattern can be detected as to when the child is most likely to wet or have a bowel movement. There may be a number of such times, but it is better if you can pick just 2 to 4 of them that are most convenient for you and the child. As with other things, too much trying can give worse results.

A great deal of patience and self-control are necessary for this training. Children are not likely to perform the first time they are put on the toilet. Any such happening is probably an accident and not likely to happen again for weeks or months on a regular basis. Therefore parents should decide on some reasonable time limit for keeping children on the seat—1 to 5 minutes is probably the range—and should remove them even sooner if they show discomfort. Parents should never insist that children remain on the toilet until they have done something.

Children trained in the proper way at the proper time will seldom backslide. However, any child may occasionally soil or wet slightly, especially at a time of great excitement or when he is too involved in playing to get to the bathroom. In addition, serious stress in the child's life—physical as in an accident or illness, or emotional as in loss or separation—may cause even the strongest child to relapse. If these lapses persist then parents should seek help from their doctor.

Children who are trained in the daytime are equally ready to be trained at night. There are no physical reasons why children who are dry in the day should wet their beds, and it may be mainly the parents' different attitudes toward the two times of day that makes the difference. Parents who become convinced that this is true will then be able to make clear to their children that the child has just as good control at night, asleep, as during the day, awake. Most children will respond by staying dry.

Physical problems are almost never the cause of bedwetting. Prolonged bedwetting is almost always a sign of psychological immaturity, and it should be handled as such by both parents and doctors. Children as young as 3 and 4 can, and probably should, learn to stay dry at night. They feel better about themselves and their development if they do so. If children continue to wet much beyond that age parents should seek some advice about the problem.

Note of Caution. One thing parents should not do to the child at any age is manipulate the rectum. Times have changed. Equipment such as enemas, suppositories, even rectal thermometers, should never be used at all unless a physician has ordered them—and then only for the shortest possible period of time. If children cannot, or will not, have bowel movements on their own, parents should seek help from their doctor. Occasionally a physical problem may be present, but some psychological problem is far more likely to be the cause of such chronic constipation.

RELATIONSHIPS

Brothers and Sisters. Although parents are the most important part of the child's life between the ages of 1 and 6, the child's brothers and sisters are also a major influence. They live in the same house, share the same food, upbringing, and often the same toys and clothes. Thus they form a regular part of the child's world and daily life. But even more importantly they share the same parent or parents and compete with each other for a share of the parents' attention and love. Although children in a family share many things, they also differ in many ways—their place in the family, the age differences between them, their ages at the time of important events in the family's life, and so on. Describing all those possible combinations is more than a book like this one can undertake. But certain facts and principles stand out for parents to be aware of.

Because of their common interests and experiences, children in a family have the ability to unite and support each other at times of crisis, loss, or loneliness. In that way they are an important mutual resource in times of need. But parents must also understand that children will be angry with each other from time to time, will be jealous of each other, and will even fight with each other at times. Given all the strains of family life and the deep feelings family members have for each other it is inevitable that things will not always go smoothly.

Most of the time children allowed to work out their differences among themselves will do so better and with less confusion than if you try to interfere or referee. The exceptions occur when there are big age differences and the younger child gets the worst of it, or when all the other children gang up on one child. If those things happen you may need to interfere to protect life and limb, but there is usually a reason for such events and you will do well to try to find out quietly why such uneven match-ups came about. In most families where children feel good about themselves and feel they have been treated fairly by their parents, such mistreatment of one child by another rarely happens.

Which brings us to the next point. Treating your children fairly does not mean treating them all alike. All children are different from each other and need to be treated as individuals. Some children are bold and some are shy. Some are physically skilled and graceful and others are clumsy. You couldn't possibly treat all those children the same. What you can and should do is to treat them each in a way that respects their special needs and reflects their special personalities.

Children understand the differences among themselves even better than adults do. They will respect those differences if you do, and will understand the need for different treatment. What you then have to be careful of is not to let this factor make you always favor one child's needs over another's. It is true that you may not love, or even like, all your children in the same way. Almost nobody does. But that shouldn't interfere with your determination to treat them all equally well and fairly. All your children can be wanted and loved for being the unique persons they are.

Finally, you should be sure to treat your children as children, especially in this age group. Don't make some of them maids or baby nurses or assistant parents—or anything else. It is useful to both you and the children for them to begin to have regular duties and chores in the household. But as much as possible these should be reasonable in number and extent, and they should not often be of the kind that gives one child control or responsibility over another. Children don't make good parents for other children—both of them often suffer in the process. If you find that you seem to be asking one or more of your children to assume what should be your responsibilities you might do well to talk to some friend or counselor about the situation.

Parents and Children. Parents who are angry with each other often involve the children in their fights. Sometimes they try to set up a special, secret alliance with one or more of the children and try to turn them against the other parent. Such behavior on the part of parents is very confusing for children and much too painful and difficult for them to handle. This is true for children of all ages, even up to adolescence, but it is particularly difficult for the child between 3 and 6 who is trying to find her or his way toward more grown-up role models with parents of both sexes. In this age group the additional stress of parents deliberately putting each other down makes it more troublesome for children to find useful and acceptable ways of beginning to behave like adult men and women. It is important for parents not to put down their children, either, when the children attempt to act more mature and more parent-like.

Friends. If you are like most parents you probably expect your young children to be able to do more with other children than they can do. Most children aren't capable of playing well with others of the same age until they are about 3 years old. Between 3 and 4, children can begin to plan activities together and to look forward to seeing each other. They can, in short, begin to remember and talk about their friends. Even so, they often are not ready to visit friends' houses for any long play period until they are well past 4.

This doesn't mean it isn't important for children to have other children to play with. It is important. Children learn a lot from others their own age. If there are no children around the neighborhood for your children to play with, it is probably worthwhile for you to look for a day care center or nursery school where they can learn to play with other children under supervision. Before you send your children to a center or school, though, you should visit it while school is in session and make sure that it is a place in which you would want your child to spend time. The building and the kinds of equipment are important, but even more important are the people. You should pay special attention to how closely the teachers supervise the play and safety of the children, and how they seem to like the children they work with. The Checklist on page 31 in Chapter 2 offers some useful suggestions for judging a day care home or center. See also the School Readiness discussion at the end of this chapter.

It doesn't matter if your child plays with children of different ages part of the time. In fact it is probably good for older and younger children to play together now and then as long as the span between the age groups isn't too large and as long as some responsible adults are watching. Older children enjoy teaching younger ones, and the younger ones enjoy the prestige of playing with older kids. Nevertheless, it is better if more of their play time is spent with children about their own age.

It is worth remembering that although two children may play together, three children are more likely to fight among themselves. Two against one is the usual pattern, and often the same child tends to be on the short end. It is better for play groups to be arranged in larger groups which can then divide up in their own ways. Things will not always go smoothly even between children who normally get along well together. There are bad days between children just as there are between adults.

It is not a good idea to insist that young children share their things with other children. Such forced sharing only makes children feel powerless and resentful. As they get older they will learn to share more willingly, especially if they know that you expect sharing and approve of it. In the meantime, it is a good idea when you go visiting to take along with you some of the child's own toys. This makes it possible for your child to have something to play with even if the other child doesn't feel like sharing at the time. It also makes children more likely to be willing to share if the sharing goes both ways. Besides, the child who has some familiar things along is likely to feel more comfortable in an unfamiliar setting.

While your children are still young you can control which children they play with by keeping them away from children whose habits you don't like. But as they get older, especially after they go to school, you cannot control things so well and they will inevitably make a friend you wish they hadn't. The friend may be a bully or have other habits you don't want your child exposed to. You can seldom break up the friendship by criticizing the other child or the bad habits. It may be those very habits which attracted your child in the first place. Such friendships may be a way for your children to learn how to deal with these bad habits in another person, or, perhaps, in themselves. If you can stay cool but still point out to your children that these are habits you would prefer they didn't pick up, the message will usually get through successfully.

Relatives. A common minor tragedy in many families occurs when favorite relatives come to visit and the children refuse to welcome them or treat them specially. Often both you and the visitors may be hurt and upset by their refusal. But you must understand that unless relatives live with the child or are seen regularly and often, there is no way for the child to know that these are different from other strangers who come by from time to time. It is true that they will pick up some of your very strong positive feelings about the visitors (and secret negative feelings, too, if you have them) but they will not necessarily transfer those feelings to themselves. They will treat the relatives like other visitors—hanging back and watching for a while before they decide how to react. The worst thing you or the relatives can do is to try to force the children to kiss the relatives or say they love them. That kind of pressure will almost always make the children more uncomfortable and stubborn. The best thing is for everyone to hang loose and let the children find their own way to react with the relatives after a while. If the relatives can't understand this then the problem is theirs and there isn't much you can do about it except give them this to read.

Another common problem is deciding who will do the disciplining when you and the children go to visit the grandparents or other relatives. Most of the time it makes sense for the house rules to apply and you can decide with your children that some behavior may be all right in grandma's house, but not all right when they get home again. But grandparents should never undercut the authority of the parents. It is very important for grownups not to use questions of control of the children to fight out their fights with each other. As the parents you are the protectors of your children, even against the grandparents or other relatives. You also have to protect your children from the unrealistic expectations or standards that relatives may have for them. In general, if you can't work out a good arrangement with your relatives about the way your children are handled, then it is probably better to avoid visiting them too often.

SEX

In this age group the word sex refers to children's interest in bodies, particularly their own, and the feelings which arise from them. Most parents help their children learn a great deal about their own bodies with both pleasure and enthusiasm. They do so by teaching them the names, locations, and even the uses, of almost all the parts of the body—hair, eyes, ears, nose, mouth, chin, arms, fingers, chest, tummy, belly button, legs, feet, toes, and so forth. Around this teaching there is usually a lot of touching and pointing to the various parts, and obvious pleasure and excitement when the child learns a part correctly.

But very few parents do anything about teaching their children about the parts of the body we call the genital organs. If those get any attention at all they are usually lumped together in some vague and uninformative term like "middle," "privates," "personal parts," or the like, instead of the proper words like penis, testicles, vagina, labia, and so on. What are children to make of that? Just what you might expect—that there is something very different, mysterious, and bad about this part of them. They learn not to talk about it because their parents so clearly don't want to. And they learn to feel sneaky and guilty because they have already become aware in the first year that touching and rubbing their genitals gives them special pleasure and excitement.

It would be much better if parents could overcome their own lack of knowledge and their embarrassment and matter-of-factly include the genitals in their regular inventory of body parts. Then children would find those parts no more mysterious than any other and would actually pay less attention to them, rather than more. However, parents must realize that it is quite normal for all children to pay some attention to their genitals. The good feelings which arise from touching them are too good for children to ignore, just as they are for adults. The touching and rubbing are a form of masturbation, but it does not have the kind of sexual meanings and fantasies it has for adolescents and adults. It is a way for children to get some pleasure from their bodies and to relieve tension at times. Occasional masturbation in young children is not harmful to them and does not interfere in any way with normal growth or development. Sometimes, though, it may become a major, rather constant, activity and preoccupation of a child. That is only likely to happen if other things are not going well in the child's life and the masturbation becomes a substitute for other pleasures or gratifications. When that happens you should get some help from a doctor or other advisor.

Often the masturbation is not a problem for the child but is for the parents. They tend to get embarrassed and uncomfortable when their children rub or hold their genitals. They are especially likely to feel this way if the children do this in public. Parents' comfort is important. It is probably not possible to make children stop masturbating entirely—no matter what you do—and it certainly isn't advisable to try. But it is reasonable to use the subject as a way of teaching children the difference between public and private places and behaviors. Most children will easily understand that the behavior they enjoy is all right for them to engage in only in the privacy of their own rooms.

The issue of privacy is certain to arise in other areas as well. Young children are also curious about bodies other than their own, especially their parents'. Many parents are not aware that children can get excited by the sight and feel of their parents' naked bodies. As a general rule, the more eager children are to see their parents nude, the more exciting it is apt to be, and also the more upsetting. The way the parents feel about being seen also contributes to the excitement and the upset. Some parents can be quite casual about this while others are uptight about it. Usually it is better for the parents to exercise their preference for privacy—to dress and undress in their own rooms—but for them not to panic if the children happen to come in while the parents are undressed.

Some children get particularly insistent around the time of toilet training about accompanying the parent into the bathroom when the parent wants to use the toilet. There is no useful purpose to be served by this and many parents find it uncomfortable and have a right to claim their privacy. Of course, that means that parents must be willing to respect the child's right to privacy as well when it is reasonable and appropriate to do so.

When children are excited or overstimulated they behave a good deal like children who are overtired—they get irritable, have temper tantrums, have trouble settling down to sleep, and so forth. When parents see their children behaving in this way they will do well to look at the possibility of overstimulation as an underlying cause. If it seems a possibility they should make every effort to modify and limit it.

Some time during the first 6 years of life children begin to ask questions about adult sex. The first questions are most often about differences between boys and girls, grownups and children and where babies come from, but they may be about almost anything. How you answer those questions for your child will depend on the age of the child and the nature of the question. In general, it is a good idea to give as short and simple and accurate an answer as possible. For most children that kind of answer will be enough, especially if it is given openly and without embarrassment. Some children will want to know more and will ask another question which should be answered in the same way. Your children are very tuned in to your feelings, and if you seem to hesitate and dodge questions they will come back at you from different directions trying to find out what your problem is. If you are equally uncomfortable and have trouble answering at all, your children will get the message that there is something not nice but rather upsetting about sex. That is not a good feeling for them to get because it may well lead to problems in their own handling of sexuality as they get older. It is, therefore, a good idea for you to check out whether you are ready to hear and answer these questions in an informed and easy way. If you are uncomfortable with the subject and think you need help, you can turn to a doctor, nurse, or other child care expert, or to one of the many excellent books and pamphlets written especially for parents of children of varying ages.

DE-EMPHASIZING SEXUAL STEREOTYPES

Many of the differing expectations about the behavior of boys and girls are learned rather than inborn, and the way children are brought up has a lot to do with those differences.

We certainly know now that all children will do better if both their parents are involved in their care from the very beginning. Fathers can't breast feed infants but there isn't anything else they can't do. There isn't anything "unmanly" about fathers holding their babies or changing them or feeding them bottles. Nor is there anything 'unwomanly' about mothers working or getting into outdoor sports with their children. When half or more of all mothers are working and involved in many activities that once only men did, it doesn't make sense not to examine new concepts of what mothers and fathers can and should do. Parents may want to follow traditional or new parenting ideas, but it is important that they respect each other enough to agree.

It still is not clear what kinds of roles and relationships will be worked out in the future. But certainly it will be easier for the next generation to feel comfortable with the wide variety of roles each sex is capable of if today's children can be raised with less emphasis on the traditional roles assigned to boys and girls. For example, there is no good reason for offering different kinds of toys to infants and young children of different sexes. All infants like the same moving objects and then the same soft and cuddly toys. As they become toddlers all children like things they can take apart and put together—whether they are boys or girls. Given the chance they will all like bicycles, balls to throw, running, jumping, swings, books to look at, playing house, and so on. The differences in activity and capability between individuals of the same sex are certainly greater than the group differences between the sexes.

When they are tired or frightened or hurt, boys need to be held and hugged and kissed just as much as girls might need to. When there are trucks to be played with and sports to be learned, girls should be right there along with the boys. In time, when competition in sports becomes important to some, differences in speed and strength will sort out individuals and sexes both.

Each child needs to be loved and told so. Each child must be allowed to try out all the skills and activities which his or her development makes possible. In the long run the payoff for this will be respect for self and respect for others as individuals instead of biases that are based on group stereotypes.

SCHOOL READINESS

This subject usually refers to readiness for regular public school —kindergarten or first grade. There is a general belief in this country that children should begin their formal education in the period between 4½ and 6 years but not much earlier. Therefore, most states or communities have rules or regulations which require that children enter public school by a certain age—often 6 years—and prevent them from entering before a certain minimum age—4 years 8 months, 5 years, or thereabouts. However, children are as different in their readiness to go to school as they are in everything else, and none of the rules really helps you to know what is best for your child. There really aren't any simple rules or landmarks to tell you whether your child is ready to start school. Many things have been used—age, IQ, number of teeth, height and weight, drawings by the child, and so on. But no one of these things in itself will give you an answer.

Going to school is more complicated and threatening to the child than it sometimes seems to us. It involves the child's maturity in a number of areas.

- Physically the child must be healthy and strong enough to enjoy the challenge of going to school and to bear up under the increased strains and stresses involved.
- The child must be capable of separating from you and spending a number of hours each day in a place that is unfamiliar, with adults and children who are largely unknown at first.
- In most schools the child must be able to obey directions even when not watched every minute.
- The child must have a long enough attention span to be able to sit still for fairly long periods and concentrate on one thing at a time, gradually learning to enjoy the practicing and problem solving activity involved.
- The child must be able to tolerate the frustration of not getting immediate attention from the teacher or others and to wait for and take turns.
- The child must have some of the basic hand-eye skills necessary to the learning of reading and writing. These include skills such as handling a pencil, turning pages, recognizing shapes and colors, and so forth.

No single rule or test is going to be able to help you decide whether your child is really ready or not. What, then, can you do? One thing is not to push your child into school at the earliest possible age your school allows. Although a few children who are both very bright and very mature socially may be ready at the earliest possible age, many children aren't. Remember that one year of age difference in the 4-6 year age group is an enormous amount of extra living and learning time on a percentage basis. It amounts to one-fourth to one-fifth of the child's entire life. That amount of extra time between the start of one school year and the next may be just the time your child needs to get it all together—to integrate physical, psychological, and social skills to the point where entering school becomes exciting instead of frightening. On the average, girls will be more mature and therefore are more likely to be ready for school than boys of the same age.

Beyond this, many people would advise that you think about helping your child to get ready for school even before the 4-6 year period. One way is to have the child spend some time in a preschool program of some sort—a parent-child center, nursery school, or day care center. Although these programs may be different in many ways—the number of hours the child spends there is an important one—they are alike in that they provide a place where your child can learn to be with other children, in groups, under the supervision of adults other than you or your family. They provide experience for the child in learning to separate from you, to get along with the group, to wait his turn, to concentrate in the midst of confusion, and to understand and respect authority outside of the home. Usually, he will also pick up some specific skills such as drawing, recognizing pictures, colors, listening to a story, etc. That's a lot.

Children will not, however, learn all those things merely by attending just any preschool program. Helping young children take advantage of all the possibilities of such programs is a skilled job, and untrained people, even with the best motives, cannot do it. So one of the things you should look for in such a program is that it is run by a person or persons who understand the basic needs of young children and the problems which may arise, and whose program gives them the time and patience to deal with these problems. They need training in recognizing the special needs of each child and in how to arrange a program to meet those needs most effectively. This does not mean that such people must have a certain title or training, but they should have either that or a good deal of experience working with someone who has had such training.

You should certainly visit any program to which you intend to send your child. In addition to watching how the staff works with the children in general, you should be prepared to ask some specific questions about their policies. One of these is how they handle new children coming to school for the first time. Many children are likely to find the new experience overwhelming, if not frightening, and will probably need some help in separating from you. Most good centers or schools will want you to stay in school with the child for the first few times, and then to stay for shorter and shorter periods until your child seems at home and doesn't mind your leaving. Even with children who don't seem to mind at first it is probably a good idea for you to stay around for a while at the beginning just in case. This approach is better than just dumping the child in a new place with a 'sink or swim' attitude. Some children will manage in that way, more will not. But all of them will get more long term benefit from the experience if you are there to help. Be cautious of a school that forbids you that chance.

Other things to ask about are the kinds of activities the school encourages for children of different ages, how they handle fighting among children if it occurs, how they will discipline your child if that should be necessary, and so on. You will probably want to see if their answers to those questions agree with the way you want things done for your child. If not you should talk to the staff and find out their reasons for the way they do things. They may convince you that their way is better or that it is all right for your child to learn that rules at school and at home can be different. But if there are major differences between you and the people in charge of the school then you are probably better off taking your child somewhere else.

All of this assumes, of course, that you have looked at the actual building and outdoor and indoor play spaces and equipment and found them satisfactory. Though these should not be as important to you as the kind of people and program involved, they may give an indication of the values and attitudes of the school you are trying to evaluate. Those values and attitudes and the people who put them into action will always be the most important factors for you and your child.

Preschool programs by themselves probably aren't the whole answer, either. Most good programs of the kind described above will probably help you to learn things you can do at home to provide additional support for your child in acquiring good learning habits, tools, and experiences. Many people feel that that kind of home based experience ought to begin late in the first or early in the second year of life—even before your child is likely to be enrolled in such programs. The point of all this is not to turn you into a school teacher, or to have you try to teach your child actual reading, writing, or arithmetic at home. The idea, rather, is for you to make sure that your child will be ready to go to school when it is time, equipped to make the most of the learning opportunities the school offers, and convinced that you believe that school and learning are important. That is one of the most valuable things you can do for your child.

6
Special Problems

FEARS

During the first week of life babies normally have a startle reflex which makes them jump, stiffen out, and cry if they hear a loud noise, if they feel they are falling and, sometimes, for no apparent reason at all. Many parents take this to mean that their baby is a "nervous baby," although babies are never "nervous" in the way adults are. Unfortunately, when parents believe something about one of their children they tend to treat the child in such a way that what they believe to be true actually becomes true. This is especially so of behavior parents don't like or worry about. "Nervousness" is one of those behaviors. Parents worry that children who are nervous or afraid will cling to them all the time. They also worry that such children will be made fun of by other children and adults. Because of this parents are often very impatient with children when they act afraid. They tease them, refuse to listen to them or comfort them, or even punish them for being afraid. When parents do that it makes the children even more afraid. They come to feel that fears are never to be talked about, but to be suffered alone and in silence.

It is very important for you to learn to take your young child's fears seriously, even though the cause of the fear may seem silly to you and the child's reaction to it may seem out of proportion. You don't have to pretend the fear is real for you, but you should accept it as real for the child. That acceptance, accompanied by your reassurance and your own lack of fear, sets a good pattern and model for children and helps them to deal with their own fears. As they follow your model they become less dependent on you in meeting and handling new experiences.

Some infants seem to react fearfully to strange people, places, and things fairly early, but the first major source of fear common to all children comes near the end of the first year. This is the child's gradual awareness that the best loved person, usually the mother, is actually a separate individual and could possibly be lost forever. This discovery, often called 8-month anxiety, because it usually appears around that age, seems to be earthshaking for some infants. Until this time, everything in the surrounding world, including people, seems to the baby to be a firmly attached, permanent part of him. Suddenly it becomes clear that things are not firmly attached and the most important part of that outside world can disappear or be lost.

At first the reaction of most babies to this discovery is not too marked. They may look worried or startled when strangers approach, or they may even cry. They are particularly likely to do this if the strangers approach too quickly or try to pick them up or hold them right away. Sometimes the babies will seem upset and cry if they look around and do not see the favored parent immediately. A baby at this stage may be unwilling to stay with previously accepted babysitters or relatives.

As time goes on this behavior worsens and develops by a year or so into what is called *separation anxiety*. This is reflected by more marked changes in behavior. A baby who has previously been good-natured and even-tempered suddenly cries up a storm when the favored parent leaves the room or otherwise disappears from sight. A baby who has always gone to sleep easily and slept through the night suddenly refuses to go to sleep at all or wakes repeatedly during the night and cries. These are upsetting changes to parents and many of them get angry because they feel that the baby has become spoiled or "bad." But the behavior only indicates the baby's fear that the temporary loss or disappearance of the parent may become a permanent one. Instead of getting angry, parents need to understand why the baby is acting up and to show their understanding by taking sympathetic and reassuring action.

One thing parents can do is to help babies get experience with separation—first with very short periods and then with longer ones. Peek-a-boo is a good game for this. The brief covering of the baby's eyes, or the parents' brief disappearance, is short enough to prevent the full development of the fear and the baby is pleased and reassured when the reappearance occurs. The child who is older and more used to some separation may start to fret when the parent is in another room. Often the sound of the parent's voice will stop the fretting. If not, the sight of the parent briefly popping back into view will often reassure the child for some time.

But whatever you do you must realize that this type of behavior in the 10-18-month-old is based on real fears. If the parents take them seriously and handle them with patience and care they help the child overcome his fears and go on to other stages of development. Parents who do not help the child overcome separation fears at this time let themselves and the child in for long term difficulties. Such children are often fearful of new people and new situations, are unwilling to go to, or stay at, day care centers, nursery schools, or regular school, or have difficulty forming permanent relationships with people as they get older.

It is difficult for adults to see the world the way small children see it. Objects and sounds that seem perfectly obvious to us may look or sound very strange to the young child. Children may be terrified at such things as a flush toilet, a sudden movement, thunder, an animal (small or large), being locked in a room, and so on. Sometimes children aren't quite sure what they are frightened of. It is a good idea for you not to jump to conclusions about what is frightening your child. Comfort him and allow him time to talk about the fear. This is likely to bring out useful information which you and the child can deal with at a later, calmer moment.

Very young children usually react fearfully only to something going on at the time in their immediate surroundings. As they become older, though, they remember and imagine situations, places, and times which are scary and unpleasant and react to them even though they are not part of their immediate surroundings. At this time, often around age 3 or 4, children begin to become afraid of the dark, of animals they have never seen, and events that have never happened to them. At such times they are often unable to tell the difference between reality and their imagined fear. They may say things which sound to you like a whopping lie.

"A lion was going to eat me!"
"There was a man in the corner of the room and he was going to take me away."

These aren't lies and they shouldn't be treated as such. For the children those stories are real and frightening. They need sympathy and your understanding that they felt frightened by something they imagined or worried about. At 3 to 5 years thoughts often feel like happenings. Don't worry about setting the story straight right then and there. The children will do that themselves in a quieter moment.

Most children have fears at one time or another, but some children have more fears than others. The way children have been treated by the people and happenings in their lives makes a big difference. For example, some studies show that children who sleep in the same bed or the same room as their parents are more likely to have excessive fears. This is also true of children whose parents fight all the time, either with loud words or actual blows. It is especially true if the fighting seems to be about the child or the child's care. Other studies also show that children are not happy if their parents don't ever correct them or set limits for them. Such children, those who are allowed to run wild and behave any way they want, also tend to have more fears than other children.

The specific fears children develop may come from a variety of sources—from inside themselves or from real situations in the outside world. Many children develop their fears by accepting those of their parents. Fear is contagious and children are particularly sensitive to their parents' feelings. Parents who know they are afraid of certain things will do well to let other adults introduce their children to those things. For example, parents who are afraid of heights should let someone else take their children sightseeing on tall buildings or other high places.

A relatively new source of fears worth discussing is television. At a time when children are still too young to read and learn about frightening happenings or ideas through books, they are exposed to all sorts of such things on the tube. Despite repeated warnings

Special Problems

parents continue to use TV as a babysitter without paying any attention to what the child is watching. Children up to the age of 4 or 5 are often unable to tell the difference between reality and make-believe unless it is carefully explained. It is almost never explained at all on television, and children end up accepting dramatic shows as just as real as the news or what happens in their daily lives.

Sometimes adults frighten children deliberately for a number of reasons. The adults may hope to influence the child's behavior:

"If you don't eat your supper I'm going to have the doctor come and give you a shot."

The adult may hope to promote safety:

"Don't go play in the empty lot because a giant rat will eat you up."

But sometimes adults are just being cruel or mean because they don't feel well themselves. It is important to set limits for children, and it is important and necessary to warn them about hazards in their environment, but not in a way that confuses or terrifies them.

A final note. Sometimes children who are frightened don't react by crying or showing fear. Sometimes they act up and become fresh and sassy instead. Just as adults often get blustery when they are afraid, so do children. Remember—children who are acting up may not be acting bad—they may just be afraid or tense.

If all children have fears at some time, how can you tell when children are more fearful than normal? Most fears last only a short time and go away with sympathetic handling. When the fear or fears interfere with the child's ability to do ordinary, daily activities, or when they interfere with the child's normal course of development, then the time has come to do something more definite than already suggested. Hitting children is no more a treatment for fear than it is for anything else. Sometimes it may be advisable to help children avoid whatever it is that is frightening them, and to reassure them quickly and constantly when they can't avoid it. If this doesn't work you should look for advice from your doctor or some other person who knows about young children.

Some things that happen are so upsetting they could cause fears in any child. Separation situations continue to be especially difficult, particularly when the separation is sudden and unexpected or when it lasts for very long. The situations which follow are all special kinds of separation situations needing careful attention.

SEPARATIONS

Moving. Moving to a new home, especially if it is any distance from the old one, is an upsetting experience for young children. They tend to like to do the same things in the same way day after day, and losing the old familiar surroundings is not a pleasant experience for them. They have difficulty remembering the old home in any but fragmentary ways—little bits and pieces—and this, too, can be frightening for them. The new home, even if nicer than the old, is not likely to look that way to the young child at first. There are some things parents can do to help reduce the upset and confusion:

• Take the children to see the new place often if you can arrange it before you move. This will help introduce it into their lives more comfortably.

• Don't move during the school year. Leaving old friends and the familiar school is hard. Moving into a new schoolroom at a time when the class has been together for a while and everybody knows everybody but you is even harder.

• Let the children help with the move. Let them pack some of their own things—or even better carry their favorite things themselves from the old house to the new. Let them have some part, but don't try to make them sit through the whole process. Moving is an exhausting experience even for adults.

• Try to make the child's new room as much like the old one as possible—particularly the bed in relation to the window or door so that shadows will be the same—even if it isn't the best arrangement for the new room. The child will be reassured by the familiar relationship among things and once you have all settled down you can slowly rearrange them if it seems necessary.

• Remember that neither you nor the child knows where all the dangers are at first. So be extra careful and watchful for a while after you move.

The pressures around moving time are among the things that may make children go back for a while to acting like younger children. Don't get upset. They will catch up again once they get used to the new place.

Vacations. When you take a vacation away from your young children it causes a separation that they don't understand. If you stay away for a day or two they will be unhappy. If you stay away longer they will be hurt. If you stay away long enough, or they are young enough, or both, the hurt may be permanent. Children cannot understand why you should want to be away from them, inasmuch as they don't want to be away from you. Very young children also have no sense of time and no way of knowing when you will return or if you will ever return.

The situation can be made a little easier while you are gone by having the children stay in their own home with someone else they know well and like—a favorite grandparent, for instance. But even that will not relieve all the problem, and you should be prepared for some upset when you return. Even though it is clumsy it is better if you can take vacations *with* your children when they are still young. Instead of trying to travel with them you will do better to find someplace to go and stay for the period of the vacation. If you are going away without them it is important for you to work out short periods of separation first—a few hours, then, perhaps, overnight once or twice before you actually go. This will help the children realize that you can and will come back.

Hospitalization of a Parent. This may also upset children. If the admission is a planned one so that you have some warning about going, you will find that the children will do better if you can try to do some of the same training for separation as that described above. If you are going to be hospitalized for any length of time it will be better for the children if they can be brought to see you occasionally.

Divorce. The process of divorce is a difficult one for adults but it is even worse for the children involved. This does not mean that it necessarily makes sense for parents to try to stay together 'for the sake of the children.' When parents really want to be separated the tension involved in their staying together may have a worse effect on the children than their separation will have. But, in any case, it is very important for families involved in divorce to try to understand just what it means to the children.

Children never come through the divorce process unharmed.

How badly they are affected depends to a great extent on how the parents themselves manage their relationship with each other and with the children. The more anger and hate involved, the worse it is likely to be for the children. The less the parents talk to the children about their feelings and about what is going on the worse it is for the children. The most common mistake is for parents to assume that the children can't understand what is happening or even that anything is wrong. Actually, that is often not what parents really believe but what they choose to believe because they are having enough trouble facing their own feelings. Facing what they are doing to their children is too uncomfortable for most parents. Children are, of course, extremely sensitive to their parents' feelings and always know when tensions are high. They often don't say anything because they are afraid that if they do they will make matters worse. They are often right.

Children in the younger age group are quite likely, at least in their fantasies, to feel guilty and responsible for the divorce taking place. This is particularly true if the care of the child or children is one of the areas over which parents have disagreed in the past. Children in this period of their lives still tend to feel that their world revolves around them and that they are in some way responsible if their world falls apart. This feeling has to be dealt with by parents leveling with the children as to why they, the adults, couldn't get along and live together any more.

This is one area in which parents really have to work together if at all possible. Even though parents cannot agree about anything else in the divorce, they will salvage a great deal if they can agree on what to tell the children, and when and how to provide for their future custody and relationships with each of the parents. This is very hard to do because when parents are angry at each other they often tend to use the children as weapons against each other without meaning to and without being aware they are doing it. Because of this, it is useful for the parents to get the help of a trained third person in working out the arrangements for the children. Generally it is desirable for children to stay with one of the parents and to be helped to maintain a good relationship with the absent parent through regular and sensible visiting plans.

Death of a Parent. Death, of course, is the ultimate separation. Parents go away and don't ever come back. Children begin to understand the finality of death about 4 or 5 but even before that age it is important for adults to be honest with children and not try to sugar coat death with terms like 'going on a long trip' or 'going to sleep.' Both these terms just make the child's other fears even worse—that going to sleep or on a trip does cause permanent loss of the people you love.

Whichever parent dies, the other parent is bound to be caught up in his or her own grief and feelings of loss. This may make it very hard for them to respond to what the children are feeling and to be able to help them. When the adults themselves are having trouble accepting the finality of death it is very difficult for them to talk to children about it. Nevertheless it is fairer and easier for children in the long run if adults can do this.

Often children, especially young children, will not show much outward grief or sense of loss when a parent dies. They have a different timetable for mourning than the adults do, and they have a different way of showing their mourning. They have trouble understanding the permanence of the loss—every loss is a problem to them—and it is only after a time that they fully realize what has happened. In the meantime many adults accept the child's apparent unconcern as an evidence of lack of feeling or caring. Nothing could be further from the truth. Children always care deeply and will suffer greatly from the loss of a parent. But children who cry so easily at small things seldom do so at the major catastrophes in their lives. Those take so long to sink in that the children find other ways of showing their reactions at a later time. If the adults in the family cannot talk easily to the children about the death it may be helpful to ask for some help from some professional who knows the family well. Doctors, ministers, or others can all be useful at such a time.

Hospitalization of the Child. The best advice on this subject is not to hospitalize young children at all if you can help it. It is terrifying for young children to be in the hospital. They view it as abandonment and as punishment for things they may have done or thought and are afraid of the strange and painful happenings as well as the separation. However, it is sometimes necessary that children be hospitalized. When this is inevitable you should be sure that you can be there too. You should allow your child to be hospitalized only where they will let you stay with him. Some hospitals will actually provide you with a cot to sleep on in the child's room or down the hall. Others will offer a reclining chair to sleep in and some will offer nothing at all. Nevertheless, given what we now know about the effects of hospitalization on young children there is seldom a reasonable excuse for any hospital to refuse to let parents stay.

This can be a difficult and painful experience for you, too. When the child needs holding you will not always be able to do so because of equipment in the way or because of the needs of the child's treatment. You will not be able to protect him from painful experiences like shots or blood-drawing or pain after surgery. But you will be there to talk to the child, to let him know you haven't deserted him, and to help reassure him that things will get better and that the day to go home will come. Don't worry or be embarrassed if your child cries with painful procedures or even just from fright. Anybody with any sense would be afraid of most of the things that happen in hospitals. Your child is just being open in admitting it. It will also mean fewer problems for the future if your child can let feelings show at the time. Most studies show that the children who are too afraid to cry, who accept everything without expression, are the ones most likely to have long term psychological problems from being in the hospital.

FIGHTING

Young children, in the first few years of life, rarely fight. But some children, as they get older, will react to frustration by fighting, hitting other children or adults, provoking fights by teasing and calling names, or by using bad language. This is the way some children show or express their feelings. Whether they continue to use this as a way of settling problems or taking out their disappointments depends very much on how the parents handle it. Obviously, hitting children is not a good way to set an example to stop them from hitting others. Instead it is most important for you to set firm limits and indicate your disapproval of that sort of behavior without getting violent about it yourself. Children's behavior most often reflects what they see going on in their homes. Usually when children can't control their tendency to fight it is because something at home is going badly. Parents whose child is always fighting will do well to look at the way in which they are treating the child and each other.

Children do imitate each other's behavior and some children learn bad habits from other children. But they imitate their parents even more. If they hear shouting and see fighting at home they will tend to do the same things in their play and other activities. The child who is always fighting and bullying others is in trouble. Such children are usually feared and disliked by other children and adults. They find themselves more and more left out by other children, which makes them angrier and even readier to fight. Children have to learn other ways of dealing with difficult situations. Parents have to help them by setting a useful example.

The child who is always a victim—always being bullied or picked on by other children—is probably also repeating behavior learned at home. These are often children whose parents are never satisfied with them and are always belittling them. In the same way the child who is always being beaten at home may learn no other way of relating to people but to be beaten by them in one way or another. Both kinds of children have a very poor opinion of themselves. They can seldom handle problems in a calm, strong way because they have no confidence in themselves. Instead they either become victims or they strike out in rage from time to time in their frustration at always being the victim. In either case they seldom get what they want. Children like this find it difficult as they grow up to do well in school, at work, in marriage, or in other important life experiences.

Parents who want to avoid having their children grow up in such a way must watch their own behavior. For parents who have always been shouters, name callers, and hitters this may be difficult to do. Some parents don't even recognize that they are that kind of person until they see their children imitating them. No matter how difficult it seems, the effort to change this pattern is worthwhile. It can help spare children a lifetime of frustration and difficulty. You can tell when you are in trouble when your child is doing something that you cannot stand and cannot stop. That is the time to get some professional help.

7
Health Care

WELL-CHILD CARE

As we said in Chapter 3, every child should have a regular and dependable source of health care, whether that be an individual doctor, a group of doctors practicing together, a clinic or some other kind of program. It is essential that you take your children there when they are well, not only when they are sick. Although children do not need checkups every month, it is important that they have them on some sort of schedule that is decided upon by your doctor and you. There are several reasons for this:
• Workers in a child health care service should be able to help you answer questions about your children's growth and development, education, and other parts of their lives as well as just about their illnesses. They can do this more easily when the children are seen regularly when they are well. You will find it easier to ask questions at such times.
• Your children need immunizations against diseases like whooping cough, diphtheria, tetanus, measles, polio, and so on. (See the Recommended Immunization Schedule in this chapter.) They can only get these immunizations when they are well. Usually

these have to be given in a series and the time between the doses is important.

• When your children are sick the doctor or nurse can do a much better job of recognizing how sick they are if they know how the children act when they are well.

• You and your children will have more confidence in the treatment prescribed for an illness by a doctor or nurse if you have known them over a period of time.

The most common illnesses in the 1 to 6 age group are infectious and contagious diseases. All these diseases are passed on from one person to another—they don't come from the weather or anything else. How often children get sick, and how seriously, depends very much on how many people with illnesses they are exposed to. Where first children live only with their parents and don't go out in crowds much or play with other children much they probably won't get sick very often. On the other hand, a child who has older brothers and sisters already in school is likely to be exposed to many more things and to get sick more often. Generally the diseases in this age group are not very serious. Those most often seen are the common cold, sore throats, ear infections, coughs and such. If treated promptly these usually run their course without complications. However, the possibility of serious complications does exist with all these diseases, and it is important for you to learn when to be concerned, when to call for advice, and when to make sure your child is seen by the doctor or nurse.

Chapters 13 and 14 offer some helpful advice for handling a variety of illnesses and accidents.

IMMUNIZATIONS

Not too many years ago, almost every summer brought parents the fear that an epidemic of poliomyelitis (known as "polio" or "infantile paralysis") would paralyze or kill their children. Throughout the year, parents dreaded attacks of measles, mumps, chickenpox, diphtheria or whooping cough which, though less likely to cause death, were still capable of making children quite sick and of causing permanent crippling or handicapping. Parents worried that children who got deep punctures might develop a fatal infection called tetanus or lockjaw. Then scientists developed, over a period of years, vaccines against most of these diseases. These vaccines, some given by shot and others by mouth, can totally prevent the development of these serious diseases.

As preventive vaccinations (called immunizations) were developed and given to children the diseases listed above almost disappeared from our country. *There is still no reason why any child in the United States should have any of those diseases ever again.* But in recent years diseases have been coming back again. Why? Because today's parents, doctors, and nurses aren't seeing to it that children get the vaccines. The parents grew up during the time when these diseases were almost gone and they don't themselves remember how serious these diseases can be; therefore they don't understand the importance of preventing them. As a result thousands of children every year are getting serious diseases with serious complications which their parents and doctors working together could have prevented. Don't let your child be one of them.

Most immunizations can and should be begun in the first year of life. (See chart) If you don't have a regular doctor to take your child to, then go to your local health department or well-baby clinic and ask them about shots for your baby. A few trips to the doctor or clinic in this period can save you and your child a lot of sickness and possible tragedy.

Recommended Immunization Schedule

At Age	Vaccine
2 months	DPT. Oral Polio
4 months	DPT. Oral Polio
6 months	DPT. (Some doctors also recommend an additional dose of oral polio.)
15 months	Measles, Rubella, Mumps
18 months	DPT. Oral Polio
4–6 years (before school)	DPT Booster, Polio Booster
14–16 years	TD (Tetanus-diphtheria toxoids, adult type)
Thereafter	Tetanus-diphtheria (TD) booster should be given every 10 years or following a dirty wound if a booster has not been given in the preceding 5 years.

GETTING HELP FOR YOUR CHILD

There are often times when your children have problems that you can't seem to handle all by yourself. This book gives a number of examples of such problems and then often suggests you call your doctor for advice. But not every doctor is equally interested in every kind of problem. There may be times when you feel that your doctor isn't paying enough attention to your worries, complaints or fears about your children. When that happens there are several things you can do. You can make it clear to your doctor that you aren't satisfied wtih the answers you have been given. Sometimes, when doctors are busy they don't realize they haven't really answered the question in a way you can understand. Telling them so may help get a better answer. If it doesn't you might ask your doctor to refer you to someone else for that problem or you might start looking on your own for another person or place where the answer might be available. Most parts of the country now have children's agencies or clinics or groups of parents or other citizens which exist just to answer the kinds of questions this book talks about and which you may find hardest to answer.

The important thing is for you not to give up if you are not comfortable with answers about your children. Whether your fears or concerns are real or imagined, your children will probably not do well until you are more comfortable. So whether it is your child or you who needs the advice you should keep trying until you get some answers that make sense to you. The reassurance that "the child will outgrow the problem" is not often good advice or even true. Children don't often outgrow their problems—only their clothes. If you think you and your child need help, keep looking until you find it.

SAFETY

Accident Prevention. Accidents are the most common cause of injury and death in young children. Children fall, get cut, are hit by automobiles, are electrocuted, are burned, drown, take poison or overdoses of medicine by mistake by the thousands every year and are injured, permanently crippled, or killed as a result. Yet almost all of these happenings can be prevented if adults in general are more careful of the kinds of dangers that are left around for children to get into, and if parents in particular are very watchful in helping their children to avoid such dangers.

Even the youngest infants may manage to roll over or wriggle off a table or other high place if left unstrapped and unwatched. But it is particularly when children begin to crawl and then to walk that parents must begin to think carefully of all the dangers around them. Sharp objects and other dangerous things should be kept entirely out of the reach of small children. Young children should not be left alone in the bathtub or allowed to go near pools, lakes, streams, or the ocean without a parent close at hand. Children 1-6 should never be left at home without a responsible adult. Electric outlets should be covered. Parents should remember to test how hot the bath water is, to keep pot handles turned in on the stove and cup handles turned in at the table, and to keep matches out of reach.

Young children should not be allowed to play or ride tricycles or bicycles on the streets alone. Children can safely be left alone only in places where you know all the dangers have been removed. Children do need the opportunity to explore and try new things, but they also need to know that their parents have made things safe for them while they are exploring and are there to protect them in one way or another.

In short, you have to take a careful and thorough look around your house and neighborhood from a child's-eye point of view to see what kinds of danger it is possible for your child to get into.

Accidents and poisonings involving children tend to happen most often at times when you are tired or preoccupied with other things. Children have a knack for sensing when you are paying less attention, and that is just when they will zip off and get into some mischief. That is why it is especially important for you to develop a regular habit of always putting dangerous things away immediately when you are finished using them—and always keeping them safely locked or guarded. If you don't do this your children are more likely to come upon serious danger at times when you aren't watching closely.

Poisoning. Most poisonings in childhood are caused by substances brought into the house by the parents or other adults. Certainly you should never leave medicines, cleaning solutions, fuel oils, paints and paint removers, chemicals, insect or animal poisons, sprays, weed killers, or any other possibly toxic materials or liquids anywhere that children might get at them. Even high places are not safe once children learn to climb, and they will often learn overnight before you are aware of it. The best rule is to keep all dangerous things under lock and key and to keep the key yourself. Even some house plants may be dangerous for children to chew or suck on. If you grow plants take the trouble to find out which kinds are poisonous.

Poison control centers are located around the country and they usually provide 24-hour information services on the contents, toxicity, and antidotes for almost all products available. It would be a good idea for you to find out whether such a service is available in your area and to keep the number posted next to your telephone with other emergency numbers.

Children may suffer either *acute* or *chronic* poisoning—which kind will depend on the exact amount and kind of the particular poison involved. Chronic poisoning builds up slowly over a period of days or weeks. Acute poisoning occurs within minutes or hours of the time the child first swallows the poison and is rapid in its course. It needs immediate attention. The most common cause of this kind of poisoning is the swallowing of large numbers of aspirin tablets—either the children's or adult type. One adult aspirin is equal to four children's and is therefore even more dangerous. Chronic poisoning is different. It results from prolonged exposure over a period of time to some poison in the environment which requires a long build-up to cause trouble. It is more common in some parts of the country than others. The most important example in our country today is *lead poisoning*, which affects mostly young children who live in the older neighborhood of our cities. Children get poisoned by lead by eating, chewing or inhaling things which have lead in them. There are many such things—auto batteries, the fumes from automobile exhausts, the ink in funny papers—but the most common of all is old paint. Before World War II almost all housepaints were made with lead as a base, so houses that were built in that period were originally painted with lead-based paint. Although the more recent coats of paint in these houses are probably free of lead, when the paint chips, the bottom layers come off with the top layers and many children eat these chips of peeling paint and plaster. They are sweet to the taste.

If children take in too much lead they begin to show various signs or symptoms of lead poisoning. They become anemic, they may be either listless or hyperactive and irritable, they lose their appetites, they have difficulty learning and, most seriously of all, they may suffer convulsions and possibly permanent brain damage. If you live in old housing and your children ever eat the peeling paint or plaster you should check with your doctor. Through a simple blood test the doctor can find out if your child has taken in too much lead. The doctor can then recommend treatment which will help get rid of much of the extra lead in the body and so prevent your child from suffering the serious consequences listed above. Also, you can get some help in understanding why your child will nibble on paint and other materials so that the habit can be overcome.

Inside the Car. Almost all parents warn children not to play in the street and to avoid running in front of cars. Actually, more children have been hurt *inside* cars, as passengers, than outside cars, as pedestrians. A lot of attention has been given in recent years to safety procedures and restraints for adults, but very little has been given to the same sort of safeguards for young children. Ordinary seat belts are not useful for infants or young children and may even cause internal damage. Also, most car seats available on the market for young children are not designed to provide protection in accidents at any speed.

Recently new equipment has begun to be designed and manufactured. There are now a dozen or more devices which will really protect children in accidents. Brand names differ, but some rules will help you pick the good ones from the not-so-good. For infants, the best seat is one in which the baby rides facing backwards. It should be held firmly in place by the car's seat belt. For toddlers and slightly older children the key points to look for are that the seat can be fastened securely by the seat belt and, in the case of tall seats, that the top can also be anchored to keep it from toppling forward. Belts or harnesses should be designed so that they do not hit young children across the stomach and cannot slide up into that area under use. Each of the major car manufacturers now has an

Health Care

adequate car seat which should be available through their dealers. However, many dealers don't know such products are available and you may have to insist that they look it up. Some department stores and some children's furniture stores now also sell well-designed car seats. It will take you some time and energy to find the right equipment and to use it once you find it, but it will be well worth the effort in terms of lives saved and serious injuries prevented.

Injuries. Some children seem to get bumped and banged and bruised and scraped more than other children, but it is a rare child who never gets any injuries at all. For short descriptions of some of the most common problems, see the alphabetized listing at the back of the book in Chapter 14.

Six to Twelve Years

8
Personality and Physical Development

Most children from age 6 to 12 are in full bloom. At this stage, your child is no longer a baby, and the rewards and demands of adult life are far away. It is a time for slow, steady growth; for your child's gradual development into a separate person who is getting to know more and more about himself and his world. As your youngster reaches these middle years of childhood, he has won the freedom of an individual who can take care of himself in many ways. He is well past one period of rapid growth—and is now preparing for the spurt that will come just before adolescence. He still has the protection of adults who generally view him with kindly consideration because, after all, he is young and tender.

As he grows from age 6 to 12, his life, and yours, won't be all love and peace. He is an eager adventurer who often finds, to his and your dismay, that he still has a lot to learn. You and your child will often have different beliefs and desires. But together you can discover how to deal with the excitement, surprises, arguments, joys, and disappointments of everyday living in your family. Being human, in this sense, is not easy at any age. But it is surely worth the struggle.

Your child is a unique individual in your unique family, and there can be no sure set of rules for raising him. But there are certain principles of child growth that apply to all youngsters. How your child grows will depend partly on the self he inherited from both sides of his family, and partly on the experiences he has had, is having, and will have, inside and outside the home. It will depend, to a very great extent on the understanding and direction that you give him. Your child also learns by imitating you. He may copy his mother's actions, his father's, or, most likely, he takes bits and pieces of both parents, adds a few fancy touches of his own, and spices the whole with dashes of brother, sister, grandmother, friend Susie, neighbor George, and other people who are special to him.

YOUR CHILD'S INDIVIDUAL STYLE

Your child's personality is made up of many forces working together to make him act as he does. They operate in their own particular pattern for each individual boy or girl.

Perhaps your child is somewhat like Sammy who is quick to see when someone else feels hurt. He is all sympathy and gentle pity. But it works the other way, too. Tender Sammy turns to bellowing boy when his own feelings run into the barbed wire of "Don't" or "No."

Is your child, perhaps, more like Alice who sulks or rejoices so quietly that it is hard to realize what she is feeling? Or like Phil, who skips along on the joyous notion that all is always fine?

Your child may be something like Alice and Sammy and Phil, but he also has his own special emotional style. All human beings share the joys and burdens of powerful emotions, which they express is different ways. These emotions are at the very core of your child's life. They give him the push to live, to grow, to learn, to save himself from danger, and they are tied to the most basic human needs. Your youngster is aware of these needs in his own special way. He learns to have his own particular feelings about them—and he learns to act upon these feelings in his own way. Like all human beings, a child's needs are for:

- Food, sleep, air, shelter, and protection from danger.
- A chance to be loved and to love.

- An opportunity to be an independent person, but able to depend on others also.
- A feeling of importance and value as an individual.
- Freedom to explore, to grow, to learn, and to create.

When your child's emotional needs are met, he is contented and cooperative. He expresses his good feelings in his own way and brings pleasure to his family. But when your child feels unimportant, perhaps because of a low grade in school, doesn't like what you are having for dinner and gets scolded for not promptly setting the table, he may be very unhappy. The way he expresses his unhappiness will be his own way, too. He may be openly angry and generally naughty. Or he might feel sick, restless, sulky, or bored.

How does your child act when he is upset? What upsets him? What pleases him? How does he show pleasure or anger? These sound like simple questions, but the answers can be complicated. As you watch and listen to your child, you may learn more about the needs and feelings that cause his actions. This will help you to guide his behavior in a way that is good for him and for others.

Physical Makeup

A child's inherited physical makeup also has quite a bit to do with how he reacts to different experiences. Your child has his own built-in abilities to feel, hear, see, smell, and taste. One youngster may find that carrots have a sickening taste; to another, carrots may be delicious. One youngster may hear the faint trill of a blackbird on the other side of a meadow; another seems to hardly notice the shattering wail of an ambulance siren. One screams with pain when he skins his knee; and another only seems mildly curious over the flow of blood.

Although your child has his unique ways of feeling, he must learn to meet his needs in a socially acceptable way.

Abilities and Limitations

As you teach your child the never-ending lessons of living, you will find that he learns some of them better than others. He may be slow in learning to pick up his toys, but he is likely to discover—and never forget—where the peanut butter is. He is apt to find bed-making a mysteriously difficult art, but conquers roller skating with astonishing skill.

Naturally, a lot depends on how much a child wants to learn a particular lesson. Wanting to learn, however, doesn't always guarantee success. A lot depends on individual abilities. Your child learned to walk and talk in his own fashion—and in his own good time.

Your child has talents all his own, but he also has some limitations. These gifts and limits are somewhat a matter of his particular stage of growth. For instance, he might learn to read at age 8 instead of age 6, perhaps because of the way the nerves and muscles of his eyes are developing. He might struggle in vain to learn to skip at age 6, but become an all-star skipper at age 7.

It is far too early to decide that your child can achieve certain skills and not others. It is always too early for you to decide what he will make of his life. With your help and that of others, he will gradually find his own way as he grows.

What he needs now is your interest and belief in him as an individual. He needs a chance to explore, to experiment, to think, to talk, to look, to listen, to work, and to play. He needs a chance to study life in all these ways without being pushed too hard to succeed. He needs to feel you will love him whether he wins or loses. He needs to know you know he can't learn everything equally well.

Your Child's Self-Image

The ways in which your child is like others and still like himself are partly a result of the picture he forms in his own mind. Your child, like others, carries around within him an image of himself, which is an important force in his personality.

Bobby pictures himself as an especially naughty little boy. He half expects to be blamed for everything that goes wrong. He knows that he is smart and strong. He feels that he can do almost anything he tries. He is the first to climb and then jump off a high fence. He will fight with any kid who dares him. He is the champion stunt artist on his bike. He is active and carefree except for the aching belief that no one really approves of him.

Ginny sees herself as a lovable 9-year-old girl who has both her good and bad points. She is proud and happy that she is a first-rate artist, yet gym throws her for a loss. Ginny thinks this is too bad, but not a disaster. She views herself as someone who gets along pretty well with almost everybody. She believes she will be a success at many things and is eager to find out more about what she can and can't do. If she fails in one thing, she knows she'll get along all right in another.

Your child's self-image may or may not be quite what he really is. He has built it up, over the years, from many experiences. These include the way you feel about him and the way you treat him; the way other people feel about him and treat him; his failures and successes.

His self-image will change as he grows. This has both its advantages and disadvantages. Since your child tends to act according to his self-image, which changes through his experiences, the job of parenthood is, indeed, an especially challenging and exciting one.

Your child needs, for the most part, to have a pleasant picture of himself. It will help to give him courage and self-respect. This self-picture also needs to be true to what your child really is, and true to what his world really is.

LEARNING TO BE INDEPENDENT

In middle childhood your youngster is like a commuter to the outside world. He travels back and forth between it and the smaller, more personal world of your family. At age 6, he makes short trips and comes home often. As he grows, his trips become longer and he checks in at the home station less often.

Your growing child has an increasingly strong urge to be independent. This is part of his long journey from being a helpless baby in your family to being the responsible parent of his own babies. He must grow from being dependent on you to being more dependent on himself, from being weak to being strong, from being frightened to being brave, from knowing little to knowing much, and being able to learn more.

You have your own confusing feelings to cope with as your child grows up. Although you are proud and happy in his growth, you probably sometimes think wistfully of your once-little child. As your youngster succeeds more and more in handling life on his own, you have to find ways of handling your life without his needing you quite so much.

Conquering Fears

As your child grows in self-confident independence, he will gradually conquer his fears. When he is 6 or 7, he is likely to have imaginary terrors. There are many reasons for this. One of them is lack of knowledge and skill. He has a lot to learn about how to handle potentially dangerous realities—such as electrical appliances, automobiles, fire hazards, and so on. There are other fears the child has that are not real, but he thinks they are, or could be. The ghost in the closet, or the bear under the bed, or the dragon in nightmares are all examples of typical fears at this age. Six- and 7-year-old children often have fears of this kind because they are overwhelmed by the feeling that they cannot be as good or strong or brave as they want to be, or perhaps as you expect them to be.

Although you can't banish his fears, your child is likely to find comfort in talking them over with you. It also helps if he learns, with your firm, calm guidance, to face some of them. Success in conquering small fears can build courage for coping with bigger ones. Girls in our society generally tend to feel that they can show their fears more than boys do, but children of both sexes will need your understanding and help with their fears.

The Urge to Explore

As your children grow toward more independence and as they gradually overcome their fears, the urge to adventure and explore also grows. This natural push is encouraged by books, television programs, school lessons, companions, and so on.

Not all adventures take place near home. Especially as your children reach 9 and 10, they will want to range farther and farther in their explorations, on bike trips, for example.

THE IMPORTANCE OF PLAY

Your school-aged child probably has a wonderful time racing around the neighborhood. He climbs, jumps, hops, skips, turns himself upside down and inside out. He wants to get places in a hurry and so he takes to scooters, wagons, bicycles, and skates. He would fly if he could. Sometimes he feels as if this were possible, for his young energy fills him with a sense of soaring power and his rapidly developing bones and muscles give him new strength and skill.

As he plays, he practices and practices. Over and over again, he mounts his bike, rides a few wobbly feet, falls with a crash, rises from the wreckage and tries again. As he practices, he builds skills that are important to him now, and for the rest of his life. He develops nerves and muscles. He learns the many games that are a passport to the world of other children. He explores his talents and comes to accept some of his weaknesses. He plays by himself and with other youngsters. He plays in his own style because he is a special person, but he plays by the hour because he is a child.

Your child has a natural urge to develop his mind as well as his body, and words are vital to him as he learns to express his ideas, feelings, and desires. Much of a child's learning, in school and at play, comes in word packages. One reason that he talks so much, tells so many (to adults) silly jokes, and revels in riddles is that he is excited over learning to use words.

Part of a child's play at this stage takes on a kind of magic ritual. He likes counting games. He likes to chant the same nonsense over and over. He likes to jump over the sidewalk cracks so as not to "break his mother's back." He enjoys counting the palings in a fence, white cars, blue trucks, and panes in the church window. Wishing on a star or a wishbone gives him a comforting sense of power.

Your child often works out bothersome feelings through his games. Feelings of fear, for instance, may be dealt with in imaginary games about ghosts and witches. Terrors of the unknown can be partly conquered when your child, in play, catches and "kills" the "wicked giant."

Children between the ages of 6 and 8 usually play quite informally. They are apt to like games without too many rules, making up their own as they go along. They may care very little about team spirit. Instead, they gather in small neighborhood clusters made up of both boys and girls. These clusters of friends are apt to change from day to day.

Around the age of 9 or 10, however, children usually play in larger, more definite groups. They prefer games that have exact rules—rules which are handed on from one children's group to another. Your youngster probably cares very little about your ways of playing baseball, for instance. His ways are the ways of his gang. He belongs to his own generation, and this is as it should be. Parents cannot relive their childhood through their children.

RULES

Six- to 12-years-olds passionately insist on "justice." "It isn't fair" is a familiar complaint in many homes. When he is quite young, your child is apt to insist that a rule is a rule is a rule. No ifs, ands, or buts about it, especially when the rule works in his favor. As he gets a bit older, he becomes somewhat less severe and can see that rules sometimes change, depending on people and events. When he gets still older, he begins to see that rules are tied to basic principles.

Six-year-old Mary is outraged when she doesn't get her regular bedtime story, and she likes the same one over and over again. It makes no difference to her that there is company for dinner and her parents are tied up taking care of their guests. "But, you said I could have a story every night and now you broke the rule," she sobs, in outrage. By age 9, the same Mary can understand that the bedtime story depends a bit on how busy or tired her parents are when the moment arrives. (It helps, too, that she can read one herself.) By the time Mary is 11, she can understand that having a time to share her interests with parents is the important thing. It no longer has to be a story or even a special visit at bedtime. She becomes willing to consider many shared experiences, such as a TV program, a game of checkers, an activity with her father, and so on.

SELF-EXPRESSION

Your child learns in many ways besides talking and listening. He is full of curiosity. This can be both a pleasure and a problem to him and to you. His curiosity leads him to take clocks, radios, and sewing machines apart; to attach a homemade parachute to the family cat and launch the poor creature from the second story window; and to spread paint, paste, pins, and scraps of paper all over the living room.

As one father said, "It isn't children that I mind so much—it's what goes with them that will be the death of me." Six- to 12-year-olds can be pretty overwhelming as their curiosity calls them from one experiment to the next. They need limits put on their boundless enthusiasm for seeing, making, and doing. But they also need opportunities for self-expression.

Curiosity can often be channeled into constructive hobbies. Your youngster probably is a devoted hobbyist. His room may bulge with the deserted loves of yesterday and the ambitious plans for today and tomorrow. The guppy-raising project now has only a cracked fish bowl as a monument to that phase. It is filled with horse chestnuts that no longer gleam, broken crayons, old playing cards, and an ancient teddy bear clearly in need of surgery. The bow and arrow that he couldn't live without, now is limp and deserted. The blocks that have been airports, apartment houses, stables, railway terminals, and the North Pole are neglected bits of wood.

But not all is ruin. On his desk is the latest passion—the new stamp album with bits of pink, green, yellow, and blue lovingly mounted in the correct places. Here is the match book collection, neatly arranged by type—birds, restaurants, hotels, and flowers.

Stay your hand. Don't clean up a thing without the help of your young hobbyist. Everything you see, including yesterday's clutter, has meaning to him. Your child has evolved out of this confusing maze. Gradually he has found out a good deal about himself—what he can do and what he can't; what interests him and what doesn't.

As you close the door to his room, maybe you notice, for the first time, the sign "Private. Keep out. This means everyone over 12 and under 9." This means his brothers and sisters, his mother and father.

Why such a strong need for privacy? Mostly because he is growing up. Your school-aged child is working hard at building up a separate sense of self.

This passion for privacy was, perhaps, only a small spark at age 6 when he was still largely dependent on you. But the spark becomes a steady flame by the time he is 9 or 10 and it provides considerable heat during the years to follow. His passion to be himself is revealed, too, by his collections and personal belongings. They help to add to a sense of "me and mine."

Your child probably insists on having a pet. One of the reasons for this demand may be that having an animal of his own adds to his sense of power as a separate individual. As your child seeks to be less of a baby who takes love and more of an individual who gives love, he reaches out to animals as objects of his affection. One 7-year-old, when offered a goldfish instead of a puppy, mourned, "But I simply have to have something I can hold on my lap and love."

Another way your child shows he is a person is through his work projects. Your school-aged youngster has the chance of his lifetime to be intensely occupied with learning and doing. He has gained the basic skills for taking care of himself and he can get along without the constant attention of his parents.

Sometimes, however, his ambitions outrun his abilities. It is good for him to have failures if he can overcome most of them and learn how to do better the next time. Or if he can learn to give up when he is trying to do something that is too hard. But too many defeats are not good for him. They may make him feel like an all-around failure. Children vary in how many stumbling blocks they can put up with, and you will have to judge for yourself how much help your child needs in meeting the problems that are sure to come his way.

SELF-CONTROL

Your growing child learns in many ways to control his feelings. He not only "hangs on to his mads" (as one child put it) better than he used to, but he also becomes more generous and cooperative. When he was tiny, he had just one thing on his mind, himself. As he gets older he grows in his ability to give, as well as take, love. He can put off getting what he wants for quite a period of time, such as waiting until his birthday for the box of paints. Sometimes he can even settle for not getting everything he wants.

Your growing child won't be self-controlled all of the time. Children vary in how much they can think of others rather than themselves. A good deal depends on their experiences, their natural ways of feeling, and their state of health. When your child doesn't feel very well or is upset about something, he is apt to act less grownup than at other times. It is natural for him to move forward and backward in the way he handles his feelings.

Your child still goes back and forth, too, in his understanding of right and wrong. As he explores the many parts of his larger world, he finds out that some people lie, cheat, and steal. He may be tempted to do likewise. He finds out there is prejudice and he wonders about this. He learns new words that have the effect of dynamite when he casually drops them at home. He learns there are many ways of thinking about God and the purposes of life. Parents are given plenty to think about as their growing child asks questions about his many new experiences.

Your standards have probably become a part of him. He can hear them inside himself even when you aren't there, and now that he is 6 or 7, you can trust him more than you could earlier. Temptation, however, sometimes speaks louder than conscience. Your child will need loving guidance and firm discipline for a number of years before he can "go it alone."

SEX

As your son and daughter grow, their interest in sex takes on a different slant. When they were younger, they probably were mostly concerned about where babies came from. Your son also grew to realize that some day he would be a man, and your daughter, a woman. But this seemed to be far in the future. Your child probably was very curious about how people looked with nothing on and went through a stage when he seemed to have no sense of modesty.

Your youngster is apt to have come a long way in controlling interests such as these. He generally keeps his clothes on, asks fewer direct questions, and seems less curious about the human body. This display of self-control may mislead you into thinking that he only has school and games on his mind.

Although these topics are very important to him, he hasn't forgotten the subject of sex. Especially as he reaches the age of 9 or 10, he and his friends may discuss it a great deal among themselves. But they also discuss the importance of keeping some of the "facts of life" from adults.

While it is good for your growing child to have some areas of privacy and independence from you concerning his sex interests, this does not mean that the subject should be a closed one between you and him. Far from it. Ideally, you will have answered his questions about sex as they came up when he was younger. By the time he is 6, you have probably given him some basic information about the physical differences between boys and girls, about how pregnancy occurs, how babies grow within a mother's body, and how, in general, they are born. If you have not already talked with him about these things, the experts agree that it is best for you to do so now.

They warn that children who do not learn about sex from their parents are likely to get many frightening and upsetting ideas from their friends, from misleading books and magazines, or from other sources. They also find that children who are free to talk about sex and matters related to it with their parents, when they are young, are far more likely to bring problems of this kind to their mothers and fathers when they are older.

Some parents hope to "protect their children from sex" by withholding information until their child reaches adolescence. Actually, this practice is apt to expose the child to dangers rather than protect him. His natural physical growth urges him to want to know about himself and his world in its many aspects, including those related to sex. Also, today's children live in a society in which sex is emphasized. They see and hear about it on every side. Much of what they see and hear gives them a false impression of excitement, glamour, and the purely physical aspects of this function.

The place of sex as one way of expressing mature love and as the basis for creating new life is a healthy point of view that you as a parent can give your child both by what you say and by what you do. As you talk with your child about marriage, pregnancy, and childbirth, you may want to add that it is wise for parents to plan the size of their families and to space the birth of their children so that each child can be properly cared for as he grows up.

It is generally recommended that both parents answer their child's questions as he asks them and that they keep their answers simple and honest. Some children fail to ask questions. There can be many reasons for this. If your child has not asked for information, you can take the lead when the moment seems ripe. For instance, your youngster may comment that he would like to have a new baby brother or sister as a Christmas present, or he might observe that a neighbor, who is expecting a baby, has become very fat. If you are alert to your child's interests, he will probably give you cues of some kind as to questions he may have.

Especially as your child reaches the age of 9 or 10, it is important to explain how boys and girls grow into adolescence. They should be prepared for these physical changes long before they occur.

These questions will come up over and over again. It takes a long time for children to understand such matters. Actually, it takes them a long time to understand many topics, but parents, finding sex-related subjects to be more difficult than some others—such as "what makes a clock run?"—are more likely to feel that the subject of sex comes up especially often.

Guiding your child toward a healthy, satisfying life as a boy or girl growing into manhood or womanhood is far more than a matter of giving sex information. It is also a matter of your child's total life as part of your family and of his larger world, first as a person, and second as a boy or as a girl. Your son learns about being a man partly by loving and copying his father and other men he knows and admires. Your daughter grows toward becoming a woman partly by being close to her mother and other women. How you, as parents, feel about each other and behave toward each other as a married pair and how you feel about and behave toward your children as boys and as girls are part of this process.

How and what to tell your child about sex can be a complicated matter. There are a number of excellent pamphlets and books on this subject. Your library, church, temple, or school may have them available for loan.

Concerns about Sex Play

Although your child probably is not quite so interested as he was earlier in playing games that include direct sex behavior and talk, interests of this sort are apt to continue. However, youngsters of this age usually are a bit more careful about what they do and where they do it. Even so, boys and girls may continue to be interested in seeing and touching each other's nude bodies. Games such as "playing doctor" and "playing father and mother" are quite common.

Many parents get upset when their children act in this way. While you have your own values about such activities, it may help you to know that most experts on child behavior believe that sex interests of this kind are natural. It is a good idea to explain to your child that our social customs require boys and girls not to show their bodies to each other and not to touch each other's sex organs. But it is generally wise to avoid making your child feel as if he had done something extremely wrong or sinful if he behaves in this way. He will probably be less interested in such activities if you let him know that his behavior is natural, but that it should be controlled.

Answering any questions he may have will probably help, too. Moreover, if your child is sure of your love and approval of him as a person, he is more likely to want to control his behavior in this matter as well as others. One more point. Children who have plenty of interesting, satisfying activities at home and in the neighborhood are generally more apt to be less fascinated with sex play.

Most boys and many girls handle their own sex organs. Although many people believe this is wrong or dangerous, most specialists in child behavior do not agree with this point of view. They find that this activity generally hurts children only when undue attention is called to it and they are made to feel guilty about it.

Children usually have less desire to get pleasure from their own bodies when they feel sure of their parents' interest and affection, when they have been able to talk about sex at home, when they have plenty of other interesting activities, and when they have a chance to make and keep friends.

Sometimes a child may become deeply upset by other problems in his life. He may express these upset feelings partly through a great deal of sex interest in words and behavior. In cases like this, it is often a good idea to talk the matter over with a child guidance expert.

PHYSICAL DEVELOPMENT

Your child's physical growth is apt to be slow but fairly steady from age 6 to age 10 or 11. Probably this slow physical growth gives him a chance to "spread himself" in interests, skills, and knowledge without being hampered by the exhausting physical changes which come with preadolescence and adolescence.

Your child will grow at his own rate, although he will follow a general pattern. How much and how fast he grows depends on his inheritance, nutrition, and physical and emotional health. Girls generally are 6 months to several years ahead of boys in their physical development. If your child is healthy and making progress, it probably doesn't make much difference whether he is a fast, slow, or average grower.

Health is not determined by size. Some youngsters are naturally tall and slender, some short and chubby, and others square and muscular. Since each child has his own natural body build, it is important to consider your child's size in terms of his natural physical style. Your doctor can tell you whether he is growing as he should, especially if he has records of your youngster's height and weight gain over a period of years.

Your 6- to 12-year-old child still has fairly soft bones and a flexible skeletal system. This is one reason that he can practically tie himself into knots. Because his bones are growing, they can be misshapen by shoes and socks that do not fit correctly, by poor mattresses, and bedding that is too heavy.

Your child's muscles are also growing at this time. He grows in his ability to move more quickly and accurately. After the age of 6 or so, he can more readily move one part of his body at a time without throwing his whole self into the act. He also becomes stronger and can go for longer periods without rest. Good food, enough sleep, and plenty of exercise will help your youngster's muscular growth.

Your child's ability to see clearly and accurately will probably continue to improve until he is 7 or 8. Your 6-year-old's eye movements may be slow and it is likely that he will have trouble seeing small print. This is apt to be truer of boys than of girls. Early reading problems are sometimes related to the fact that a child's vision is not yet fully developed. These problems may disappear when he is a little older and his vision has matured.

You will want to take your child to the dentist at least twice a year in order to know whether his teeth are in good condition and whether they are growing correctly. Early correction of dental problems is important to his present and future health and appearance.

Your child will probably be in flourishing general health during these middle years of childhood. Although he still needs good physical care, he is apt to have greater resistance to illness than was true at an earlier date. Colds and common contagious diseases may come his way especially in his first few years in school. But if immunizations are kept up to date and his general health is good, these illnesses are not likely to be serious. You should check with your doctor and follow his instructions.

If your child has a physical handicap, you will want to have it attended to early in his life.

Also, vision and hearing tests should be repeated every year or so—more often if it seems that your child may have problems along this line. Many physical problems can be cured or made less burdensome if a youngster gets skilled medical care when he is young. (See Chapter 12.)

A WORD ABOUT PREADOLESCENCE

If your child is 10 or older, you may find that he has outgrown many of the childlike qualities that we have described. This may be especially true of your daughter, for girls generally grow into adolescence somewhat earlier than boys do.

Your child moves gradually into puberty: the onset of menstruation in girls and of seminal emissions (commonly called wet dreams) in boys. Before these events occur, glandular changes take place in a child's body which gradually prepare him or her for adolescence. These changes usually bring about a certain amount of strain, as well as pride and pleasure for both you and your child.

How your child reacts to this stage depends a good deal on what kind of a person he is already and on the kind of understanding you offer during these years. As your own understanding grows, it is a good idea to share much of your knowledge with your child because most boys and girls are a bit puzzled and worried by the changes in themselves at this stage in their development.

Your Daughter's Growth

On the average, girls have their first menstrual period at about age 13, but it is normal for this to occur anywhere between the ages of 10 and 16. About 3 years before this event, your daughter starts to grow faster. About a year before menstruation, she is apt to add several inches in height, develop feminine curves, and begin to grow pubic hair.

If you have not already explained menstruation to her, you will surely want to do so during her preadolescence. It is important to answer honestly any questions that she may have about her own growth and that of a boy. Her feelings about her own growth and her interest in boys are just as important as are the basic facts.

Your Son's Growth

As a boy approaches puberty, his body shape becomes more masculine, and hair begins to grow on his face and other parts of his body. The average boy reaches puberty at about age 15. Your son's growth in height is more apt to come after his maturation, rather than before. It is important to explain to him, in advance, that he will have seminal emissions (wet dreams) and that they are a natural result of the development and accumulation of sperm and seminal fluid in his body. As in the case of your daughter, your son should learn from his parents about his own growth and the growth of girls.

Understanding Your Preadolescent

As some of the changes described above take place in your child's body, he may become more moody, restless, and rebellious. His growing interest in the opposite sex and in his own appearance is a function of many changes within his body, his feelings about them, and the kind of society we live in. Most young people at this time feel unsure of themselves. They feel too old for the pleasures of childhood and too young to belong to the society of teenagers, whom they so much admire.

Your preadolescent may be something like 12-year-old Marjorie, who appeared dressed for the school dance with her slip showing. When her mother pointed this out, she responded, "Yes, I know. I did it on purpose. It gives me something to worry about that I can fix."

Your preadolescent is apt to move backward and forward between being very independent and self-confident at one moment, and astonishingly childish the next. It is likely to help if you take these rapid shifts in behavior as calmly as possible with the understanding that he will become much steadier in time. It helps, too, if you realize that he is probably trying very hard to be a mature young person, but simply can't play the part all the time. If you show that you believe in him, he is far more apt to believe in himself.

9
Family Life

Family life is like a delicate balancing act. A lot of personalities have to be considered at once, and at the same time, you have to tend to practical matters like the family budget, mealtimes, bedtimes, school- and work-times. Everyone in the family has his own needs, interests, rights, duties, and wishes. Each individual must somehow be in balance with every other one, and the total family must fit into the larger world of other families, schools, businesses, churches, and so on.

It takes many kinds of parental abilities to bring about a certain amount of family harmony. Your family gives you and your youngsters a sense of counting for something. Each of you thrives on the knowledge that who you are and what you are make a tremendous difference to others in the family.

Although your school-aged child is less a family belonger than he used to be, he still needs family life very much. Because he is young, he has less inner strength than an adult has to shield him against loneliness. If he feels that he belongs to his family, he will have a source of inner strength no matter what happens.

Belonging to his family also gives your child a chance to practice membership skills. He learns how to share, to take turns, to be loyal, and to adjust to the feelings of other people. These lessons help him when, especially in the 6-12 age group, he moves into groups outside his home.

FAMILY RELATIONSHIPS

Close personal relationships are part of the joy of family life. You and your spouse need this intimate sharing. Your sons and daughters also need the give and take of sharing feelings, experiences, and ideas with each other and with you, their parents.

Close family relationships give every family member an important outlet for his feelings. Anger drains away when you have a chance to "blow your stack" to someone who can understand and sympathize. Successes are more triumphant when they are brought home. Failures are more bearable when you know that your family still loves and believes in you.

This personal closeness is not, of course, all sympathy and understanding. Because family members care so much, they can upset, as well as soothe, one another. And because all human beings become angry when they get hurt, family life is apt to contain plenty of tears, temper, wounded silences, heated quarrels, and gloomy thoughts of revenge. Such upsets are apt to be more common for children than for parents because it takes years of living to learn self-control. And few, if any, adults ever achieve this completely.

Another reason your family is apt to be an emotional storm center is that children and parents, alike, are expected to hold in their feelings when they deal with the outer world. These feelings build up during the day and, like dammed waters, must have an outlet. If family members can pour out their feelings at home, they probably can be more calmly reasonable at school, work, and play.

Maybe you can't smooth your child's ruffled feelings, no matter how you try. Perhaps your spouse is better at calming Johnny, or more successful with Marjorie than you are. Sometimes one parent gets along especially well with one of the children and the other parent with the other youngster.

Different Personalities

Husbands and wives are likely to have different personality traits, which can help to make a well-balanced family. It can lead to disagreements as well, but difficulties are also likely to occur when each partner has the *same* strengths and weaknesses.

Children are apt to show the same differences as their parents—and add a few of their own. Thus, Bill might see eye-to-eye with his mother on most issues while Joan may side with her father.

These differences between fathers and mothers, sons and daughters can make for a strong family team. They can also make for some strong family arguments. It is easier to stand the difficult moments if you bear in mind that differences in your family are good and necessary in the long run.

It also helps to bear in mind that most personality traits have two sides, a good and a bad one, and you have to take the bad to get the good. A breezy, happy-go-lucky father might forget to pay some of the bills and he might leave the snow tires on the car until August. But, easy-going dads like this are usually good fun, rarely lose their tempers, and can often be counted on to be generous.

Different kinds of parents not only help balance family life, they also help children see that there are many ways of being a fine person.

Brothers and Sisters

The job of parenting becomes at once harder and easier when you have several youngsters in your family—harder, because each has his special personality, stage of growth, particular demands and interests; harder, too, because most brothers and sisters compete with each other at least some of the time. When you give special attention to one, the other may feel left out. "You love her more than you do me," "It's his turn to set the table, not mine," "If he's going to stay up late, I am too" are familiar words in many families.

But how about the easy part? Brothers and sisters have a lot of fun together. They also teach each other many important lessons. Older children can set good examples for the younger ones. The younger child helps his big brother or sister to feel wise, strong, and important when he looks to them for wisdom and strength. They can even teach each other lessons when they are fighting. It helps your children to learn how to argue, to defend themselves, to stand up for their own rights, and to make peace.

Peace may become quite an issue in some families. Brother-sister quarreling sometimes becomes unbearable. Some of it can be borne more easily if you realize that often your youngsters are competing for your attention. Each wants to be your adored child. Therefore, quarreling can often be cut down by showing and telling each of your youngsters how much you love him.

Then, too, your children may be fighting mostly because they are hungry, or tired, or just because living together and sharing a home often means giving up something they want for themselves. Food and rest at the right moment can help. Also, quarreling can often be reduced by encouraging your children to talk about what angers them. This, at least, gets matters out of the punching, pinching, and hitting stage.

However, talk can go too far. Angry words occasionally build up into a traffic jam of insult-trading. One way to break up the jam is to get each youngster off the "center" and set him speeding along his own road. Such as "Johnny, you go outdoors and ride your bike. Janie, you go in the living room and paint me a picture. Judy, I can see you are tired, I want you to take a nap."

Separating brothers and sisters for a while cools down heated feelings. Letting restless ones have a chance to blow off steam through exercise or creative activity drains off tensions. Putting tired youngsters to bed helps them to feel less cross. Just what directions you give each of your children depends, of course, on what you have found works for each and what is causing each to behave as he does.

If you can manage to be fair, firm, and calm as you settle family bickering, your youngsters will appreciate it. They set great store by justice. They like a sense of order and control. They want you to save them from being too free with their anger and jealousy.

To this end, some families have a system of rules, work assignments, regular treats, and so on. Some families make charts, after discussion with the children, so that each youngster knows exactly what his jobs are for each day. In this way, arguments are cut down as to "Whose turn is it?" Of course, systems can be overdone. They tend to work best when they can be changed for special reasons.

Favoritism

Even though you do your best to promote good feeling in your family, one or more of your children might accuse you of playing favorites.

It might be worth your while to think this over. Maybe, without realizing it, you do show more favor to one child than to another. You might have especially high standards for one because he is so much like you. Perhaps you understand him best, but perhaps you also get particularly cross with him when he shows traits that you have—and wish you didn't—like a hot temper, for instance, or a tendency toward shyness or carelessness. It may well be that you are more severe with this child than you really ought to be.

Or you may have a special sympathy for one of your youngsters. If you were once a middle child, for example, you may be unusually kind to your own in-between. You might, without realizing it, be paying off your own big sister and little brother of years ago by favoring your middle ones. Naturally, you don't mean to do this. If you find yourself truly favoring or overblaming one of your children more than the others, you can sometimes correct yourself by facing this fact and searching for the reasons. This doesn't always work, because none of us can hope to understand and control all of our feelings and actions. If you realize you have made a mistake like this, it might also be a good idea to tell your child and, at the same time, try to mend your ways.

PARENTS AS FAMILY LEADERS

Your 6- to 12-year-old models himself after both of his parents and looks to them for inspiration, advice, and help in self-control. You are wiser, older, and more experienced than your children, and both you and your spouse are of equal importance, although one may be a better leader in some cases than the other. When parents share leadership, families are more likely to gain a healthy balance.

Good leadership naturally requires a bit of skill. The most successful leaders know how to suggest rather than demand. When they say "no" they mean it, but they say it calmly; punishments are sure, but mild. Good leaders are reasonable and fair, taking into account the particular strengths and weaknesses of their followers, and making allowances for special circumstances. They respect the rights of each individual, give clear directions and praise for work well done, and they are willing to do the same things that they ask others to do.

As a parent and family leader, you are human. At times, you may lose your temper and say and do many unwise things. Even though you may know you are being anything but a model parent, you can be swept away by your own feelings of anger or despair. Maybe you are tired or ill, or extremely worried. Sometimes "everything is just too much." All is not lost if you lose your self-control now and then.

Your children can forgive and forget your slips, if they don't happen too often. It is very possible that your child may benefit from a few parental mistakes. Children can find it mighty discouraging to have a perfect mother or father.

Your 6- to 12-year-old child can be a real help to you on your "not-too-often" off days. He is old enough to understand some of the pressures that bother you. As times goes by, your youngster should develop enough self-control to understand and to consider your situation as well as his own.

But it is dangerous to pile too many burdens on him. Much of his self-confidence still depends on believing in your strength. He still needs you as a self-disciplined adult who can help him discipline himself.

Discipline Designed to Fit Your Child

The discussion of Discipline on pages 70–77 offers some valuable advice that is applicable to children in the 6-12-year-old age group.

If your child is a rather gentle, shy person, he might "hop to it" under the force of a harsh scolding, but he will probably go about his tasks in a half-hearted, resentful way. He will keep his unhappy feelings to himself and brood silently about how to find ways of doing what he wants without your knowing about it.

When you push a timid child around, you may push his small, inner self into a dark lonely closet of worry, shame, and fear. He will hide from you and you will know only the part of him that he dares to let you see.

On the other hand, if your child has a "firecracker" response to commands, he is likely to resist direct orders every inch of the way. No brooding silence and outward obedience from him. He is a fighter who needs a firm but gentle hand. You might be able to control him with your greater strength and size when he is young, but the time is coming when he will be as strong and as big as you are. When this happens, your small firecracker may become a cannon—and his explosions will be dangerous to you, to him, and to other people.

So, whether your child is the easily led (but secretly resentful) type, or the "won't give an inch" rebellious kind, you aren't likely to get far by criticism and commands. Although you often have good reasons to want to handle your youngsters with an "I'm right, you're wrong" approach, in the long run you will be wrong instead of right.

The question of how to discipline your child also depends on his age. Six- and seven-year-olds are still quite dependent on their parents and are likely to believe that mothers and fathers are (mostly) right.

As your child gets older, he may question your discipline more often. This is largely because he is encountering different customs outside his home, and also because he wants to prove his independence from his parents.

The whole matter of discipline can get pretty wearing at times. Some parents, discouraged by struggling with their children, are tempted to surrender to them. Other parents underplay discipline because they believe that children thrive on self-expression. And some, unsure of what they think, find it hard to take a stand and hold to it.

Despite the effort, good discipline does pay excellent returns. Children do need to express themselves but they also need to have limits on this freedom. Parents need to establish family rules together, to discuss these rules with their youngsters, and to be prepared to stand by them.

Children who are given almost complete freedom to be themselves often grow up to become, charming, creative, friendly people. But they may also become irresponsible, lazy, and self-centered. This is usually as hard on them as it is on other people, partly because they will find themselves disliked and unwanted in most groups. On the other hand, youngsters who are cramped by too many rules and too much pressure for hard work may grow up to be dull, timid, and afraid to think for themselves. Or they may rebel and "run wild."

Making Rules

It is necessary to have some rules, but having too many of them is bound to create trouble. You can hold your child to the important ones.

Children like to know the reasons for rules. They like to discuss the pros and cons and to have a part in making them. You may find that your youngster makes some excellent rules when you give him a chance to suggest them. Although you have the final say, you will find it helpful to talk over practical matters of family do's and don'ts with your youngsters.

As they get older, children grow out of some rules and into others. All kinds of daily details change with your changing child. He continues to need limits, but these need to be adjusted to his growing skills and interests.

Punishment

There will be times when your child steps off limits. This calls for some kind of action on your part. Before you punish him, however, you will want to find out why he did something wrong. Some children are disobedient through ignorance. If your child misbehaves through ignorance, you will want to explain to him where he went wrong and help him make up for his misdeed.

Children are sometimes disobedient because temptation is simply too much for them. There is, for example, the lure of the nearby creek when, in early spring, the weather seems to jump into midsummer. Of course your child shouldn't give in to this temptation, but perhaps explaining to him again, a little more firmly than last time, why he shouldn't swim in the creek ("Because you might catch a bad cold and then you won't be able to play baseball") may be just what he needs. If he persists in this misbehavior, then stronger methods of punishment may be warranted. The important thing is to discipline your child with understanding as well as with justice.

Some children are particularly naughty when they don't feel well or when they are upset about a secret fear or worry. If your generally well-behaved child suddenly "goes off the track," you might check as to the state of his health or the state of his feelings. Poor appetite, restlessness, whining, and fatigue may suggest a physical problem. In this case, perhaps he should see a doctor.

You might be able to get at inner fears or worries that can cause bad behavior by gently suggesting to your child that he talk to you about what is bothering him. Think over what may have recently changed in his life. One 6-year-old boy, for example, became very naughty after his grandmother came to live with the family. She was given his room, and he was rather hastily moved in with his sister. His behavior straightened out after he freely expressed his resentment and his parents gave him more space for his things.

Some children are upset over a change of teachers, or by moving from one neighborhood to another. If parents are sympathetic and a little easygoing for a while, the child often gets used to the changes and settles down. A youngster sometimes suffers from a sense of shame over a secret wrongdoing (such as taking money from his father's wallet). He may worry about what he has done, and his worry can lead to more misbehavior. Or feeling guilty, he might do something wrong hoping to get caught because he feels he ought to be punished.

If you can find out what is bothering your youngster and treat the cause of his naughtiness, this is likely to be better than punishment when your child misbehaves because he is troubled.

At times, though, your child misbehaves because his naturally eager desire to be doing something is hard to contain. What he wants to do may cause so much trouble that his activities have to be limited. When you do apply these limits, it is best to do so right after he misbehaves. This helps to connect, in his mind, why what he is doing is the wrong thing to do.

Here are a few other points to remember when punishment seems necessary:

• Mild punishment is better than severe. Some children can be checked by a sharp look or a few firm words. Children are angered by such extreme measures as hard spanking. It is best never to hit a child or hurt him physically. If this happens, children are apt to feel as if they have been treated unfairly and without love. Also, they can be so upset by harsh punishment that they fail to understand why they are being disciplined. Severe punishment brings with it severely upset emotions—and these get in the way of learning and thinking.

• Punishment that fits the misdeed is likely to help your child learn his lesson more clearly. For instance, Sally, who put red house paint on the steps, can be told to scrub them with turpentine.

• Punishments should be short and simple, especially when your child is young. They should be in keeping with his size and understanding as well as with his personality.

- Punishments also should be something you can manage. In the heat of your dismay over your child's behavior, you might, for instance, rule that he can't play with his best friend for a week. That week can get dreadfully long and you might want to give in before it's over.

If you say "no" to your child, it is almost always a mistake to change your mind. He learns fast that sometimes you don't really mean what you say, and so he pays no attention to your threats. Therefore, before you try to control your youngster, think again and be sure you are ready, willing, and able to follow through on what you say you will do.

- Frequent punishments lose their effect. Children seem to build up a "don't care" attitude if they are scolded over and over again. Some come to believe that they will always be in trouble with their parent and so they might just as well act as they please, take their punishment, and continue misbehaving.

A Final Note

Discipline for your child includes the fact that, by word and deed, you set standards for him. He takes your standards for his own more through love and admiration for you than through punishment. As he works, plays, and talks with you, he "soaks up" your knowledge, skills, beliefs, and interests—your standards.

If you reward good behavior as well as correct your child's mistakes, he is particularly apt to want to behave well and to remember how he should behave. Rewards don't need to take the form of presents, treats, or money. Praise, a loving word or hug, a warm "thank you" can mean more than money or gifts.

PARENTING AS A PARTNERSHIP

Fathers and mothers are apt to go about the job of parenting somewhat differently. One reason for this is that they are usually different kinds of people to begin with. Another reason is that men and women, like boys and girls, are likely to approach life differently. They might do this naturally, but they have also been taught that fathers should act in a certain way and mothers, in another.

Many couples nowadays are starting to question past assumptions about the way men and women should behave and the roles they should play in family life. Fathers are less likely to be seen only as breadwinners, and mothers only as caretakers of the household and the children. Responsibilities and expectations are increasingly based on parents' individual needs and strengths, rather than on the traditional roles that society has dictated for men and women.

Husbands and wives really need each other as partners in family leadership, and children need the companionship and guidance of both parents. A family is in for rough times if husband and wife are not comfortable with the roles they play, if they see their life together as a game which one person must win and the other must lose, or a debate in which one side is right and the other wrong. The family circle will be smoother when parents think of themselves as a pair of leaders, balancing each other with different ideas, gifts, goals, and interests.

Family Discussions

Problems can often be worked out by "talking things over." Many couples find it helpful to talk together when the children are asleep or away from home. Bothersome feelings can be relieved by discussing the annoyances, worries, and problems of the day, and such discussions can lead to a new feeling of closeness—a closeness that includes children as well as parents.

The day's troubles frequently relate directly to how each parent has acted toward the other or toward the children. A father might more easily see how a mother behaves toward the children than she can herself, and vice versa. However, husbands and wives don't always agree on what they see. In fact, they sometimes get pretty critical about each other's fathering and mothering. Talking about these problems is not so easy. Feelings often get hurt, pet ideas may be attacked, and angry words may be spoken. But often, after differences have been faced and complaints are out in the open, a couple can plan together on how to tackle a problem as a team.

Family discussion certainly doesn't have to be centered on miseries. Far from it! There are plenty of good things to talk about, including what each person has done well and how much you care for one another. Expressed pride and affection does wonders. The practice of often telling each member of your family something nice about himself, perhaps as they set off for work or school, is like clothing each of them in an invisible lifejacket. You may even collect in return a whole set of lifejackets for yourself, like David's offer to shovel the snow off the walk or Patsy's home-from-school present of a bunch of droopy dandelions.

FAMILY ACTIVITIES

Most youngsters between the ages of 6 and 12 thoroughly enjoy taking trips. An outing can be fun even if it isn't fancy or far from home.

Preplanning is likely to improve the family jaunt, and it is a good idea to discuss outings with all members of the family. Of course, this may produce a heated argument. Three-year-old Barbara wants a place to wade. Six-year-old Jack wants to explore caves. Nine-year-old Sammy would like to climb mountains. Father dreams of a fishing trip. And mother may be secretly pining for a chance to go shopping for summer sales.

Clearly, one outing will not satisfy these different goals. Perhaps wading, fishing, and caving can go into this trip, while mother and Sammy wait their turn for mountains and shopping centers.

Since everyone cannot be satisfied at once, parents have to make the final decision.

It is quite likely that you are already a veteran trip-taker. You have probably found out that family journeys need to be short and simple; that plenty of food adds the light touch to difficult moments; that even on the hottest days taking along a sweater for everyone may be indicated; that someone is bound to fall into a creek and will need a change of clothes. The trip had better be budgeted ahead of time, too. If everyone knows in advance how much money can be spent on the outing, pleas for "extras" are less frequent. Also, it is wise to remind your children of some basic rules of trip behavior before you start; such as how to behave in public, how much time the outing is likely to take, and how to be safe and still have fun.

Chances are that your child's trip behavior is apt to be better outdoors than indoors. If you don't live in or near open country, you may be lucky enough to have a good park not too far from your home.

Although careful planning helps, a 100 percent perfect family outing is just about impossible. A few minor crises are bound to occur. If your outing has some nice high points, the low ones can be overlooked—especially after you are all safely home again.

Although your 6- to 12-year-old is apt to particularly enjoy outdoor trips and they may be the easiest kind for your whole family, you wouldn't want to limit yourself to nature jaunts.

Your children will enjoy and profit from many other kinds of family expeditions; for instance, trips to such places as stores, factories, railroad stations and trains, the firehouse, banks, restaurants, the court house, and so on. Excursions like these are popular with most youngsters. And teachers find that boys and girls who have been to many kinds of places usually are better students.

Your children, quite obviously, will also benefit from trips to museums, libraries, concerts, and theaters. This is particularly true if you choose events that are especially planned for children and if you let them have a part in choosing what they want to see and do.

Seeing and doing with your children can provide you with some pleasant surprises and joyous memories. As you introduce your child to the world, keep your ears open for some delightful childish reactions. For instance, your child might think yellow autumn leaves drifting to the ground look "just like fall butterflies."

Activities at Home

Families with 6- to 12-year-olds can also have fun at home. Popular activities usually make use of your child's drive to develop new skills, to have hobbies, to make things, and to feel close to family members.

Some families read aloud together. There are books, short stories, and poems that appeal to persons of almost any age. You might also ask your librarian for suggestions. Along with the enjoyment that families can find in sharing a good book goes the extra dividend that "read to" youngsters are likely to become good readers.

Then there is family music. It isn't always much to listen to, but it usually provides great enjoyment for the performers.

Not all special events or family activities need to include everyone. It is a good idea for each child to have his special times alone with both parents, or one parent. This gives a chance for another kind of important closeness and the expression of particular interests that not everyone in the family may enjoy.

As in other areas of family life, the balanced, middle-of-the-road way is generally best, with some home-made and some professionally-made entertainment.

Television, Radio, Movies, and Comics

You may question the quality of some commercial entertainment and with good reason. Many parents worry about how some movies, comics, TV, and radio programs will affect their children.

Your own 6- to 12-year-old is apt to be an enthusiastic "looking, listening, and comic-reading addict." Interest in these activities is likely to reach a peak around the age of 10. Within three or four years, your child will probably become considerably less enchanted with these forms of entertainment, especially if he or she is getting along successfully in school.

Television is not likely to hurt a child's eyes if he sits in a somewhat, but not completely, darkened room, not too close to the screen. Nor does it necessarily interfere with school work—especially if rules are observed about finishing homework first. Younger boys and girls who look at television a great deal often have an unusually large vocabulary when they enter the first grade, but the children who spend little or no time watching TV soon catch up.

It is unclear as to whether television, radio, movies, and comics have a harmful effect on children. No study has proved that these "mass media," in themselves, cause youngsters to have adjustment problems or to become delinquent. Recent research, however, does suggest that many programs give a false and overly simple picture of life. The best protection against such false ideas is the standards a child learns from his parents. How a child reacts to these programs depends on his particular makeup, previous experience and information, and the beliefs and values that are already a part of him.

While television viewing does not in itself seem to cause a youngster to have adjustment problems or to become delinquent, it is possible that unsupervised viewing can deepen or stimulate an expression of the problems that the youngster already has. Children who feel unhappy, lonely, or angry generally tend to look at

TV more than do those who are more satisfied with themselves and their lives. The same is true of radio, movies, and the comics. It is a good idea to try to help such children discover more active and creative ways of finding relief from their feelings.

All of these forms of entertainment offer your child a quick, easy trip to adventureland, far away from the disappointments and boredom he may meet in everday life. Some escape from the real world can be helpful. Carried to extremes, however, this kind of escape can stand in the way of facing up to important problems in real life. For a child to spend all or most of his free time at the TV set may be a signal that he is seriously upset and may need help from a professional counselor.

"Horror stories" on TV or in the movies do seriously frighten many children, especially when no adult watches with them. Bad dreams and continuing fears are apt to haunt the boy or girl who watches these shows. Therefore, if your child wants to see these programs and if you think he should have this privilege, you should be part of the audience, too. You may notice that he is more likely to be upset when he watches such a program late in the evening when he is tired.

Many mothers and fathers observe that their youngsters often become restless and fussy from prolonged sitting and looking. Your growing child needs plenty of exercise. This is one reason why it's a good idea to put a limit on how much time is spent on TV and other forms of inactive recreation.

However, you are likely to find it rewarding to share some of your child's reading and watching interests. You can have the fun of observing your child's growth in understanding as he reads, looks, and listens. Moreover, you can talk with him about the ideas that are being shown and help him to see that they often give a false, too simple picture of life.

You can also help your child if he becomes confused about what he reads and sees. As you show a sympathetic interest in your child's entertainment world and as you explain parts of it to him, you will gradually raise his standards. Your standards, however, can't be forced on him. In your sincere desire to give your children "nothing but the best," you might "oversell" programs and books that are labeled "educational" or "classical."

Your youngster is apt to find many of these a bit stuffy as a regular diet, especially if such fare is chiefly for older boys and girls or adults. In general, he is likely to follow your lead if you show, by example, that the "best" programs and books have real meaning to you, and give him the opportunity to learn that they hold real enjoyment for him.

At times you may want to ban certain books, movies, and programs. You may feel strongly that your child, and other children, shouldn't see them. In these instances, you may want to join with other parents to take group action.

Some families set standards for their children's entertainment by establishing a few basic rules. Some limit the amount of time their youngsters can spend each week in looking at TV, listening to the radio, going to the movies, and reading comics. Admittedly, this takes planning, since each child has to work out a schedule with his parents. It can be done, especially through advance discussion and the use of program guides.

You may also want to make rules about whether your family dinner hour will feature TV with a side dish of food. Since your evening meal might be one of the few times when everyone is together and since it probably is the heartiest meal of the day, it is best to stress family conversation and healthy eating at this time.

Rituals and Celebrations

Good times in your family are not always built around fun and entertainment, of course. As a family, you can mark a particular religious event with a particular celebration.

Your child will gain in many ways by taking part in special ceremonies observed by your family at home, school, and church. They mark for your youngster the passage of time and a sense of family growth. They provide him with a chance to give, as well as to receive.

These events don't have to be fancy. Feelings that go with them—of joy, importance, and love—are more vital than how much money is spent on them.

School celebrations to which parents are invited also have some of these qualities. If you attend the school pageant, music night, or graduation day with your child, you show your pride and belief in his world and in his place in it.

Your child is also apt to glory in the excitement and beauty of special holidays, such as Thanksgiving and Independence Day. National holidays carry with them a sense of the importance of history. Appealing songs, readings, stories, and symbols are attached to these days. Words and visions plant themselves in your child's mind with a kind of lasting splendor. Then, too, your youngster gets a sense of belonging to something far bigger than himself by taking part in these celebrations. He gets a sense of himself as being related to long ago, now, and to the future. He is apt to absorb values such as George Washington's courage, Abraham Lincoln's honesty, and the passion of the first settlers for responsible freedom.

Religious holidays and observances also have these important values—and carry with them an even loftier and deeper idealism. For religion concerns itself with the deepest issues of life: the basic purpose of living, questions of right and wrong, the relationship of one person to all other persons, birth, growth, and death, and the nature of our universe. Religious rituals have always been used by human beings all over the world as a central part of worship, celebration, mourning, rejoicing, and as a guide to how each group member should behave.

Perhaps you feel that the meaning of special holidays is in danger of becoming lost under the modern pressure to celebrate them with expensive gifts, cards, decorations, and fancy food. Homemade decorations and mementos can increase your family's sense of a personal, deep sharing in the occasion.

Parents who want their children to be guided more by ideas and ideals than by dollar signs and material things should make a particular point of discussing the true meaning of these holidays with their youngsters. They should join with them in attending special celebrations to mark the meaning of the day or season. When parents and children share such experiences, a sense of family closeness is increased. The child's love for his parents and his sense of worship are permanently woven together.

Time Alone

Although you and your child share many activities, you don't have to do everything together. Each member of your family will probably appreciate having some time alone.

How much "aloneness" each person wants depends a bit on

what each is like as a person. Especially as your child becomes older (around 10 or 11), he is likely to claim more privacy for himself. His interest in being a separate individual generally grows stronger. He also may develop a feeling of modesty about his body.

As his desire for "separateness" grows, he normally will want a room of his own. If you can't arrange this, at least you may be able to give him a corner of a room that belongs to him. Shelves, boxes, or a chest of drawers that can hold his personal belongings are almost a "must." One 10-year-old girl, driven to desperation by her prying younger brother, like a little squirrel, dug a hole in the backyard in which to hide her special treasures.

Mother and father need privacy, too. You need a time and place to be together as a couple, separate from your children. Also, both of you will want a chance, sometimes, to be completely alone.

WORK AND MONEY
Household Duties

It is probably better for you—and your children—if they share the work as well as the fun and benefits of family life.

As you think about how much work you can and should ask your children to do, here are some things for you to consider. It is probably kindest to children, in the long run, if you require them to do a certain amount of work about the house. They learn necessary skills in this way. They get the feeling of doing their share as they develop attitudes of responsibility and self-discipline. By sharing the work, they release you from some burdens. This gives you more time and energy for good times with your family. You may want to carry out a share-the-work program. A child responds much more readily and happily to "work plans" if these include the parents working along with him. Too often, we assign lonely as well as unpleasant tasks to our children instead of really sharing.

A discussion of jobs to be done, including who, when, and where, is a good start. Holding your child to the task also improves his work. When it is well done, lavish the small producer with praise.

You will also find it useful to try to adjust home jobs to your youngster's age, personality, skills, and interests. One child might be an enthusiastic polisher, for instance, once you get him started. Another might be a whiz at cookie baking, while another takes to the washing machine with pride and skill.

Despite their special abilities, your sons and daughters are apt to prefer a variety of jobs. Who, after all, wants to be a dish drying specialist day after day? As your children get older, you can step up what you expect of them and ask them to do more and more complicated jobs. Often parents do not realize how much their youngsters can do, given enough training, challenge, and praise.

Not all jobs, of course, center in your home. As your child gets older, he may want to expand his earning and learning power. Your 11- or 12-year-old may be able to find small jobs in your neighborhood, especially if you have trained him well at home. There is work like lawn-mowing, snow-shoveling, and plant-watering for vacationing neighbors. Since he is still so young, you will want to guide, teach, and protect him in his first jobs. For his protection, you will want to know the people for whom he works.

All of these jobs require your child to be responsible and skillful. He will have to be on time and do his work well. He will have to stay with it until he finishes. He will need to plan his time and energy so he doesn't find himself scheduled for homework, a party, and a job all at the same moment. As the parent of a young worker, you are apt to find yourself busy, too, providing a bit of supervision.

If your child learns to be a responsible employee early in life, he is more likely to develop into a valued full-time employee when he is older.

Your Child and His Money

Some kind of allowance system usually works well if it is carefully planned in discussion with your child and if you and he stick to it. Just as in any kind of budgeting, you and he will need to figure out how much he must spend each week and how much income is possible. There is also the matter of how much he would like to spend. Here, again, you will doubtless have to set some limits.

Planning his own income and outgo can teach your child important lessons about money. How well he does, however, depends on many things. Just as in other areas of behavior, his money ways are related to his age, experience, kind of personality, and values. Also, of course, you will have to supply parent leadership, which includes setting a good example for your child by the way you handle money.

A Perspective on Money

Although your child needs some money of his own and some of the things that money can buy, family happiness does not depend on having a large income. Money and things will not take the place of warm, close feelings. One child complained wistfully, "My father gives me everything I ask for but I hardly ever see him. I want my dad more than my bike."

Here, again, it is a matter of balance. Our modern world offers such a tempting array of things for home and family that conscientious parents can find themselves carried away in a scramble of money-earning in order to give their children "the best in life."

Money helps, of course. But, within limits. If a family has enough to eat and wear, and a place to live, more money and more things do not add up to more real happiness. Families can stretch their money if they stretch the imagination and skill of their members. A creative approach to homemaking and plenty of do-it-yourself activities can provide a richer environment and delightful memories for both children and parents.

Real poverty, of course, hurts children and parents. But families who get along with few luxuries are not injured by this fact. Unless, of course, the parents believe that they and their children cannot be happy without them.

How you feel about money and how well you handle it is more important than how much you have.

Working Parents

Children whose parents both work may get along just as well as children who have a parent at home, if a reliable, well-trained, and kindly person is in the home to care for them while the parents are away. It is also important that all the members of the family are in favor of both parents holding a job. Couples should talk together about what they think is the best plan for their family. There are a number of psychological and practical considerations to take into account when both parents plan to work.

If you are a parent who feels forced to go to work against your better judgment, and you continue to feel angry or worried about this, it may have a bad effect on your youngsters. If you are unhappy in your job, your unhappiness can affect the way you get along with your children. On the other hand, if you enjoy your work, your sense of contentment can make home life more pleasant for everyone. Nowadays more and more mothers are taking outside employment. Experts who have studied this subject have not found any clear connection between delinquency, poor school work, or other aspects of children's adjustment and the fact that their mothers do or do not work. Women who enjoy their work, however, sometimes find themselves in the difficult position of feeling guilty about this. Neighbors and relatives, for instance, may criticize them for not staying at home "where they belong." When mothers feel guilty, this, too, can cause upsets in the children.

The question of substitute care for the children is another primary consideration for working parents. Common sense and expert opinion point to the importance of good supervision for children when they are out of school. A safe, dependable plan is necessary, such as employing a kindly, responsible adult to always be with the youngsters when parents are not at home. Such adults are not always easy to find—or pay for. If this is true in your case and you would like to work, perhaps you can get part-time employment for the hours that your children are in school.

Day care centers for children of working parents are available in some communities. Although most of the centers put their emphasis on care for preschool children, some run after-school and summer programs for older ones. (For a general idea of what to consider when judging a day care center, see the Checklist, p. 31.)

Some husbands and wives arrange their jobs so that one parent or the other is always at home. This can be a good arrangement. On the other hand, if both parents hold full-time jobs at different hours of the day or night, they may find that, as a couple, they have far too little time together.

If you have a choice, and you are thinking about whether it pays to have both parents working, you will want to think about extra costs such as those of child care, transportation, working clothes, extra taxes, possibly more expensive, quick-cooking food, and

Family Life

more automatic household equipment. Balance this against what you will earn. How does it all add up?

There is also the question of whether or not you will have enough time to enjoy your children. These younger years of childhood are, after all, few in number. When your youngsters become teenagers, they probably will be at home much less than they are now. If you don't have to work full-time now, you might find it better, from every point of view, to stay at home either full- or half-time during what is, actually, a short period of your life. Some parents, eager to be good supporters, may even work overtime day after day or take two jobs. Couples will want to think seriously about whether having more time with the family or more dollars will bring the most happiness.

10
In the Outside World

FRIENDS

Although your particular child will approach his social life in his own way, people outside his family will become more important to him as he gets older. He will probably become more deeply attached to best friends, and be more selective about them.

Your 6- to 8-year-old is most likely to select his friends from the immediate neighborhood. As his interests and acquaintanceships expand, he may choose his pals from his school or club groups—friends who live miles away from your home. You may feel concerned because you don't know their parents. If your child feels strongly about wanting to spend time with this far-away pal, it may be wise to arrange get-acquainted visits between the two families.

It is sometimes hard to realize how much these childhood friendships can mean to your child.

Fighting

It is not unusual for your child to get into quarrels with other children. Small storms frequently occur when children play. Battles are apt to be intense, wild, and brief. This is part of your child's strenuous effort to learn to live with other people without giving up too much of what he is and wants.

Six- to 12-year-olds are apt to lose their tempers easily and the younger they are, the more this is likely to be true. Temper-holding and quarrel-settling by reasonable conversation are slowly acquired arts. Your child's ability in this respect will probably grow over the years. The experience of fighting and suffering the consequences of his quarrels may teach him a bit about the virtues of self-control.

It helps to accept occasional blowups as part of childish social life. If you take these blowups calmly, your youngster is more apt to do his share of quarreling and peacemaking without getting too upset.

You may find, however, that one child stands out among your youngster's friends, because it seems that every time they play together, explosions occur. It is natural, under such circumstances, for you to decide that this companion should be barred. This may or may not cure the problem. Your child may be just as mischief prone as his friend. Children are rarely made bad by bad companions. Their own trouble-making capacities may be sparked by some child, but rarely are they caused by another youngster. If your child frequently gets into difficulties when he plays with a certain friend, you may find that you can shield them both by seeing to it that they have plenty of approved, but exciting, things to do. Many young mischief-makers are merely highly active, imaginative youngsters.

You will need to spell out some ground rules regarding activities for your child and his companions and see to it that these rules are obeyed. If you can do this with a calm, light, friendly touch, you are apt to be especially successful in keeping their goodwill as well as holding their behavior within bounds.

Being a good supervisor of youthful activities does not always do the trick. It is likely that in your neighborhood, as in most, you will have at least one youngster who always seems to stir up trouble. When another child's behavior is extremely troublesome, you may decide that you simply must forbid your child to play with him. Often, however, your child, of his own accord, decides that this difficult youngster is simply not for him.

If you feel that a particular child is behaving badly because he has certain kinds of problems rather than because he wants to be bad, it may seem cruel to ban him from friendship with your youngster. However, a really difficult boy or girl needs the help of trained specialists. In extreme cases, you may be forced to keep seriously unmanageable youngsters away from your own.

The Importance of Friendships

Your child learns much about how to be a boy, or a girl, from his friends. Before your child is 8, he is apt to play happily in a group of boys or girls. After the age of 8, however, it is sometimes hard to believe that boys and girls have any feeling at all for the opposite sex other than one of scorn.

This seeming scorn for the opposite sex is more likely to be a beginning attraction between boys and girls. Since they don't know what to do about this new turn in their lives, they escape to the familiar comfort of their own sex where they can freely talk about the mysteries of the other. With their own sex, moreover, they can practice the arts of making and losing friends without losing too much of their pride in the bargain.

If your child prefers playing with members of the opposite sex, this may be perfectly natural behavior. He, or she, may live in a neighborhood that is mostly one sex, so far as youngsters are concerned. Your little girl may have a need for exercise as demanding as that of most boys in the neighborhood. Perhaps at this time her interests are also more like those of the boys she knows than those of other girls. Or, perhaps she worships an older brother whom she wants to imitate. However, if your daughter seems to deeply resent being a girl (or your son, being a boy), you may wish to consult a child guidance expert.

Although 8- to 12-year-old boys generally play with boys, and girls with girls, most of them cherish a special fondness for a particular member of the opposite sex. This fondness is often kept as a secret from parents and other adults, especially when youngsters get to be 9 or so.

Your child has a lot to learn about how to get along with the opposite sex. Through this day-by-day work and play with both boys and girls, he is slowly gaining knowledge that will help him during the dating, courtship, and marriage days that lie in the future.

Friends give other lessons, too. From them, your child learns that friends can be friends and still have many different ideas and customs. Your child and his companions are apt to explore a host of subjects together: school, parents, do's and don'ts, likes and dislikes, God, food preferences, fears, wishes, and so on. Together, they explore the whole range of life as they know and wonder about it.

BELONGING TO A GROUP

Membership in Clubs

When your youngster comes racing into the house, aglow with the excitement of "our gang has a club," you will know he has reached another mile-post on his journey toward becoming an adult. You may be invited to come see the marvelous "hideout" which the club members are building. It probably won't look like very much to you. But it seems splendid to him.

One such "clubhouse" bore a somewhat wobbly sign, boldly painted with skull and crossbones and this inscription: "Friendship Club. Keep Out."

Despite the fact that these clubs can get to be a nuisance, absorbing your child's time, interests, and your household equipment, you will want to give him freedom to be an active member. He is learning many lessons in how to take part in group life.

But, since your young citizen still is inexperienced, you will, naturally, keep ears and eyes open as to what the club is up to. As in all areas of parenthood, "freedom within limits" is the motto to remember.

Parental Guidance

Doing what everybody else does is likely to become more popular with your child with every passing month. Fathers and mothers need to think through together what their standards are for themselves and their child. As parents consider these standards, they will find it helpful to decide which values are of basic importance and which can be changed a bit.

The job of setting rules for your child will be much easier if you get together with other parents and, through discussion, work out a behavior code. Some schools foster such action through parent-teacher organizations. In many instances, children, themselves, should be brought into the discussion.

Although adults should have the last word in making rules for 6- to 12-year-olds, youngsters appreciate putting in some words of their own. They are much more likely to see the justice and wisdom of adult guidance if they are offered a chance to give their side of the story.

However, you may have tried, without success, to work with other parents in setting up guides for children's groups. When, for one reason or another, this approach does not bring results, you may have to say to your child, "Regardless of what 'everyone else does,' I can't let you go with the group. You are not 'everyone.' You belong to our family and we don't believe that the group is right." Stands like this are hard to take—hard on you and hard on your child. In the long run, it is likely that you and your youngster will gain a sturdier self-respect and self-confidence if you have the courage to stand up—alone, if need be—for what you believe to be right.

Popularity

It is easy to carry concern over "group adjustment" too far. Particularly before your child reaches age 10 or 11, group membership is likely to shift from week to week. He may go through a bewildering series of ups and downs with his group. He might, for instance, be thrown out of the Explorer's Club one week, and be elected President the next.

However, being left out of the group is not always this simple. For example, a child who has many personal difficulties may be disliked by other youngsters. Simply belonging to a group is not apt to solve his problems. In many cases, a child has to get right with himself before he can get right with the group.

Being outside the group, on the other hand, doesn't necessarily mean your youngster has personal difficulties. Sometimes the group, not your child, has the problems. For instance, a group built on prejudice against people of other races, religions, and nationalities is one which you would not want your child to join. Then, too, some groups of children band together to cause trouble in the school or neighborhood.

All in all, group membership and popularity can be bought at too high a price. Contrary to frequently held beliefs, the popular youngster does not always become the successful adult. The question may be: successful at what? Certain kinds of jobs (as in some businesses) demand that a person develop qualities of being generally well-liked and hailed as a leader. Many other jobs, however, require other qualities, such as being particularly skilled in a certain field. Being successful in marriage and parenthood probably has very little, if any, relationship to being popular.

None of this is meant to say that popularity is wrong. Our society does need popular leaders as well as other kinds of people. The qualities which make a youngster popular in the first grade also appear to make him popular in the sixth and on into high school. Popular children are often healthy, friendly, affectionate, easygoing, cooperative, and full of energy. They also seem to be especially able to see quickly what members of the group desire and to behave accordingly. Youngsters of this kind can easily adapt themselves to whatever group they find themselves a part of.

Your child may enjoy this kind of life, but then, again, he may not. Some perfectly well-adjusted youngsters prefer to stay by themselves for the most part or with one or two close friends. This is sometimes true of especially bright or creative children who are busy with their own ideas and activities. They may not want to give these up for the sake of "belonging."

Some children choose to be by themselves or with a few people partly because they feel overwhelmed by a large group. Even though some youngsters are "loners" by choice, others are made unhappy by their troubles in making and keeping friends. If this is true of your child, he may need your help. Although you can't make his friends for him, you may be able to give him a boost up the friendship ladder. A lot depends on what causes his lonesome state.

Helping Shy Children

Some children lack friends because they are shy. Shyness is more common with 6- or 7-year-olds than with older children and more common with girls than boys. Shyness sometimes comes about from lack of practice in building friendships or from moving into a new school or neighborhood. Such "skin-deep" shyness is apt to wear off after a child has been around other youngsters a while, particularly if parents and teachers help him feel at ease with other boys and girls. If your child needs help with surface shyness, the following suggestions might be useful:

- Encourage him to give a party. In general, small, simple parties lasting no longer than a few hours are best for 6- to 12-year-old children. This is particularly true for shy ones. Simple, outdoor parties, such as picnics, often work well.
- At party time in particular, give your youngster some guidance on dress and manners. Although these things are not of first importance in making friends, they can smooth your child's way in social life. When you teach him about the right things to wear, check on where he is going.

Nearly all children want to look pretty much like the others in their group. This is true of shy youngsters and especially true of older ones. Within the limits of your pocketbook and your own standards, you may be able to boost your child's self-confidence by paying attention to what other youngsters wear and getting generally similar clothes for him. Let him do some of the choosing—under your guidance, of course.

- Give your child a chance to develop skill in games which are popular with other youngsters. You can, generally, find out what games are the thing in your area simply by keeping your eyes and ears open. Naturally, you wouldn't force your child through a series of lessons in the various sports. Nor would you count on skills of this kind to make him a social whiz.

Unfortunately, shyness is not always cured by surface changes. Some youngsters remain basically timid. If this seems to be true of your youngster, and if he appears to be unhappy about the situation, you may find other approaches that help.

Perhaps he needs more opportunities to talk over his feelings with you. Perhaps he needs more praise and affection. Perhaps, without realizing it, you have been a bit too strict with your discipline or have set overly high standards for him. This can make him feel as if he never will amount to very much.

Children Who Fight Too Much

On the other hand, some youngsters seem to get into a fight almost every time they play with other children. Some, in fact, declare war at the drop of a marble or jump rope. They seem to be looking for trouble and have no difficulty in finding it.

Children like this may have learned far too little about the importance of self-control. If you have a chronic fighter in your family, it is possible you have been a little too easygoing in letting him express his feelings. Perhaps he might benefit from firmer discipline. Now that he is getting older, he may need somewhat higher standards of peaceable behavior set for him.

Some quarrelsome youngsters, on the other hand, are reacting to too much strict discipline without enough outlets for their emotions. This is especially true if they are punished often and severely, and especially if this punishment is the off-again, on-again variety. Children punished in this way may become confused and angry. An angry child may look for a chance to punish other youngsters.

Keeping angry feelings under control is harder for some people than for others. If your child has many violent quarrels at home, school, and in the neighborhood and if he shows little or no improvement in this matter, it may be wise to get the help of a child guidance specialist.

Organizations

Many organizations have sprung up throughout the country to meet the needs of children for group membership. You are probably familiar with many of them: Boy and Girl Scouts, YMCA's and YWCA's, Community Centers, 4-H Clubs, Boys' and Girls' Clubs of America, Catholic Youth Organization, and so on.

The majority of youngsters who participate enjoy and benefit from these organizations because they are based on an understanding of children, their interests, and their needs.

No one organization is necessarily better for your child than another. Your child may, or may not, find satisfaction and an opportunity for growth in a particular organization. Let him try out different groups and find out himself what works best for him.

Of course, you may have to encourage him to give whatever he tries a fair trial. He can hardly tell from one Boy Scout meeting, for instance, that he does or does not like this organization. Shy children, particularly, may benefit from making a number of tries at fitting into a club. As they feel more at home in a group, they are apt to like it better. On the other hand, you may have a youthful joiner who needs to be discouraged a bit from overdoing his memberships. He may need help in facing up to the fact that there is only one of him and he has only 24 hours in a day and 7 days in a week. It is a good idea not to stress badges and rewards too much. Some youth groups and camps build their programs around competition. This is an easy way to keep children active. But children can get pretty anxious over the pressure to come out on top. Learning to swim, tie knots, cook, pitch a tent, name birds, and apply first aid are fine accomplishments in and of themselves. Such learning is apt to soak in deeper and last longer when the reward lies mostly in the joy of knowing and doing.

Many physicians, psychologists, and other experts warn against the highly competitive nature of many organizations sponsoring such games as baseball or football for young boys. They believe that young boys lack the physical and emotional strength to readily bear the severe strains put on them by such extreme competition. While many agree that active team sports are excellent for most young boys and girls, they advise that play for the sake of play is to be preferred.

One of the greatest rewards that your child can get out of his organization is the opportunity he may have to meet fine adult leaders. Your child learns how to be a grown man or woman mostly from you. But other adults he knows well also can set an important example for him. This is the chief reason why all adults who work with youngsters should be mature, kindly, responsible people as well as people who have specific knowledge and skills.

Using the Library

Use of the library is a fine way to enrich your child's life. It is not possible, or even practical, for parents to provide a child with every book that might interest him. Thanks to libraries, this isn't necessary. Nearly all communities have a free library, though some of the smaller towns have traveling ones. If your community does not have a free library of any kind, or if you think yours is inadequate, you may wish to join with other citizens to see what you can do about this.

When you take your child to the library, you may feel strongly tempted to choose his books for him. Although it is fine to give him suggestions, remember that part of the joy of going to a library is browsing through the books and choosing some for yourself. Since your youngster may end up with a selection that is not satisfying to him (too advanced books, for instance), you may want to seek the librarian's help.

See to it that your child knows and obeys library rules and that he learns how to take care of books. If your library is not too far from your home, he should, before long, be able to handle the matter of book borrowing—and returning—by himself.

It is best to introduce your child to the joys of reading without insisting that he and books become daily companions. Each child learns in his own special way. Books may be especially good for some children and not so much so for others.

Summer Camps and Community Playgrounds

If your child is like most, much of the time he simply has to move at a fast, complicated pace, in the company of others near his own age. When making plans for the summer, it is important for you to provide safe and rewarding outlets for his long vacation period.

Some communities run free or low-cost all-day recreation programs for children. How good these are depends mostly on the quality of their leadership.

Good day camp or playground leaders like and understand children and have training in such skills as sports, music, arts and crafts, games, and dramatics. At least one staff member should have training in first aid. All staff members should be responsible people who can control their own feelings and behavior. Senior leaders should be at least 18 years old, and it is probably best to have at least one leader for every 20 to 25 children.

As in the case of other club programs for youngsters, the better recreation centers put their emphasis on a good time for every child rather than on competitions and rewards.

Although the staff and program of a day camp or playground are more important than its location and equipment, this doesn't mean, of course, that you simply overlook what the place looks like. Certainly children need a big play area so they can run without running into each other. They need safe drinking water, sanitary toilets, and a shelter from the rain and hot sun. Swings, slides, sand boxes, seesaws, jungle-gyms, baseball and basketball areas are familiar playground needs. Many recreation specialists also recommend playground supplies such as huge blocks, which stimulate a child's imagination. Then, too, craft supplies and musical instruments enrich a playground program.

Some playgrounds include wading and swimming pools. When this is so, it is essential to have qualified lifeguards on duty. Adult leaders also have to give safety supervision when children play on other equipment, especially swings, ladders, and slides.

If your community does not have a good day camp or summer recreation center, you may want to join with other parents in asking your city or county government to provide one. Some public centers of this kind partly finance themselves by small fees paid by the users. Also, some states provide part of the cost of financing local recreation programs.

These summer programs may also be organized and financed by such youth organizations as the Scouts, church groups, 4-H Clubs, and so on. Sometimes, adult organizations, such as men's and women's clubs, plan and pay for children's recreation projects.

Going away to an overnight camp can be a wonderful experience for your youngster. But, again, it depends on what kind of camp and on what kind of child. Generally, older youngsters thrive on a chance to leave home for a while and live an active, outdoor life. For city youngsters particularly, there is a thrill in having the freedom to run across an open field without the fear of traffic, and to breathe deeply of air that smells of clover or pine.

Camp may, or may not, be like this for your child. Camps vary tremendously. And so do children. Youngsters below the age of 8 are likely to still need the nighttime protection of home and family and probably should be in day programs only.

The American Camping Association has set up basic standards for the staffing, equipment, health and safety provision, and other desirable features of children's camps. If you are choosing a camp for your child, it is probably a good idea to find out whether the one you are thinking about has been approved by this association. Much of what we have said about day camps applies to overnight ones, only more so. Safety provisions must be even more adequate and there should be not more than 8 or 9 children to a counselor. Good camps are not necessarily the expensive ones.

Religious Organizations

Your child's community life is not all play and social activities, of course. The church or temple may well be one of the most important factors in his total development.

Although you, along with other parents, approach religion in your own individual way, there are a few general principles you may wish to think about.

If your child is like most, perhaps he has already asked you many questions related to religion. And he will ask you many more, such as: "Who made the world?" "What happens when I die?" "Why should I be good?" "What makes a dog, a dog?" "Frank doesn't even pray and he has a better house and more money than I do. How come?" "What exactly is sin?" And so it goes.

As a couple, you have learned long ago that it is best if you agree on important things like these or, at least, to have reached an agreement to respect your differing points of view. You have also learned that you have to think out what you do believe so you can give clear, honest answers to your child.

You may have found that young minds cannot cope very well with ideas about religion. These ideas have to be expressed in a simple, practical manner. As your child gets older, you can talk to him in more abstract terms.

If you hold religious beliefs, but don't know how to answer your child's questions, it is a temptation to simply send him to church or temple and put the whole matter in the hands of an expert. But you are an active member of your child's health and education team, and you can't leave his spiritual life entirely up to the professionals. Because your youngster tends to model himself after you more than after anyone else, his religious training is not likely to "take" unless you take part in it, too: by living according to the teachings of your religion; by sharing your beliefs with him; by going to church or temple with him; or by worshipping with him in other ways that seem right to you.

Although regular attendance at classes in religious education can play an important part in giving him knowledge about his religion, such attendance does not guarantee that he will act according to religious teachings. Your child, like all of us, needs more than knowledge to guide his behavior. He needs an inner sense of conviction that certain ways of thinking and behaving are good ways. He needs to feel that he wants to behave in a certain way because he wants to be like the adults he loves and admires.

AT SCHOOL

When your child is ready for the first grade, you and he are likely to have many different kinds of feelings. He probably is bursting with excitement at one moment over his great adventure, and a bit frightened about leaving home, the next. You, too, may have mixed feelings of pride and worry.

You know how schools can differ. Some are staffed by teachers who love and believe in children, teachers who are devoted to opening up young minds to the power and excitement of facts and ideas. Some are staffed by teachers who believe that youngsters have to be firmly controlled and pushed through the unpleasant business of numbers, words, rivers, presidents, and no-running-in-the-halls.

Then, too, each student is different from every other one. All that he has been, is now, and hopes to be sits with him at his desk—his particular feelings about himself, the skills he has learned, his state of health, his special ways of knowing and learning, his rate of growth, his faith, or lack of it, in other people.

You can't do his learning for him, but you can help him in many ways. When you send him off to school after a good night's rest, a healthy breakfast, and a loving goodby, he carries a sense of well-being with him. With your help, he can store up the strength to meet the small victories and defeats that come his way in the schoolroom and on the playground.

There are other, more direct ways you can help him, too.

Leading Your Child to Learning

You can help your child to feel that learning is important and satisfying by building on his natural urge to explore, to grow, and to develop new skills. At his age, he likes to be busy. He enjoys an increasing sense of strength and independence as he learns to read, to use numbers, and to write. These skills help him master himself and his widening world. If he develops this feeling during his middle years, he will find it easier to settle down to serious work later in life.

The more your child knows of his world, the more he is apt to want to learn about it. You can provide him with many valuable experiences, some of which need take you no farther from home than your living room. For example, when you sit down with him and read him a story, you foster his sense of enjoyment in reading. As he gets a little older, he can begin to read to you. Children who have experiences like this at home almost always do better work in school than those who don't. Even if you can read together only 10 minutes a day, it is likely to make a big difference in his feelings about books and learning.

There are other very simple ways in which you can help your child gain knowledge. One 9-year-old girl and her father sat in their yard on a summer evening. She asked, and he answered, about the Big Dipper and the Milky Way, the half moon that would soon be full, the big stars and the little ones. The little girl slowly mused, "What I wonder is how can there be so much to wonder about."

Family excursions keep your child's sense of wonder alive. There are trips to stores, public buildings, the countryside, and other towns. All of this adds to your child's knowledge and desire for more.

He learns from talking and listening. One reason most youngsters between 6 and 12 are so eager for a home audience is that they want to practice the new words they are constantly learning. Most of them love riddles, chants, and jokes. They tell long, complicated stories that are partly fact and partly dreams and wishes. Most of them love to hear you tell stories too; about when you were little or about "once upon a time."

Family talk has many values. Talking and listening add to your child's sense of self-confidence. Through home conversation, he builds up his power to understand and use words. This power is vital to his success in school.

You can also encourage your child to be a good pupil by setting an example for him. If you are a reader, this impresses him. If you talk about facts and ideas that interest you, he notes that parents also grow in knowledge. This may sound like a tall order for busy parents. But, on the other hand, you will find life livelier when you cultivate a few interests of your own. As your child grows older, you may have more time for this.

Your young student will learn how to learn partly by imitating you, but he also wants some direct help. Listen to his stories of life at school and look at his papers. It is a good idea to play up what he has done well and play down what isn't so good, although there are times when school problems can't be overlooked. If he isn't doing good work, you will want to find out what the trouble is.

Time Out

Although it is important to encourage your child in his learning process, he can have too many rich experiences just as he can get too much rich food. Some youngsters feel that their minds cannot digest all their parents offer. Some feel that they can never live up to what their parents expect. They sometimes lose self-confidence, and may become afraid, worried, or angry. When this happens, learning problems may develop. So try to set standards your child can reach.

Health Is Important

Your youngster may seem well and still not be in first-rate physical condition. He needs plenty of sleep, exercise, and nourishing food if he is to be alert. It is also important to have his eyes and ears checked carefully.

If your child has signs of illness such as a heavy cold, a fever, or a rash, you will want to check with the doctor about keeping him at home until he is better. He can spread disease as well as become sicker himself if he leaves the house.

Growth Affects Learning

Since each person grows at his own individual rate, each child is a bit different from others in a classroom. Because abilities develop at different rates, at one age a child may struggle hopelessly to acquire a certain skill, such as writing. If he is given time to grow, he may acquire it easily when he is a little older.

If your youngster is a "slow developer," he may be 8 or 9 years old before he is ready to do well in school. A number of youngsters, especially boys, are not ready for such skills as reading until they are about 9. This doesn't mean that such children are less intelligent than others. It can mean that some have grown slowly and that, when their growth "catches up" with them, they may do much better work.

This matter of different rates of growth in children is so important that some experts are now urging that children not start the first grade until they are clearly ready for this experience. This depends on many things, such as physical size, ability to work with a group, capacity to speak fairly clearly, and interest in working with words and numbers.

If your youngster has gone to kindergarten, his teacher may be able to tell you whether he is ready for the first grade. About one-fourth of the first graders today (twice as many boys as girls) do failing work. Failure is not easy to accept at any time. It is harder to accept when you are a beginner. You may be able to save your child from much unhappiness by giving careful thought to the best time for him to start school. Most children should not begin the first grade before they reach the age of 6, and some may do better if they wait until they are a bit older. Some are ready earlier than age 6. Whether a child is likely to succeed in first grade depends a great deal on his total growth, not on his exact age. Some schools study each child carefully and advise parents as to when he seems to be ready for the first grade.

In the primary grades, he must learn to read, write, and handle numbers. His future education is built on these skills. If he is having serious trouble with these "tools for learning," you will want to talk to his teacher. Perhaps he needs individual help.

As we stated above, boys usually develop more slowly than girls, especially in the skills that are particularly valued in school. Six-year-old girls are generally better talkers than 6-year-old boys. This tends to make it easier for them to learn to read and write. Also, their small muscles, which are so useful in reading, writing, arts and crafts, tend to be in a more advanced stage than is true for most boys of the same age.

Boys have superior big muscle development and this is fine on the playground.

But in the usual classroom, the boy is apt to feel restless. He also is apt to feel inferior because, in many ways, most of the girls are ahead of him.

Boyish resentment is further fanned into flames when the boys are compared with girls or teamed up against them in contests that the males are sure to lose, such as spelling, singing, and reading.

If a boy goes home and is scolded for having lower grades than his sister, his sense of inferiority and anger sometimes becomes unbearable. He concludes that school is for sissies and the athletic field is for "he-men."

If your son has more school problems than your daughter, this probably is not because he is less intelligent. Boys and girls are equal in their intellectual ability.

Intelligence Tests

Most schools study each child in a number of ways to find out how to guide him, his parents, and his teachers in making the most of his educational experience.

If your school gives intelligence tests, it is unlikely that you will be given your youngster's exact score. You may be told that he has below average, average, good, or excellent intellectual ability as measured by the test. One reason that schools hesitate to give exact scores is that they can be misleading. Intelligence tests, especially group ones, do not always give accurate results. Also, scores may change from time to time as a child is tested over the years. A good deal may depend on what test is used, how it is given and scored, a child's state of health, and how he feels about himself and school at the time he is tested.

When used carefully by trained persons, intelligence tests may be useful as one of many guides to your child's capacity to learn in school and to understand most school subjects, especially those which are based on reading and the use of words. These tests do not tell much about his special talents. Moreover, children who think in original and creative ways may not do as well on intelligence tests as might be expected.

The special aspects of a child's intelligence are least likely to be discovered when he is tested as part of a group. If you think your child is not getting all he might from his education and that more should be known about his mental ability, you might be able to arrange for him to have an individual test at school or elsewhere.

Parents often have strong feelings about intelligence and other tests. There is so much pressure today for success in school that it is common for everyone concerned to put too much emphasis on scores and grades. When parents get overly worried about these matters, children are likely to get upset, too. Upset children do not do as well on tests as their intelligence merits, and some do not enjoy or make the most of their education. It is more important for your child to be interested in what he is learning and to experience the joy of knowing than it is for him to get good test scores and honor grades.

Achievement Tests

Your child's measured intelligence is only one guide to his ability to learn in school. Other things, such as his interest in education, his health, and his self-confidence, play a big part in what he can and will do at school.

You can find out a good deal about what your child has learned so far through the scores that he gets on achievement tests. Many schools give these after a child has finished one or several grades. These tests are given in such fields as reading, use of words, number reasoning, and so on. Achievement test scores may be a useful guide as to what kind of individual help your child may need. However, the same warnings given about how intelligence tests are used apply to achievement tests, too.

Your child may need no help at all with his school progress. If he gets average or better scores in achievement tests, all may be well with his education. However, if his measured intelligence is high and his achievement scores are average or below, it's worth trying to find out why. Some very bright children coast along in school because they don't have enough to keep them interested or because standards are not set high enough for them. Some do poorly because their parents push them too hard.

One the other hand, some children get higher marks on their achievement tests than would seem likely in terms of their measured intelligence. There may be no reason to worry about differences of this sort unless your child seems to be working too hard and is anxiously pushing himself to be a school success.

Getting Used to School

Some youngsters react to their beginning months in the first grade with such symptoms as nightmares, stomachaches, and bedwetting. Some seem to become more babyish for a while. Many people—adults as well as children—become more childish under pressure or a trying new situation. If you give your youngster a chance to talk over his feelings about school, if you see that he has an affectionate, easygoing time at home, and plenty of rest, he will probably soon learn to feel better about himself at school.

When your youngster starts each new grade, he may have a period of unhappiness before he settles down. You can help smooth his way by realizing that some children naturally act like this and by giving him support while he gets used to his new classmates and his teacher.

As he reaches the fourth, fifth, and sixth grades, he probably will feel more sure of himself. School often becomes more interesting to him at this time. He has probably mastered some of the basic education tools, and is ready to learn about more ideas and a wider range of facts. His mental abilities have also grown so that he is better able to understand ideas. He is apt to come home each day overflowing with new information.

Teachers Play a Big Part

Your child's teacher is especially important to him in the lower grades. Before he is 8 or 9, he is still apt to be quite dependent on adults. It is hard for him to get along all day without you. His teacher serves partly as a mother or father to him during his school day.

If he loves his teacher, it is usually a compliment to you as well as to him or her. From you he has learned to love grownups—and he is broadening his love to include another adult who is important in his life. This is good for him in many ways. It makes him want to learn. It also encourages him toward independence and maturity.

It upsets him if home and school are very different. Then he is torn in his loyalties. This is one reason why it is a good idea for you to visit school and work in partnership with his teacher.

As your child moves on to the third or fourth grade, he will probably be less impressed with his teacher and busier with his own age-mates. His teacher is still important to him, but more as an inspiration and an example than as someone to be dependent on and love.

Talking with Your Child's Teacher

Teachers, like parents, are human. Like parents, they can get angry or sick or worried. Unlike parents, they have 20 or more children to take care of. Also, unlike parents, they don't have the same deep, personal feelings for each individual child. This has its advantages and disadvantages. Your child's teacher can be calmer than you about your youngster's failures and successes. On the other hand, you have a more personal interest in your particular child than his teacher does.

Parents and teachers sometimes get irritated with each other. If your youngster does poorly in school, no one likes to take the blame. His teacher may find it easier to think you are at fault, while you may prefer to blame the teacher. Your youngster may blame both of you. Probably all three parties—home, school, and child—contribute their share. The problem is likely to get worse unless everyone concerned can get together and try to solve it.

If your child is having trouble, visit his school. It is best to call for an appointment. Some schools set aside special times for parent-teacher conferences.

When you visit, perhaps old fears and resentments from your own school days come sweeping over you. But pull yourself together and meet your child's teacher, person to person.

Think, too, for a moment about how the teacher may feel. Many have vague fears of parents. Enraged parents have been known to stir up principals and other parents. Unfortunately, teachers hardly ever hear from satisfied parents. This is hard on anybody's self-confidence.

You will want to know what the teacher thinks of your child's school work. If it is poor, the teacher should be able to give you some idea as to what is causing the trouble. Perhaps she can make suggestions as to what you can do to help. Try to meet your child's teacher with an open mind and an honest view of your child's behavior—his weaknesses and shortcomings, as well as the qualities you like in him.

If she feels your child behaves badly in class, maybe you can give her some understanding of why he may be "acting up." For instance, a shy child may impress the teacher as being bored. If she realizes he is afraid to speak in a group, she may treat him more gently. An overactive youngster can create a lot of commotion in a classroom. If your child is a "wiggler," maybe his teacher can think of more active things for him to do, such as cleaning the erasers, watering the plants, and so on. If times have been troubled in your home, this can lead to poor marks or difficult school behavior. It is often wise to let your child's teacher know something about home problems so she can be more sympathetic toward your youngster.

There is no one best kind of teacher just as there is no one best kind of parent or student. Some children get along happily with a strict, "no-nonsense" teacher who insists on order, quiet, and plenty of hard work. Others flourish in a more easygoing classroom atmosphere.

Sometimes a child can be in serious conflict with a particular teacher. If this happens to your youngster and if talks with him and his teacher seem to do no good, you may find it best to take the problem up with his school principal.

Some schools also have social workers or guidance counselors who are helpful. They may suggest that your child be placed in another classroom. This is worth trying, if it is possible. For the sake of his education and emotional health, it may be wiser to take him out of a setting where he is miserable.

There may be no way of changing his class. He may have to simply put up with it. You can help him do this by explaining to him why this is necessary and by giving him good experiences at home. Let him know that you sympathize with the hard time he is having, but be firm in saying that he must go to school. Be careful not to blame the teacher too personally and directly; such attitudes can often make the situation more difficult for your youngster. The law requires his attendance and he must have an education.

Homework

Not all elementary schools give homework assignments. Proof is lacking that youngsters of this age necessarily learn more if they have extra lessons to do at home. Some educators believe children should have such lessons only when their work shows they need special practice. Children of this age need considerable time for play and exercise as well as for school work.

However, if your child does have homework, the best way you

can help him is to give him a good, quiet place to study and to guide him in planning his time. Be sure he has the tools he needs, such as paper, pencil, ruler, and so on. You may be called on to help him find reference books and other materials. If you find that your child is not understanding his assignments, it is a good idea to ask his teacher how you can help him.

Sometimes homework can trigger a crisis. There's a problem that just can't get solved, the story that isn't written, the test that hasn't been studied for. Your child is in tears or tantrums and you are tempted to rush in to save him. Ideally, you should guide him in getting his work done without doing it yourself. In practical terms, you might have to lend a hand to get him out of a "bad spot."

Teachers say, however, that when parents make a practice of being partners in a child's homework, he is likely to get lazy, irresponsible, or confused.

Extra Lessons

As your child's interests and abilities expand, he may want to join classes outside his regular school program. This can be overdone.

Some youngsters, for instance, have quite enough to do in keeping up with their schoolwork and their home and community life. If your child is not the especially energetic or highly active kind, or if schoolwork does not come easily to him, extra lessons might prove a burden.

It is easy in these times to plan too busy a program for your growing child. He should have a chance to be himself—to sit and dream, to do his own explorations and experiments, to forget the clock so that he can have time to remember who he is. As many experiences come his way, he needs the freedom to weave them into the fabric that is his own special design for living.

New Ways in Teaching

Most schools have "go-to-school" night. At this time, teachers explain something about how and what they teach. Your school also is likely to have a parent-teacher organization. Find out more about your child's school by visiting it and taking part in activities for parents.

Schools vary so throughout the country that it is impossible to give an exact picture of what goes on in your school. Some of the newer ways in education are discussed here as a general guide.

Arithmetic. In many schools, arithmetic is no longer a step-by-step march through adding, subtracting, multiplying, fractions, and percentages.

There are so many different ways used in teaching the "new math" that they cannot be explained here. A number of schools set up special meetings to explain these methods to parents. It appears that these new ways usually are far more effective than older ones in giving children a real understanding of numbers and their uses.

Reading. Reading is also being taught in many new ways. Educators have found that there is no one best method for teaching children to read. Youngsters read well or poorly for different reasons, such as their stage of physical growth, their intelligence, their general health, their eyesight, their special abilities, their life experiences, and their feelings about themselves and school.

All children learn best when they have some successes in their learning, when they understand what they are doing, and when their studies seem useful and interesting. When these principles are applied to reading, it means among other things that different children learn best from different books. These books should be along the lines of the child's interests. They also should be neither too "hard" nor too "easy" for him because, of course, each youngster does best when he is encouraged, but not pushed to read. It is also important for him to get the meaning out of his reading. It does no good, for instance, to recognize, pronounce, and spell words correctly if they don't add up to a story or idea that makes sense to him.

Languages. Foreign languages are taught in some elementary schools today. Children seem to pick up a new language more easily than older people do. Since the opportunities for travel and for work with other countries are growing, it is clear that your child's life will be enriched if he knows at least one language besides his own. And if he starts learning one early, he is more likely to master it.

Teaching Tools

Learning through class projects. Teachers know that elementary school youngsters have strong drives to create, to explore, to be active, to be part of a group, and to master real problems. Most learn best when their classwork is built on these needs. This is why some teachers use projects such as parties, plays, and trips as part of the school program.

Teaching machines. Perhaps your child learns partly through teaching machines. With careful planning by the teacher, these machines can give him a chance to learn certain kinds of facts and ideas on his own. They can give him a chance to check his own work as he goes along and to learn at his own rate. They can free the teacher to work with individuals and small groups or to lead class discussion.

Audio-visual aids. Modern education also is built partly on the use of films and records that enrich a child's understanding. Some schools now have tape recorders that teachers can use to make records for the use of small groups or individual students. Children can also use these for practice in speaking.

Team teaching and "master" teachers. Your youngster might have two teachers at once for some of his classes, or he may take part in a large demonstration or lecture given by a "master" teacher, sometimes by way of television. Then, too, he may have a specialized teacher or teachers for different subjects. Some schools teach in these ways because knowledge is increasing so rapidly that one teacher cannot be an expert in everything.

Classroom aides. Parents or other adults may serve as assistants to the teacher. Their services may range all the way from helping first-graders with snowsuits to marking papers and keeping records. These aides free the teacher to spend all of his time in the task of education.

Special Services

These school teams may include a number of special "pupil personnel services" set up to serve students as individuals. Your school may have all, some, or a few of the services which are described here.

Health services. Your school probably has a health unit. The doctor who comes to the school may give physical examinations to students once or twice a year, or he may serve as a medical consultant. A school nurse is probably on duty at least during a part of each day. School nurses tend to emergencies and also advise youngsters and their parents on some health and personal problems. They may explain the meaning of illness and the importance of getting help. They may help a teacher in planning a child's school day. Or they may work with the teacher in planning a health education program.

School social workers. The job of the school social worker is to counsel with families on personal matters that can affect a child's school progress. When parents have trouble getting along with each other, for instance, their unhappiness can upset their children. School social workers can also help with such family problems as illness, unemployment, or lack of money. If the school social worker cannot give direct help to a family, he or she usually can tell parents where to find the help they need.

Guidance counselors. Guidance counselors specialize in understanding and helping the child as an individual make the most of his learning abilities. They also help with his personal adjustment to the total school program. Furthermore, these counselors are trained to plan testing programs for a school (such as intelligence and achievement tests) and to explain to teachers, parents, and children what the results of these tests mean.

Because a child's home life, personal feelings, and health all affect how well he does at school, the guidance counselor works in partnership with the parents, the school social worker, the nurse, and the teacher. If there is no school social worker, the guidance counselor may help parents and children with their personal problems at home as well as at school.

School psychologist. Some schools have a psychologist on their staff, others share a psychologist with one or more other schools, while others may refer youngsters with special difficulties to a psychologist in the community. The school psychologist studies individual children in terms of their particular abilities and weaknesses, their feelings about themselves and others, their special interests, and so on. If your child seems to be having problems in learning or in classroom behavior, the psychologist often can help by working directly with your youngster or in advising what help he particularly needs.

School psychiatrist. Few schools have the funds to employ a full-time psychiatrist, but a number use a psychiatrist on a part-time basis. If there is no psychiatrist on the staff, troubled students may be referred to one in the community. Some communities have free or low-cost mental health or child guidance clinics which are staffed by psychiatrists, psychologists, and social workers. A small community may have the services of a traveling mental health clinic.

The psychiatrist specializes in helping children who show that they are seriously upset. These upsets usually have no relation to mental illness. They generally suggest that a child has fears and worries that are deeply troubling to him. Since it is far easier to help a troubled child when he is young it is a wise idea for him to see a psychiatrist if the school recommends this. Or, parents may decide for themselves that their youngster needs help of this kind.

Remedial reading teachers. As in the case of other difficulties, early treatment of reading problems is best. If your child's teacher thinks he needs a remedial reading specialist and there is none in your school or through the board of education, you may find one in your community. A remedial reading specialist is trained to help a youngster develop the particular reading skills he lacks and to understand why he has had trouble in learning to read in the first place.

Speech therapist. Speech problems may be caused by many things, including poor hearing, slow development, emotional upsets, and lack of practice. Since many speech problems can be cleared up with special treatment, some schools have speech therapists. Your child's teacher could probably tell you whether your youngster needs the attention of a speech specialist.

Parent education groups. A number of schools sponsor lectures and discussion groups for parents. These may be run by a parent-teacher organization, by the school, or by a group of interested parents. Such groups usually work best if both mothers and fathers are included, if there is considerable group discussion, and if some of the excellent films, plays, and publications on child development and family life are used.

11
Health Care

Good health is far more than not being sick. It is having plenty of energy for play as well as for work. It is having a strong body you can count on for running, walking, climbing, and stretching. It is being able to see the small print in a book, the pigeon strutting down the sidewalk, or the mountain on the horizon. It is being able to hear the rustle of wind in the grass and the teacher's voice in the classroom.

Healthy children have the physical equipment to make full use of the opportunities that come their way. They are more ready to learn, more skillful and joyous in play, better able to enjoy what is good in life, and to conquer what is hard.

Healthy children are also apt to become healthy adults. Their bodies grow better if they get enough exercise, rest, and the right kind of food when they are young. These factors also help them build up reserves of strength and energy for when they are older.

Food, exercise, and rest are only part of the health story, of course. You also want to protect your family from illnesses. Your doctor will guide you in the details of the specific care that family members need.

Now is the time, also, for children to learn about maintaining good health in the future. You can tell them, for instance, that smoking is a serious threat to health, and why. If they learn these facts early, they may never want to experiment with cigarettes later.

SOME BASIC FACTS ABOUT HEALTH

Cleanliness

Careful hand-washing is one of the most important rules your child should learn for his health. Even when hands look clean, they can carry germs that cause illness. This is especially true in reference to colds, many kinds of digestive upsets such as diarrhea and vomiting, and some other contagious diseases. Like many other habits, hand-washing can, in time, become so natural to your child that you won't have to check on him any more about this.

Clean clothes also play their part in keeping families healthy. Clothes, particularly handkerchiefs and underthings, should be washed thoroughly, especially if there has been sickness in the home. If a member of your family has had a contagious disease, your doctor is likely to give you specific instructions about disinfecting the clothes, dishes, towels, etc., which this ill person has used. He will probably advise that the ill person use tissues instead of handkerchiefs and that these tissues be disposed of promptly after use.

Active Play Aids Health

Planning exercise for your 6- to 12-year-old may seem downright foolish. To many parents, the problem appears to go in the opposite direction: finding a way to get their sons and daughters to sit still for more than a few minutes.

But, in our modern age, it is sometimes necessary to see to it that your children exercise actively. If you give your youngsters the space and equipment for active play, they are likely to go along enthusiastically with an exercise program, especially if it comes under the heading of sports and play rather than something that is labeled exercise.

This doesn't mean that they should have special lessons in the various sports. Nor does it mean that they have to have a lot of fancy equipment. It does mean that they should have a safe place to play, like a yard or playground.

Your children also will benefit from having a few simple sports supplies, like roller skates and a ball and bat. If you live in a neighborhood with other children, you may want to plan with their parents in pooling equipment. If you live in a yardless area, you might get together with other parents to promote a well-equipped community playground. Some schools keep their recreation spaces supervised and available to children and parents throughout the year and after school hours.

Your children can also get exercise right at home. After all, there are times when they can't be out of doors. Within the limits of your particular budget and home, you can provide activity inside your house or apartment. For instance, an old mattress on the floor makes a dandy place for young headstanders, somersaulters, wrestlers, and boxers. Games of darts, Ping-Pong, and balloon volleyball are a few possible active indoor sports. You can get more suggestions along this line from books on home recreation.

Besides having play equipment and space, your child will benefit from a bit of sports-teaching. If you have any athletic ability at all, it will probably do both of you good if you take time to play with him. This is especially true when he is less than 9 or 10.

Your child will enjoy and benefit from physical activity if he is encouraged to go about it in his own way without pressure to engage in any particular sport and without pressure to be a star performer.

Emotions and Health

Your child's health, as well as your own, is also affected by feelings. When a person is unhappy or worried, his body is less able to fight off infections. Feelings of loneliness, fear, and anger may be so upsetting that they bring about real physical pain, such as a headache or stomach cramps. The physical and emotional sides of life are partners. Poor physical health can upset behavior, and upset emotions can undermine the body's strength to fight disease. For this reason, the general well-being of each family member is promoted by a well-balanced, daily combination of satisfying experiences and good physical care.

It is important, however, not to be too concerned about your child's minor aches and pains, and emotional upsets. If you are, your youngster may take delight in the dramatic role of fragile invalid. If you pass over his complaints rather casually and stress your affection for him as a person, he will feel less need to be sick in order to find out how much you love him. He will probably discover that he "just can't be bothered" with illnesses if he has your steady love, friends, lots of satisfying play, an absorbing hobby, and a zest for living. On the other hand, if life seems to be just one long, dull, gray day after another, full of failures and disappointments, sickness can look like a wonderful escape.

Good Teeth and Good Health

As in other matters of growth, your child will follow his own timetable in the development of his teeth.

You should take your child to the dentist at least twice a year. Many grownups suffer from poor teeth because they did not get the proper dental care when they were young. We now know that cavities in teeth must be filled as soon as they develop. This is true of baby teeth as well as permanent ones.

If your children have been fortunate enough to have grown up in a community where the water supply contains fluoride, chances are quite good that they will have fewer dental defects. There is no doubt that a proper amount of fluoride in the drinking water is harmless and can reduce by two-thirds the number of cavities in children's teeth. If your water supply does not contain sufficient fluoride, a dentist may wish to suggest other techniques that also are effective, although to a lesser degree, toward preventing dental defects.

Some dentists now specialize in work with children. You may want to find out whether there is such a specialist in your community. Dentists who limit their services to children are not only specially trained in meeting a child's physical needs, but they are also particularly skillful in dealing with the well-known "dentist panic" which so many people, young and old, seem to have.

Signs of Physical Illness

It isn't always easy to tell whether your youngster is physically ill or emotionally upset. Common signs of physical illness are: loss of appetite, sudden irritability, restless sleep, extreme fatigue, pain, and a rise in temperature. However, most of these symptoms may also be signs of disturbed feelings. It is always a good idea to check with your doctor if any of these distress signals come on suddenly, continue for more than a few hours, or appear again and again.

Preventing Illness

Nourishing food, plenty of exercise, cleanliness, and rest are not the whole health story for your family. Part of giving your youngster a healthy home environment involves the prevention of illness. Although your child probably is sick less often than when he was younger, he still requires good care.

Regular medical examinations at least once a year are a part of this care. Perhaps your child is examined every year by the school doctor. If so, it is a good idea for you to be present at the time so you can talk to him about your youngster's health. If this doctor recommends more medical attention for your child, you will want to follow this advice by taking your child to your own physician or to a clinic.

Regular health care by your own doctor or through a good school health program not only helps to keep your child well, it also gives you a chance to find out early whether he has a handicap—such as poor vision or poor hearing. If your physician recommends glasses for your child, he will probably pass on to you the advice of experts to the effect that children's glasses should have shatter-resistant lenses and sturdy, flame-proof frames.

Many physical problems can often be treated successfully, and the earlier the treatment is started the better.

You also should be sure your child has protection from disease through a series of immunizations begun when he was an infant. (See the Recommended Immunization Schedule, p. 106.)

EATING RIGHT

Good food promotes child and family health in many ways. It builds strong bodies, and being well-fed also gives your youngsters a sense of being loved and protected. Food should never be used as a substitute for family communication, however. As 11-year-old Bobby said to his mother, "Every time something goes wrong in our family, you try to solve it with hot cocoa. When you think things are especially bad, you put two marshmallows in every cup." Family woes can't be drowned in a flood of cocoa and marshmallows, delicious as both are. Good family feeding takes a lot of know-how, as well as a lot of love.

As you plan meals for your family, it is important to bear in mind that each member needs certain kinds of foods every day. These include the following: Milk and foods containing milk; fruits and vegetables; meat, poultry, or fish; whole grain or enriched bread and cereals; fats and sugars.

The Daily Food Guide, which appears in this section, should be a practical help to you in menu planning. Although this list applies to your 6-to 12-year-old child, the same foods can be used for all members of the family. Some adjustments in the kind of food, size of portion, or method of preparation may be needed for those on special diets, or for the baby, or an aged member of the family.

Importance of the food groups. Each of the broad food groups included in the daily food plan has a special job to do in building an adequate diet. For example, milk is the leading source of calcium, which is essential for the development of bones and teeth. Milk also contains high quality protein and is an excellent source of riboflavin, other vitamins, minerals, carbohydrates, and fat. Milk products such as cheese and ice cream supply these nutrients but in quite different amounts. Whole milk normally contains very small amounts of vitamin D, but milk to which vitamin D has been added becomes a valuable source of this nutrient.

The foods in the meat group are important for the amount and quality of the protein they provide. Protein is important mainly as a tissue builder. It is a part of muscle, organs, blood, skin, hair, and other living tissues. Dried beans, peas, and nuts also supply protein but it is a lower quality than the protein of meat and milk. Besides protein these foods provide iron, thiamin, riboflavin, and niacin.

Daily Food Guide for Children

Type of Food	Amount Each Day
MILK GROUP	2 to 3 cups
Milk (fluid whole, evaporated, skim, dry, buttermilk).	
Dairy products such as: cheddar cheese, cottage cheese, and ice cream.	May be used sometimes in place of milk.

VEGETABLE-FRUIT GROUP

A citrus or other fruit or vegetable high in vitamin C. Grapefruit, orange, tomato (whole or in juice), raw cabbage, broccoli, fresh strawberries, guava, mango, papaya, cantaloup.

A dark green or deep yellow vegetable for vitamin A. You can judge fairly well by color—dark green and deep yellow—apricots, broccoli, cantaloup, carrots, greens, pumpkin, sweet potatoes, winter squash.

Other fruits and vegetables including potato.

Choose 4 or more servings including:

1 serving each day—usually ½ cup or a portion as ordinarily served such as a medium orange, half grapefruit.

1 serving at least every other day, usually ½ cup of vegetable.

2 servings, count as 1 serving ½ cup of fruit or vegetable.

MEAT GROUP

Meat, fish, poultry, egg.
As alternate: dry beans, dry peas, lentils, nuts and peanut butter.

Choose 2 or more servings.

Count as serving: 2 to 3 ounces of lean cooked meat, poultry, or fish (without bone), or 2 eggs or 1 cup cooked dry beans, peas, etc., or 4 tablespoons peanut butter.

BREAD AND CEREAL GROUP

Whole grain, enriched or restored bread and cereals, and other grain products as cornmeal, grits, macaroni, spaghetti, and rice.

Choose 4 or more servings.

Count as a serving: 1 slice of bread; 1 ounce ready-to-eat cereal; ½ cup to ¾ cup cooked cereal, cornmeal, grits, macaroni, noodles, rice or spaghetti.

PLUS OTHER FOODS

Other foods such as sugars, oils, margarine, butter, and other fats may be used in many ways to complete meals and to satisfy appetites.

Serving sizes may differ—small for young children, extra large (or seconds) for very active teenagers.

Vegetables and fruits are valuable because of the vitamins and minerals they contain. Vitamin A is very important for growth and development in children, for normal vision, and for a healthy skin condition. Another important vitamin is ascorbic acid or vitamin C, which is essential for healthy gums and body tissues.

Breads and cereals—whole grain, enriched, restored—furnish worthwhile amounts of thiamin, iron, niacin, protein, and food energy.

All the foods listed in the Daily Food Guide can be found in the grocery store. Usually children will get all the vitamins and minerals they need from a good, varied diet, and supplements are not necessary. Occasionally a doctor may prescribe vitamin D in some form, if the child is not getting enough through foods like milk, margarine, and cereals which often have vitamin D added to them.

Your Child's Appetite

Within limits, it is generally more important what your child eats than how much. Many youngsters overplay fats and sugars and underplay the other essential foods.

So long as your child is healthy and not seriously under- or overweight, it is a good idea not to push him to eat more or less than he naturally wants. Since each child has his own natural rate and style of growth, each will require varying amounts of food. However, if he suddenly loses his appetite, you will want to check on your child's physical and emotional health. When a normally enthusiastic eater turns down food, it can be a sign that something ails him.

Overweight Children

It is easy for your child to overeat. Some 6- to 12-year-old children are overweight simply because they eat too much and exercise too little. Most 6- to 12-year-olds are eager to keep up with their running, leaping, somersaulting playmates. It's no fun to be chosen as a natural base for the pyramid, the ballast in the rowboat, or the fat clown in the neighborhood circus.

Children need plenty of food for energy and growth, but often need to watch their weight. This could mean preventing excessive weight gain as well as losing weight. Many times, children get fat because they are taught to eat more than they need. Beginning with babyhood, parents have a responsibility and an opportunity to develop good eating practices in their children and to provide the right kind and amount of food in the family meals. If your child appears too plump, take a good look at what and how much he is eating. Often it is possible to control obesity by reducing the kind and amount of between meal snacks, cutting down on butter, fried foods, salad dressings, and rich desserts.

If your child continues to gain excessively, take him to his physican for an examination. The physician will determine if he is overweight and will recommend how to handle the problem.

Some children eat too much partly because of emotional problems. This is discussed further in Chapter 13.

Underweight Children

The underweight and the undernourished child is of concern to parents. Sometimes the long, lean type of child is assumed to be underweight when he really isn't. On the other hand, he may be underweight because of not enough food, overactivity, lack of sleep, infectious disease, or other factors which affect his appetite and food intake.

Whether your child is actually underweight or overweight should be determined by the physician who will then give advice on correcting the cause.

Family Meals

Fortunately for you and your youngster, his daily food needs and yours can be met by many kinds of foods. You can pay attention to the special likes and dislikes of your family and still give them healthful meals. Remembering that people naturally have different tastes, you can be sympathetic to your child who, for instance, may heartily dislike cauliflower. As you study your family, your food guide, and your budget, you will be able to work out meals that satisfy your family's health, happiness, and pocketbook all at once.

Planning and cooking meals is only part of the job of feeding the family. There is also the matter of setting a peaceful family "tone" at mealtimes. Food tastes better and appetites are keener when mealtimes are pleasant.

The light touch may help—such as taking it easy on the question of table manners. The art of skillful eating comes slowly. Some parents find that youngsters are embarrassed if their manners are corrected in front of the whole family. Quiet teaching goes better when you and your small amateur are alone. He surely won't enjoy his food or digest it as comfortably if he is constantly reminded about his eating techniques. If you give him time to grow and set a good example yourself, you will probably have more enjoyable mealtimes; and, in the long run, a more dependably courteous youngster.

You probably try to avoid talking about problems at meals. Parents can often set the mealtime tone by stressing interesting and pleasant happenings of the day, drawing everyone into the conversation, and giving each person a chance to talk.

Another way to avoid trouble is to use table mats that can be wiped off, unbreakable dishes, and tumblers that don't tumble. One mother found that she felt better about her children's messiness when she got a "crumb-colored rug with a pattern like grease spots."

To avoid the morning rush hour panic, it is a good idea to set the table and plan the breakfast menu the night before. Gather up the school supplies. Figure out what each person will wear. It does take organization, but it is well worth the time in terms of the crises that can be avoided.

You and your children will get along much better at breakfast and through the morning if you all eat well, without being rushed. Breakfast menus don't have to follow a set routine. For instance, if your youngster rebels against cereals and eggs, there's nothing wrong with a hamburger along with fruit juice and milk. A peanut butter sandwich, a serving of custard pudding, a glass of milk, and an orange make a pretty good beginning for the day. You don't have to have the usual breakfast foods every day. But it is a good idea to have milk in the morning meal, or growing children may not get the amount needed during the course of the day. The same is true of vitamin C foods such as oranges or grapefruit. If they're missed at breakfast, be sure to include them in another meal.

Breakfast foods are simple, and often the 6- to 12-year-old enjoys preparing his own meal. He can take this responsibility if you help him by having foods at hand that are easy to prepare or even by withholding your criticism if he decides to eat the leftover spaghetti and meat balls or make a "Dagwood" sandwich with all the trimmings.

Snacks and Treats

It appears that, unless parents firm up their "no" power, our children may become a nation of unwise snackers. Not that there's anything wrong with a between-meal pickup. There *is* danger in going overboard on soft drinks, candy, and greasy foods that add pounds but not much basic nourishment. Too many sweets, moreover, are likely to damage teeth.

One way to cut down on this overspending and overeating is to have snacks available at home. All kinds of fruits, raw vegetables, simple cookies, whole-grain or enriched breads, milk, and cheese are far better than sweets and fats.

One way to prevent "snacks unlimited" is to see to it that your child has three hearty meals a day. Another way of limiting the money flow from home to snack-counter is to put him on an allowance. If he has 60 cents a week to spend on "treats," for instance, and if you stick with this rule, he will find out before long that he has to stop and count before he spends. It might also increase his interest in the seemingly free meals to be had at home.

At the Grocery Store

Maybe your children would like to help with marketing and food planning. Going to the grocery store with your youngsters may not be the easiest way to buy food, but your sons and daughters are likely to get a lot out of the experience, especially if you encourage them to help you make your grocery list and figure out how much money can be spent. Chances are that, with practice, your child can eventually be a real help to you as assistant chief marketer. Also, with your guidance, he will learn to be a smart consumer, and that is quite an accomplishment.

Lunch for Your School-Age Child

If your child carries his lunch, perhaps he can help prepare it. You will want to at least help him plan his lunch, and inspect what goes into his lunch box. A hearty sandwich of meat, egg, cheese or peanut butter, fruit, a simple cookie, and a raw vegetable such as carrot sticks are an easy pattern to follow. If he doesn't buy milk at school, he should carry some in a thermos bottle.

Maybe your youngster eats in the cafeteria in school. Some schools have enough teachers and lunchroom helpers to guide young customers, but a bit of home discussion on the topic will help. Here, as elsewhere, parents and teachers can operate as a team.

You might live close enough to school so that your child can come home for lunch. Many parents and youngsters like such an arrangement. This is a time when you can give him the foods he particularly relishes, and when he can share with you the trials and triumphs of his morning.

As your child gets a bit older, he may scorn his home-for-lunch program. Like other 9- to 12-year-olds, he may vastly prefer the social life of lunch with his buddies.

REST AND SLEEP

There is no set rule for how much rest a child should have. Children usually can get by with somewhat less sleep as they get older. During the years between 6 and 12, growth slows down and a child uses up less physical energy. Typically, most youngsters at this age bounce energetically through the day without a nap and with only short rest periods.

This ready supply of energy is especially typical of children over the age of 7 or 8. Younger ones may get along better if they have longer and more frequent "quiet hours."

Dealing with Bedtime Battles

Your children will probably accept going to bed more easily if you work together on the time for "good night." Although you have the final say, the child's point of view is worth considering. Just when a child should go to bed depends on how much sleep he needs. And that depends on his age, health, the day's activities, and what kind of person he is. Your 6-year-old, for instance, probably requires about 11 hours of sleep and your 11-year-old may do nicely with 9.

If your child bounces gaily out of bed in the morning, full of zip, he is probably getting enough sleep. If he gets up long before family rising time, maybe he is going to bed too early. If you have to drag him from his slumbers, he probably is not getting enough rest.

Your 6- to 12-year-old should be able to understand why he has a particular bedtime and the importance of rest to his own well-being. But, although he understands all this, he still may balk when the hour comes.

If you let him know 15 minutes or so in advance that the time is approaching, he is likely to put up less of a fuss. No one wants to be interrupted in the middle of an activity with an abrupt "Time to quit." Another idea along this line is to help him plan his evening projects in advance so there won't be a last minute rush. Then, too, activities should take on a calm, quiet tone as bedtime draws near.

It is sometimes hard to bring about this before bedtime calm. Some children get fussier and more excitable in the evening. The more tired they get, the less willing they may be to call it quits. If your child acts this way, he will get along better if you very firmly take him in hand and start him to bed.

He will accept this more happily if special treats are connected with this hour. Perhaps a glass of milk or some fruit has a soothing effect. Younger children love to have a story. Older ones probably prefer to read their own, but may enjoy a little visit with you. It is a good time for you to listen quietly while your child talks about his today and considers his tomorrow. You may have an evening prayer, or a good night song that you sing together. Perhaps you have a set routine that your youngster demands every night.

Rituals appeal to younger children as a kind of magic protection from the perils of giving themselves up to sleep. They may also want a special teddy bear—or blanket or book—or the new pair of shoes to keep them company. Such bedmates bring comfort and surely won't cause any harm. Older youngsters usually have overcome their bedtime fears and have less need for a set pattern of retiring.

If your child has a comfortable bed in a quiet room, he is likely to relax and go to sleep more easily. He also should have a bed that is large enough for him, a firm mattress, and light, but warm bed clothing.

Even with all this in his favor, your youngster may put you through a few more paces before he is ready to settle down. After you have said your supposedly last good night, you may hear such complaints as: "I'm hungry." "I'm thirsty." "I bumped my foot." "I'm hot." If you calmly and definitely let your child know that you know these are excuses to stay up and that you aren't falling for them, he is likely to give in pretty quickly.

SAFETY

Accidents kill or cripple more children than any disease does. The chief causes of accidental death to youngsters in this age group are automobiles, drowning, fire, explosions, and firearms. As your child's play leads him on to wider explorations and experiments, you will want to keep track of his activities and teach him how to live safely.

Caution Can Be Overdone

The following section on accident prevention may stir up your fears for your child's safety too much. While it is true that you must be alert to the protection of your youngster, it is also true that too much worry on your part can be harmful to him. When children are overly anxious about their own welfare, tension can lead them to have more accidents or to be hurt more severely when they do encounter danger. Panic prevents clear thinking and skillful action when threats to safety loom.

Some suggestions for your know-how and his are given here. Ideally, parents slowly and calmly teach their youngsters over a period of time not only to protect, but also to enjoy, themselves. If you can give your child plenty of know-how, a pinch of caution, and a general sense of well-being, he has a very good chance of escaping harm and of developing courage in his approach to life.

Toys and Play Equipment

If your child is like most children, he probably strews the house and yard with his toys and play equipment. For his own sake and yours, not to mention that of his equipment, he may need to be reminded over and over again to put his toys where they belong. Otherwise, they can become booby traps leading to accidents.

Home Appliances

The modern home is full of mechanical and chemical marvels that make life easier, more pleasant, and more healthful. Now that your child is growing older and becoming more skillful, it is time for you to teach him, step by step, how to use these appliances in the right way.

Over a period of time, you can show him how to light the oven, run the washing machine, use sharp knives correctly, and operate the vacuum cleaner. As he learns more about how to use electricity, gas, and oil as sources of power, he should be learning about their dangers. He must understand the hazards of frayed electric cords, broken electric plugs, exposed wires, and using metal to take toast from the toaster. He should learn that it is never safe for a person to touch an electric switch when he is standing in water or on a wet surface, or when his hands are wet.

Fire

Even the brightest youngster needs time to fully understand the explosive powers of gas, gasoline, many cleaning fluids, and other chemicals. He has to have a certain amount of supervised experience with such things to realize that oils and greases burn very rapidly; that grass fires easily get out of control, especially on windy days; that camp fires should always be doused with water before they are left; that if one's hair or clothing catches fire, the right thing to do is to roll on the ground or in a blanket, never to start running or walking away.

Firearms

It is becoming more and more important to teach your child the correct use and the dangers of guns because there seem to be so many of them around. The National Rifle Association and your local health department offer a course in home firearms. If you give a gun to your child, be sure you know the rules and regulations that are necessary for its safe use. Teach these rules to your child. If you have firearms in your home, you will want to see that they are unloaded and kept in a locked closet. If your child is eager to learn to shoot, it is a good idea for him to be taught by an expert. Marksmanship and handling of guns and pistols can be taught to older boys and girls under safe conditions. All children need to learn that no gun of any kind should ever be pointed at any person, even in fun.

Medicines and Poisons

Most homes regularly have on hand an assortment of dangerous chemicals. Some of these are in ordinary household cleaning materials and in most insecticides. In nearly every bathroom cabinet are common drugs that can harm children.

You can do several things to lessen these hazards to your child's well-being. As stated in the Safety section in Chapter 7, all toxic substances should be kept out of reach of children, preferably under lock and key. Your older child can gradually be taught to read

Health Care

labels, and to understand and safely use common home remedies and cleansers. You will want to warn him to keep dangerous materials away from his younger brothers and sisters and never to give them medicine unless you have told him to do this. Many families clean out their medicine cabinets and utility closets regularly, destroying all unlabeled bottles and cans. The contents of these bottles and cans can be flushed down the toilet. The containers should be washed out before they are put in the trash. Medicines on the shelves for more than 6 months have probably lost their value anyway. Some drugs become poisons after they have been kept too long. Teach your child not to take any medicine without consulting you first.

Safety Outside the Home

Although safety begins at home, it certainly doesn't stop there. Your 6- to 12-year old is likely to become more venturesome with each passing month. His activities are apt to lead him to play in alleys and streets. Since this is extremely dangerous in most communities, you will have to firmly say "no" to it. This "no" will be accepted more readily if you give your child other equally interesting things to do.

Your young explorer will not be safe simply because he has a playground. He is eager for adventure, and not likely to stick to one, or even several, recreation areas. For this reason, you will want to step up your lessons in traffic safety. These lessons should include instructions on bike riding and roller skating, as well as walking. If you can join with neighbors in setting up basic safety rules, all the children on your block will have better protection and fewer arguments will occur such as, "Jimmie doesn't have to cross the street at the traffic light. Why do I?"

Most streets and all highways offer serious dangers to the foot-traveler, not to mention the bike rider, the roller skater, and small children pushing doll buggies and wagons. But many neighborhoods lack sidewalks. This lack of safe walk-ways also makes children dependent on the family car or the bus to get to school, stores, recreation centers, and so on. Since it is good for your child to learn to get safely around his community on his own feet, you may want to work with other parents to see to it that sidewalks are provided in your area.

Then, too, your child needs to be taught about other dangers in his surroundings. If he flies a kite, he should be taught to keep it away from power lines. He should be taught to stay away from dumps, quarries, torches burning at street barricades, steep ravines, pools, swamps, buildings being wrecked, and places where blasting is going on. A healthy respect for fenced enclosures and "No trespassing" signs may save his life. Since children are attracted to such places by their urge to explore, it is important to help them find safer ways to adventure, such as in parks, playgrounds, family trips, club activities, and so on.

Safety from strangers. One of your worries about your child's safety away from home probably is concerned with his being hurt or frightened by some stranger. Although adult crimes against children are relatively few, dangers do exist, especially in large cities.

Although it is important to warn your child about such dangers, you do not want to frighten him too much. Some parents tend to overcaution their little girls and they sometimes grow up with an unfortunate feeling that all men are dangerous. Such feelings may stand in the way of falling in love and marrying happily.

You may want to quietly explain to both your sons and daughters that some people—a very few, as a matter of fact—are so mixed up in their own feelings that they express their interest in sex in very peculiar ways. Your child will generally be safe from persons of this kind if he always refuses rides or treats from strangers, comes home before dark, stays with a group of children, and looks on policemen as his friends and protectors.

As you discuss such matters with your youngster, you will want to answer his questions and give him the feeling that he can tell you about any upsetting event that occurs.

If your child does have unfortunate contacts with strangers, it is best to treat the matter as calmly as possible. Get all the facts you can from your youngster and report the matter to the police. The police will be greatly aided in their work if your child can give an accurate description of the stranger. Police also stress that youngsters be trained to memorize license numbers of automobiles if they are molested or threatened by people who are in cars.

Another way to protect your child from strangers is to provide him with good times and good feelings at home and in his own neighborhood. Children who are mostly happy with themselves and their surroundings are less likely to be tempted by gifts or seeming friendliness from people they don't know.

Safety after nightfall. Even though you try to make your child happy at home, as he gets older, he is likely to want to play outdoors or wander about after dark. You can't blame him for loving the mystery and adventure of the nighttime world. In most parts of our country, however, parents or other adults need to be with youngsters after nightfall. This doesn't mean, of course, that your child can't go to club meetings or go visiting in the evening, especially when there is no school the next day. But it does mean that you should check as to whether responsible older persons will be with your boys and girls at these times. Also, if your child has to go far to reach his destination, an older person should go with him, or, at least, he should travel with a group. No exact rules can be made about this, since some neighborhoods are safer than others.

Safety in cars. Teach your child to always use the seat belt when he rides in automobiles. Be sure the family car has this equipment.

Water safety. Your child is probably enchanted by water in any form, from puddles to oceans. Therefore, it is essential for him to learn how to swim early in life. Perhaps you can teach him yourself. If not, you are apt to find that your community offers swimming lessons that are free or low in cost.

You and your child should also know the basic rules of water safety. He should understand that he must not swim in unguarded or unknown bodies of water; that it is best not to go into the water alone; that it is wise to wait for an hour after a meal before going swimming; that it is not smart to rock a small boat, especially if there is anyone in it who can't swim. Also, all nonswimmers should wear life jackets when playing on or near the water.

When Your Child Needs Help

12
Handicaps and Emotional Problems

Most of this book has been devoted to the growth and development of normal children in average families. It has not dealt with special problems of particular children because most parents cannot handle these without the help of professionally trained specialists. Although reading about serious problems of children may help you decide whether or not your child does have a severe difficulty, a book cannot lead you to the effective treatment of such difficulties. For this, you need a professionally trained specialist or a team of specialists. In the following pages we present a brief guide to some fairly common difficulties in order to help you decide whether or not your child may have a serious physical or emotional problem which requires specialized treatment.

EMOTIONAL PROBLEMS

Since children often have more difficulty than adults in knowing what is bothering them—and in talking about some of their troubles—they are more apt to express their emotional upsets through the way they behave than through what they say.

As you read the list of behavior symptoms which may show that your child has a serious emotional problem, you may become quite alarmed. The chief reason for your alarm may well be that some of the signs of serious difficulties may also be signs of temporary upsets. Most children have some symptoms of emotional problems some of the time. This doesn't necessarily mean that they have severe, long-lasting difficulties. They may be reacting only to a short-time strain, such as a new baby in the family or a move to a different neighborhood, or to something that has happened that you may not know about.

As you think about whether or not your youngster may have a serious problem, you will find it helpful to ask yourself whether or not he has one or most of the listed symptoms frequently, whether or not he has them in a slight or more extreme form, and whether he is reacting to a passing strain. It is also a good idea to check your observations with such persons as your child's doctor, teachers, and religious leaders.

While it is important not to worry too much about your youngster, it is also important to watch for early signs of trouble. If your child does have serious difficulties, he will be helped most by early treatment of them. Untreated emotional difficulties are likely to get worse, rather than better. Skilled treatment by qualified specialists is just as important as early treatment.

It is hard for most parents to face the possibility that their child may have an emotional problem. There are many reasons for this. For instance, there are the old superstitions that still are quoted to the effect that there is something shameful about emotional problems. Modern science shows that upset feelings are to be understood and treated in much the same way that physical illnesses are to be understood and treated. Although parents may blame themselves more for a child's emotional upsets than for his physical ones, it is important to realize that there are many possible causes for emotional problems. These causes may have little to do with the way the parents have raised the child. Children are born with different ways of reacting to the world around them, and they are exposed to many influences besides those of their parents.

Signs of possible emotional disturbances tend to fall into two major groups. The first group includes those youngsters who are deeply unhappy, frightened, worried, who have guilty feelings, and who tend to handle these feelings by drawing away from the outer world and from other people. Seriously disturbed youngsters of this kind may behave in one or more of the following ways.

Severely Shy Children

The first four groups of behavior patterns listed below are common with very young children; as your child gets older he should be acting in these ways less often:

- Extremely shy, fearful behavior, such as being afraid to make any friends outside the family or being afraid to try even simple new experiences.
- Extreme dislike of being away from parents for even a short time, frequent bedwetting, demands for help from parents in simple tasks, such as dressing, etc.
- Frequent temper tantrums, whining, crying over slight matters.
- Frequent nightmares or sleepwalking.
- Extreme, continued confusion over what is imagined and what is real. If a 6- to 12-year old child seems to see and hear things that do not exist, if he imagines a number of events that did not happen, he may be in real trouble. If he shows that he can see the difference between what is real and what is make-believe when this is pointed out to him, then he may simply have an active imagination.
- Reacting with panic, over and over again, to a particular object or thing that is not frightening to most people (such as a kitten or a stuffed toy).
- Showing extreme fear of being hurt even in quite safe activities or worrying in a seemingly unreasonable way over possible failure even in simple tasks.
- Absolute insistence on a number of set routines or on extreme order and neatness as well as being anxious to be considered perfect.
- Appearing to be bored, showing little strong feeling, absent-mindedness.
- Repeating simple acts over and over again in a way that the child seems unable to control, such as nose picking, thumb-sucking, rocking back and forth, nail biting, public masturbation, mouth twisting, hand wringing, and so on.

- Frequent pains, stomach upsets, skin rashes, etc., for which doctors cannot find a physical cause.

Serious Troublemakers

Another group of signs of possible problems are often observed in children who have exceptional difficulty in controlling their angry and destructive feelings. These feelings are usually expressed in a roundabout way, so that it is frequently difficult to tell what the child is angry about or who is making him angry. Often, he doesn't know, himself. Children of this kind may have one or more of the following symptoms:

- Excessive and frequent fighting, explosive temper tantrums, running away or truanting from school more than a few times.
- Frequent stealing (especially when the stolen objects seem to be of no, or little, worth to the child); frequent lying in a more serious way than simply playing games of make-believe.
- Taking serious risks with his own physical safety; extreme, continuing interest in stories focused on crime and terror.
- Frequent and noisy use of clearly forbidden swear words and sex talk; a strong and active resistance to persons in authority.
- Serious and frequent destruction of property, fascination with setting fires, cruel treatment of other children or animals, repeated acts of destructive mischief.

Children who frequently show one or more of the above symptoms are often seen by others as being "undisciplined and spoiled." Youngsters who tend to do just about whatever they wish are, indeed, often lacking in discipline. On the other hand, some children, out of their deep, inner unhappiness, act in a violent, destructive, and disobedient way. It sometimes may seem as if they wish to destroy themselves and others.

Here, again, it is important to consider how often a child misbehaves, how serious his misbehavior is, and whether his misbehavior seems to be related only to a passing event which has upset him. Although more firm discipline can often help the child who carelessly disregards rules, it is not likely to help the touchy, irritable youngster who "acts bad because he feels bad." If you have a youngster who frequently gets into serious trouble because he is destructive, rebellious, and so on, it would be a good idea to ask the advice of professionally trained experts who specialize in children's problems.

Using Trained Specialists

If you think your child has a serious emotional problem, you will want to have him checked first by your doctor. Sometimes, problems which appear to be caused by upset feelings are at least partly caused by physical illnesses or handicaps. Since emotional upsets and physical upsets often go together, it is an ideal arrangement for a team of specialists to work together, such as a doctor, a psychiatrist, a psychologist, and a social worker. Some hospitals, clinics, and schools have such a team. In some communities, these teams are able to give free or low cost services because they are supported by tax funds or other kinds of community contributions.

If your community does not have a team of specialists that work together, your doctor may refer you to a social worker, psychologist, or psychiatrist. Your doctor is likely to know whether these people have the professional training they should have in order to effectively help your child. You can tell something, yourself, about how much professional training such people have had by finding out whether they belong to their professional associations. These associations set up standards of education and experience for their members. Among these organizations are the following: the National Association of Social Workers, the American Psychological Association, and the American Psychiatric Association. You will want to check on these matters because, in some communities, people who are not adequately trained claim or consider themselves to be qualified to treat emotional problems. Be careful not to seek help from people who are not qualified.

When you have questions or want further information about sources of help for your child, check with your family physician, your local hospital, clinic, health and welfare council, or medical association. You can also write or call your local or state departments of health or of public welfare.

If you do seek treatment for your child's emotional problems, it is very likely that the specialist who is helping him will want to talk to you, too. If you seek help from a group of specialists, at a child guidance or mental health clinic, you may find that different members of the professional team may work with different members of the family. This is partly because an emotionally upset child needs particular understanding from his parents. Also, parents find it helpful to discuss their own worries about an upset child with a trained specialist who understands them as well as the child.

It is comforting to know that these specialists are guided by a code of professional ethics which pledges them to keep everything confidential that children or parents tell them.

OTHER HANDICAPS

If your child has other special problems, other kinds of specialized help are, of course, needed. In the paragraphs below, you will find brief statements about some of the more common kinds of difficulties which affect some children.

Mental Retardation

If a child is mentally retarded, it means his intelligence is considerably less than average. Thus, he cannot learn as fast as other children, nor can he learn as much. Some retarded children are only mildly handicapped and can get along fairly well at home, at school, and in their community, especially if they are in a special school class for retarded children and if life is kept simple for them at home. Others have more serious handicaps, ranging from being unable to learn school subjects but able to tend to many of their daily needs, to being so retarded that they seem like helpless babies.

Parents who have children of this kind have serious and sad problems to face. With less severely retarded youngsters, a child's handicap may be unknown until he starts having trouble in the first or second grade. If you or your child's teacher think your youngster may be mentally retarded, it is important to have him very carefully studied by a doctor—perhaps a team of doctors—and a psychologist. A child sometimes seems to be dull because he is ill, has physical handicaps, or is emotionally upset. Although your child might seem to be retarded when he is measured by a group intelligence test (such as most schools use), tests of this kind usually cannot show whether a child has a special physical or emotional problem that may have a lot to do with a low intelligence score.

There are many causes of mental retardation. Not all of them are known. Very often the cause is not related in any way to the kind of care that parents give a child. The earlier a child gets special help for a problem of this kind, the more likely it is that the help will be effective.

You can find out about special treatment service for retarded children by talking to your doctor, clinic, school, health and welfare council, local and state departments of health, of public welfare, or education.

Speech Problems

As your child becomes 6 or 7, his speech should be getting quite clear. Some youngsters, of course, speak well at an earlier age. Of course, your 6- to 12-year old child will still mispronounce some big words and some new ones as he adds them to his vocabulary. Generally, you can help him speak well simply by talking clearly to him and by listening to what he has to say. If you correct him too often, or in a harsh or teasing way, he is apt to find it harder to learn to talk well.

Stuttering is a common difficulty with many youngsters. It sometimes comes about because they have so much more to say than time or skill to get it said. Emotional tension and special attention drawn to a child's stuttering are apt to make it worse. Boys, with their slower development and greater pressures for success, are more likely to stutter than girls. If your child does stutter a good deal and does not seem to be improving, it is an excellent idea to have his hearing tested and perhaps he should see a speech therapist. Many schools employ speech and hearing specialists. Some communities also have speech and hearing centers. Ask your school and doctor about the programs in your own community.

Other speech problems may also suggest that your child is hard of hearing. Tremendous progress has been made in recent years in specialized hearing tests for youngsters. Many schools today give such tests. If your school does not have such a service, ask your doctor about this. Especially in the case of children who are only slightly deaf, it is difficult to know without these tests whether or not he does have a hearing problem—and if so, what kind. Modern hearing aids and special treatment can be of important help to the child who is deaf.

Problems of Vision

If your child is blind, you and he surely have a particularly difficult problem. You will need the special services that most states offer. Ask your doctor about this. You may also find it helpful to get in touch with your local or state departments of health or of public welfare.

Fortunately, very few youngsters are blind. Many, however, have imperfect vision. Improved tests of children's eyesight show that even among 6- or 7-year olds, a large percentage have slight or more serious problems in seeing. Since good vision is so important to your child, especially in his school work, you will want to have him carefully checked in this matter. Even slight problems in eyesight can affect your child's ability to read well. Perhaps he will be tested in school. If not, talk the matter over with your child's doctor.

A Word about Handicapped Children

Children with handicaps should be treated as normally as their handicaps will allow. They are often more damaged by the way their parents handle them than by the handicap they were born with or acquired. If you are unable to judge accurately what your child can and cannot do, it is very important for you to discuss with your doctor or other counselor just how much activity your child can tolerate. Most parents have a tendency to overprotect the handicapped child or to treat the child so differently from the other children that the child is set even further apart from the rest of the family, and often disliked by them for this. In time the parents, too, will begin to get angry at having to make allowances for the handicapped child. Children handled this way develop a low opinion of themselves. They quickly understand that they cannot be treated the same as other children and are, therefore, probably not considered as good as the others.

In all likelihood you as a parent feel guilty about your child's handicap. You may feel partly or fully responsible. Feeling guilty most often has nothing to do with reality or common sense, and many people continue to feel that way even when they've been told repeatedly that they are not responsible for the problems. It is important for you to understand that other children in the family may feel a similar sense of guilt, particularly if they are older than the handicapped child. Children are seldom pleased at the thought of having a new brother or sister and they often wish bad things for the new baby. When the baby turns out to be handicapped the children may well feel that their wishes came true and were responsible for the handicap. That feeling becomes the same kind of guilt which parents know.

It is just those guilty feelings that make it so hard for both parents and brothers and sisters to treat handicapped children normally. Whether the feelings are deeply hidden or are fairly close to the surface they interfere with your ability to treat your child in an open, friendly, and unguarded way. That is why it is important to understand these feelings and either deal with them yourself or get help from some counselor in talking them out. Only then can you begin to deal with your handicapped child more rationally.

Children tend to be somewhat ashamed of having a handicapped brother or sister. They may react to this in one of two ways. Some will stop bringing friends home and will refuse to go outside with the handicapped child. Others, however, may become totally devoted to the care of the handicapped child. Neither of these extremes is good for the healthy child. If you see your children reacting in either of these ways you should bring things out in the open. You have to make it clear to the healthy children that you understand the kinds of feelings they have because everybody, including you, has them at some time or other.

While you are helping your handicapped children become less dependent it is important not to go too far in the other direction and drive them to overcompensate for their handicaps by trying to do things well beyond their capabilities. You have to help them become more capable of using their assets while at the same time remaining realistic about themselves in striving to compensate for their handicap.

13
Illnesses and Other Disorders

For a discussion of some common problems and worries encountered during infancy, see also pages 41-46.

Allergies

What are they? When a person is sensitive to a normally harmless substance, he has an allergy. If he receives more of this substance than he can stand, he will show an allergic reaction. An allergy may look like a cold, an upset stomach, a skin disease, or a number of other disorders.

There is such a variety of allergic reactions that a series of tests is usually necessary to find the cause of trouble. Emotional tension may often play a part in causing increasing allergic problems. Allergies are not infections and cannot be "caught" or given to anyone else. While seldom fatal, they cause discomfort and inconvenience—mild to severe—and can lead to infections.

If your child has an allergy, he should be under the care of a doctor who will, by means of tests, trial diets, and changes in environment, find out and, in most cases, control what your youngster is sensitive to.

Four of the common kinds of allergic reactions are asthma, hay fever, eczema, and hives.

Asthma narrows the air passages and produces mucus so that it is hard to breathe. A child with asthma wheezes and coughs in an alarming way. It may be worse when he lies down, and so he has to sleep propped up. Attacks frequently occur at night, and they often change with the season of the year. Sometimes a cold precedes an asthmatic attack.

Eczema is a red, thickened rough patch on the skin, frequently on the cheeks, folds of skin at the elbows and behind the knee. It will itch, and scratching causes oozing which forms crusts. While it is not contagious, the open sores may readily become infected.

Hay fever resembles the common cold, with sneezing, itching and weeping eyes, and a "stuffed up" head caused by swelling of the membranes of the nose. It is usually caused by pollens of weeds, grasses, and trees and, therefore, unlike a cold, usually comes only at regular seasons of the year.

Hives raise welts on the skin which resemble large mosquito bites. They usually appear and disappear suddenly. A child who itches from hives can be made more comfortable by applying ice to the welts, or by giving him a warm soda bath (1 cup of baking soda for a small tub).

Bowel Movements

Slight blood streaking on the outside of a bowel movement is usually caused by a small sore or fissure in the anus, and is not a cause for alarm. In infants, the fissure and the bleeding can often be cured by keeping the stools soft with one of the remedies for constipation discussed below. If bleeding or hard bowel movements persist, your doctor will be able to help. **Do not delay** medical attention if there is bloody diarrhea or passage of fresh blood or blood clots with the bowel movements.

Constipation exists when the bowel movements are hard, dry, and difficult to pass, no matter how frequent or infrequent they may be. Prune juice (1 tablespoon), brown sugar (1 tablespoon), or molasses (1 tablespoon), added to one of your infant's bottles may correct this. If not, your doctor or clinic may suggest a remedy. **Do not** use mineral oil, castor oil, adult laxatives, or enemas without the advice of your doctor. Laxatives and enemas may gravely complicate the situation if the child's appendix is inflamed. For children and older babies, plenty of fluids and fresh fruits and vegetables do no harm. There is seldom any rush about relieving a child who is constipated. Check with your doctor before giving any medicines.

Diarrhea exists when the bowel movements contain too much water. It may occur when a child eats some irritating or spoiled food, or if he has a head cold, sore throat, or other infections. It may be caused by an infection known as *enteritis* or *dysentery,* which can be very serious.

In infants, small bowel movements that are milky or watery or odd-colored are rarely of concern, and no treatment or diet change is usually necessary. Large, watery bowel movements can cause an infant to lose more water in his bowel movement than he is drinking. The dehydration which results can be a true medical emergency. Even a single huge, explosive, watery bowel movement can be an emergency in an infant one to three months old, especially if there is poor appetite or vomiting. **Do not delay in seeking medical attention when there is one or more large watery bowel movements.**

For a child of any age, diarrhea presents much the same problems as vomiting—loss of fluids from the body and the inability to replace them easily because fluids taken by mouth pass through the digestive tract too fast to be absorbed. Sometimes, of course, vomiting and diarrhea go together and the difficulties are multiplied. In diarrhea it is important to keep track of the number, the frequency, the wateriness, and the explosiveness of the bowel movements. When all these signs are present the child should be watched for the same signs of dehydration noted under the discussion of Vomiting. Additional signs to look for are the presence of blood and mucus in the stools in medium to large amounts. These are also signs that the problem may be serious.

Again the treatment is clear fluids such as those used for vomiting. Milk and fruit juices are *not* to be used. They will almost always make the diarrhea worse. You should realize that fluids taken by mouth may pass through the body very quickly and almost unchanged. For example, red jello may well come out in a watery stool still red and looking like blood. It is a good idea to avoid red liquids of that type in order not to confuse the picture.

Illnesses and Other Disorders

There are really no medicines you can buy at the store on your own which will help treat diarrhea in young children. The only effective medicines are those which must be ordered by a doctor directly. Even then, these are useful only in some kinds of diarrhea. Your doctor will undoubtedly order them when they are likely to help if you keep in touch and provide the necessary information.

The Common Cold

Colds are infectious diseases. They are caught from other people who have them. They are not caused by drafts, or wet shoes, or being dressed too lightly or too heavily. They are caused by cold germs (viruses). People who have picked up a cold germ from someone else are already contagious for a day or so while they are coming down with the cold—before any signs have even developed—and for the first day or so afterwards. Obviously, if you can catch a cold from someone who doesn't show any sign of being sick it is very difficult to avoid them. Also, there are hundreds of different viruses which cause the common cold and having one kind doesn't give any protection against having another kind. So it is possible to get one cold after another. Colds occur all year round but are more common in the late fall, winter, and early spring.

An infant with a cold will become a little fussy and lose part of his appetite. His nose will start running with clear watery material which will later become thick and sticky. His eyes may look red; he may cough frequently and make a lot of noise when he breathes. He may have a fever. The cold may last 4 or 5 days, or 2 or 3 weeks, and if a cough starts it may continue as long as 4 or 5 weeks.

Neither you nor your doctor can do much about it except keep your baby as comfortable as possible. If he seems uncomfortable with aches and pains, give him half a baby aspirin 3 or 4 times a day. Use a nasal syringe to clear his nose when it bothers him. A mixture of honey and lemon juice given 1 teaspoon every 4 hours will do as much good for a cough as many fancy cough medicines.

When You Should Worry. If he seems very weak and sick, has no energy to even cry loudly, nurses poorly, doesn't want over half of his usual bottle, doesn't wake up to be playful for even a short time—then you should seek medical care quickly.

How sick he acts tells much more about how seriously ill he might be than anything else. If he has a high fever and a cough, but takes some of his bottle eagerly and wants to play, you don't have to worry. But if he is listless, weak, uninterested in attention, play or his bottle, you should get him to a doctor quickly.

If he has labored breathing you should have him checked. This means that he has to work so hard at breathing—getting the air in and out—that he has no energy left for anything else, even for his bottle or playing. Making a lot of noise breathing is not important, but having to work very hard to breathe is!

If he cries and moans as if in pain for several hours while he has a cold, you should get him checked by a doctor. If he is just fussy and goes to sleep after you comfort him or give him half a baby aspirin, you needn't worry. But painful cries shouldn't be ignored.

You will probably want to check with a doctor the first time your baby has a bad cold, but you will soon learn what to expect with his colds and how to treat them.

During the early school years, children seem to get a discouraging number of coughs and colds and sore throats, though perhaps not so many as when they were younger. When your child comes down with a cold, check with the doctor and keep in touch with him as symptoms change. He will decide whether he needs to see your child. In this way, you are likely to avoid complications which can result when a slight infection opens the way for a more serious one.

Colds will often last a full two weeks—1–2 days of very runny nose and sneezing; 2–4 days of a very stuffy nose and beginning cough; and 9–10 days of coughing and slowly getting better. In an ordinary cold there is seldom any fever over 99–100. If the temperature goes higher it is likely that some other infection has set in as a complication. In young children the most common complication of the cold is infection of the middle ear. (See Ear Infections.)

Children tend to swallow the mucus which drips from the back of the nose into the throat. Sometimes they will vomit up that mucus but they seldom vomit seriously or repeatedly with an uncomplicated cold. Children do not have to stay in bed, but they probably should stay indoors and avoid drafts in order not to become chilled. As with most diseases, children can be relied on to control their own activity level. When they really feel sick they will be less active and get the extra rest they need; when they feel better it is all right for them to become more active.

There is no known cure for the uncomplicated common cold. All treatment is aimed at helping the child be more comfortable while the cold runs its standard course. If the child has symptoms like fever or headache, then aspirin may help. If the child is uncomfortable or cannot sleep because of the runny or stuffy nose, a decongestant medicine may sometimes relieve the symptoms. If the nose becomes sore or crusted, a little cream or ointment on the area may be soothing and may lessen the child's rubbing at the sore. When a cough is the worst part of the problem, some cough medicine may make it possible for the child to play or sleep more comfortably. When the house is especially dry, or when the nose is stuffiest, a cold water humidifier or vaporizer may be very useful. (Old-fashioned hot steam vaporizers work less well and may be dangerous to young children.) Don't worry if the child doesn't want to eat. As soon as the symptoms begin to let up, the appetite will return. In the meantime try to encourage the child to drink—especially such fluids as juice, water, clear soups, and weak tea.

The number of colds your children have will be related to the number of people with colds to whom they are exposed and to their own resistance. Resistance to colds and other infections depends on children's overall state of nutrition and health. Proper nutrition, adequate rest, the right exercise and freedom from inborn disease problems all contribute to better resistance. Finally, there is no such thing as a "chronic cold." A child who has a runny nose all the time probably has an allergy problem and should be checked by a doctor.

Colic

See page 15 for discussion.

Ear and Throat Infections

The ears and the throat are the places in the body where other common infections are most likely to settle in young children. Although they often occur as complications of the common cold or other common contagious diseases of childhood, these infections will also turn up on their own. Of the two, ear infections are more common in young children, and they are also more often seen as complications of colds.

Ear infections are frequently more painful than throat infections and often seem to come on more suddenly. Children will begin pulling on one or both ears, will complain of pain in the ear or ears and will then often begin to cry as the pain gets worse. Fever may accompany the infection. A doctor or nurse should look into the ear. The kind of infection described here is deep inside the ear and cannot be seen by parents or anyone else without a special instrument to allow looking at the ear drum. Sometimes, though, the ear drum will rupture and a discharge will run out of the ear. This makes it easier to be sure about the infection and does not mean the infection will be harder to heal. Your child may get some relief from aspirin and some decongestant medicine.

The child with a *throat* infection will probably complain of pain in the throat (although some children have trouble explaining just where the pain is), may be seen to have trouble swallowing, and may have swollen glands beneath the corner of the jaw. The throat may be red or have white patches on it but this is often very hard for parents to see. If you think your child has an infected throat it is a good idea to call your doctor. The doctor may very well want to take a culture—swabbing the throat with a sterile piece of cotton on the end of a stick—in order to find out what kind of infection is there. Usually the culture can be completed within a day or so and will not delay treatment any significant amount of time.

Strep throat is a sore throat caused by the streptococcus. Be sure to continue the medicine the doctor advises for the full period he prescribes even though the symptoms clear up quickly. To avoid later complications, it should be continued for the full course of treatment. If a streptococcus infection gets out of hand, it can lead to more serious complications such as *scarlet fever* (a red rash will be present), *tonsillitis, rheumatic fever* (see Other Respiratory Infections and Complications), and *nephritis* (see Stomach, Intestinal, and Genitourinary Disorders).

Eye Infections

Conjunctivitis, often called pinkeye, is an infection caused by a variety of bacteria and/or virus and is extremely contagious. You may be first aware of conjunctivitis when the child wakens with his eyelids glued shut by pus. It readily spreads from one member of the family to another unless extreme care is taken to keep towels, washcloths, and other toilet articles separate.

You can soothe the inflamed eyes with warm compresses, but

check with the doctor about treatment. Neglect may damage the child's vision.

A child's eyes and eyelids may become reddened for a variety of reasons. Allergy sometimes causes red or inflamed eyes. Consider the possibility of eyestrain if a child blinks, squints, or is generally irritable. Even very young children can be fitted with glasses.

Styes on the eye are caused by bacteria infecting the hair follicle of an eyelash. Pimples are related infections. Do not open a sty, and don't allow the child to rub it when it is coming to a head, otherwise the pus germs may spread to other hair follicles. When it erupts, wipe the pus away with a sterile pad.

If a child has a series of styes, get advice from the doctor.

Fever

This is one of the most common symptoms in young children and one of the most worrisome to parents. But fever is not necessarily harmful. It is the body's way of reacting to invading germs. With some diseases, the common cold for instance, the temperature seldom rises very high. However, with some other diseases there is often quite a bit of fever.

Many babies will have a fever with every cold. Many have a fever for a day or two with no other signs of illness except tiredness and fussiness. Young children run high temperatures much more easily than older children or adults. Temperatures of 100 or so are common with minor illnesses and it is not unusual for 2- or 3-year-olds to run fevers of 103 to 105 degrees with throat or ear infections or even with those virus infections that seem to go around town all the time.

Many parents become skilled at estimating their children's temperature merely by feeling them. However, that is not always accurate and, in any case, it is often necessary to follow an illness by actually knowing the exact temperature. For most parents the best way to do this is by taking what is called an axillary temperature. This means lifting the child's arm, putting the bulb end of the thermometer in the child's armpit, and then holding the arm snugly against the child's side for two minutes. Adding two degrees to the reading will give you the internal body temperature. Although the armpit method is a little less accurate than the rectal method it is easier, safer, and less likely to cause complications.

In general it is not just the height of the fever which is important, but how the child with fever is acting. Children are usually irritable with fever and that is a far less worrisome sign than if they are very sleepy and not interested in what is going on around them. If children are fairly active and are eating reasonably well the likelihood is that their illness is not a serious one no matter how high the fever. Even then, however, if the fever lasts more than 24 hours you should follow up with the doctor. Except for those children who are known to be likely to have convulsions with fever (see Convulsions), it is not necessary to try to bring down the fever quickly or by drastic measures. However, high temperatures are uncomfortable and it is reasonable to make some effort to keep them under control.

One of the best ways to control fever is to use aspirin. Flavored "baby" aspirin are easy to take and children like them. But aspirin is a poison if too much is taken and it should always be kept completely out of the reach of children at all times. Your doctor will tell you what dose of aspirin is right for your child and how often it should be given. Some children have difficulty with aspirin and there are other anti-fever medicines available. But if your child can take aspirin, and is not vomiting, it is likely to be the most effective way of controlling fever.

Other things you can do for comfort's sake include reducing the number and warmth of clothes and coverings on the child. You can also put him in a tub of lukewarm water or sponge him off with cloths soaked in lukewarm water. Don't use alcohol to sponge the child off with. The cold alcohol on the hot skin feels very uncomfortable and is likely to give him a chill.

REMEMBER: The time to worry is when the child is very sleepy, hard to waken, uninterested in what is going on, and doesn't even want to be touched.

Infections: To Treat or Not to Treat

There are, in general, two kinds of germs which cause infectious or contagious diseases in children. Viruses cause diseases like measles, flu, and the common cold. There aren't any medicines yet to cure this kind of infection, although there are vaccines to prevent many of them. The other kind of germs is bacteria. These most often cause such infections as ear and throat infections. Bacterial infections are treatable and curable with a kind of medicine called antibiotics.

Penicillin is the best known antibiotic but there are now many antibiotics available. They are all powerful medicines and should never be used without a specific doctor's prescription for the specific illness involved. Different antibiotics work better for some bacteria and diseases than for others. None of them, not even penicillin, is good for all illnesses. The doctor needs to fit the specific antibiotic and dosage to the specific child and disease. It is never a good idea for you to try to treat all your children's diseases with the same medicines or with leftover medicines. Doing so may cover up some of the signs and make it more difficult for the doctor to find out what is really going on. It is also never a good idea to give medicine which was prescribed for one child to another child, without checking with the doctor. Many of these medicines have side effects which may affect some individuals differently from others.

When the proper medicine for the disease has been prescribed children usually start to improve quite rapidly and seem a great deal better in one or two days. But that doesn't mean you should stop the medicine. Quite the opposite. *You should always give the medicine for as long a period of time as the doctor recommended.* If you stop too soon, because the child seems better, often the disease will not have been completely cured, symptoms will come back again and the cure may take longer the second time around. If you think the medicine is not working, or is causing some other effects on the child, check with the doctor before stopping or changing. We are fortunate to have all the modern medicines we do have now, but we still should use them carefully and under the supervision of someone who knows both the good and bad possibilities of the medicine involved.

Lack of Energy

If your child tires quickly, is pale and listless and lacks energy, something is probably wrong although no sign of acute illness develops. Chronic ill health and lack of vitality have various causes. Until you know the source, you can't effectively treat the condition. Don't buy special foods and tonics. Instead, take your child to your doctor for a physical checkup.

The child who lacks energy and seems run down may be suffering from:

Anemia (lack of sufficient red blood cells) may occur when a child's diet is faulty, when he loses a great deal of blood, or has had a severe illness. Unless the loss of blood is severe, he will build new red blood cells in time. However, the doctor may feel that a transfusion of whole blood is necessary to replenish the supply quickly. Or the doctor may prescribe iron as a medicine. Otherwise, good general care is all that is needed, with special emphasis on foods rich in iron, such as meats (especially liver, kidney, and heart), egg yolk, green leafy vegetables, whole grain and enriched bread and cereals, molasses, raisins and certain other dried fruits such as apricots, prunes, and figs. Foods rich in vitamin C, such as oranges and tomatoes, are also important.

Anemia may also be caused by disease which destroys the blood or by an inherited condition. In each case, the cause will determine the treatment.

A chronic infection which drains him of vitality.

Lack of sufficient rest indicates that you should slow down the pace of your child's day, plan a midday rest for him, and arrange an earlier bedtime. It may do wonders for him, and you, too!

Poor nourishment because the food your child eats fails to supply his body with energy and the building substances he needs. If he receives a faulty diet, correct this by offering foods from the Daily Food Guide in Chapter 11. In rare instances, a child's body cannot make proper use of the foods it takes in. Your doctor will have to prescribe for such a condition.

Some children who appear to be under-par may be naturally less energetic than others. Then, too, a pale, listless child may be hampered by an emotional problem.

Metabolic Disorders

Cystic Fibrosis is a disease of the pancreas, the glands along the bronchial tubes, and the sweat glands (which produce too much salt). One of the signs of this disease is an unusual appearance of bowel movements. Large and foul stools may be passed because of poor absorption of fats from the foods the child eats. This disease, which is suffered only by a small number of children, is inherited from parents who carry the trait but usually have no symptoms themselves. Eventually, it disturbs many of the functions of the body. A child with cystic fibrosis is apt to have repeated or chronic lung infections. He usually has a large appetite, but may nevertheless gain weight slowly. Careful and continued supervision by a doctor is necessary.

Diabetes (diabetes mellitus) is an inability of the body to use sugar and starches. Any change in the child's urinating habits may indicate illness. In wet or chilly weather, he may naturally urinate more often. A persistent increase in voiding, however, may mean diabetes. Untreated, the diabetic loses weight, no matter how much he eats, and eventually dies. A special diet and use of medicine now make it possible for a child with diabetes to lead a normal life.

Overweight

(See also Overweight children, p. 187). Many youngsters tend to be overweight mostly because they eat too many high calorie foods. It is generally best to let your doctor decide whether or not your youngster is overweight, since each child has his own kind of body build. Some youngsters who may appear to be overweight merely have large bones and heavy muscles.

Some youngsters are overweight mainly because of the way in which their bodies handle the food they eat—not necessarily because they eat too much. These matters can be very complicated, and it is a good idea to try to see a doctor who specializes in problems of overweight children if your child has serious difficulties along this line and fails to lose weight with a slimming diet.

Losing weight is not always a simple matter of eating the right foods and avoiding the wrong ones. A child may tend to put on weight for a variety of other reasons, including the possibility that his glands may fail to work as they should. Perhaps he doesn't exercise enough or perhaps he is emotionally upset. Some children who feel inferior, unhappy, and unloved turn to food for satisfaction. Even though they know they are overeating and even though they want to lose weight, they may not be able to cut down on their food intake. This can be quite a complicated problem, and your doctor may recommend that you consult a child guidance specialist.

Skin Infections

Itches and bites and sores on the skin are common with children. Some can spread to other members of the family. Treat any break in the skin with care, since it offers an easy entry for germs. Therefore, try to keep any sore place clean, and discourage a child from scratching even a mosquito bite. If you trim his nails short, it may help to prevent damage if he scratches while asleep.

You'll need the doctor to treat all the following conditions. Using patent medicines may waste time, or cause further irritation. If anyone has a skin disease, be careful to keep his towels, washcloths, linen, and clothing separate from others. Launder them with very hot water and press with a hot iron.

Athlete's foot is a fungus infection that usually occurs between the toes where the skin is warm and moist. The medicine you use should be prescribed by a doctor. Keep the child's feet clean and dry. Dust them with a talcum powder. Athlete's foot is most stubborn and prevalent in the summer. Change socks daily, and air the shoes. Open shoes and sandals may cut down on foot perspiration.

Boils are caused by bacteria that have infected a skin gland. They are related to pimples. Warm, moist dressings or soaks will relieve the pain and help to localize the infection. Do not open a boil. When it erupts, wipe the pus away with a sterile pad, then apply a sterile cover.

If a child has a series of boils, get advice from the doctor.

Cold sores are uncomfortable blisters on the lip, in the mouth, or on the tongue which generally heal by themselves and respond to simple cleanliness. They do seem to appear in some children when they have colds or other illness. Rinsing with warm water containing ½ teaspoon of salt or bicarbonate of soda per glass, may provide relief for sores inside the mouth. If the child has fever, complains of a very sore mouth, or has bleeding of the gums, call the physician or dentist. These may be symptoms of "trench mouth" or other infections.

Eczema and **hives** are discussed under Allergies.

Impetigo is a very contagious skin infection. It usually starts on the face with an itchy blister which oozes pus and crusts over. The child can readily infect others—or other areas of his own body—by carrying germs from the first sore.

Prompt treatment can clear up the infection. See your doctor. If neglected, impetigo spreads rapidly and paves the way for other infections.

Lice (pediculosis) are tiny animals which attach themselves to the hair or skin and cause irritation. If the child scratches, which he's sure to do, the excretion of the lice causes further irritation. Usually, lice or their eggs, called nits, can be seen. The eggs are tiny and white, and the lice are tiny, grayish, and flat. The doctor can prescribe a treatment to destroy lice and their eggs. Keep your child, his clothing, and his bedclothes clean to avoid spread and reinfection of lice.

Ringworm is a fungus which may attack the scalp. It heals in the center and spreads outward, resembling a ring. Frequently the hair will break off. It is stubborn and quite contagious. A doctor must treat ringworm.

Sometimes a child wears a tight-fitting skull cap (a stocking is often used) which can be changed frequently and boiled to kill the germs. This prevents the spread of ringworm to others. It has nothing to do with treatment of the infection.

Another form of ringworm causes round, scaly patches on the skin. It is more readily treated. Athlete's foot is another form of ringworm.

Scabies, sometimes known as "the itch," is caused by a tiny animal which burrows under the skin to live and lay its eggs. The intense itching is apt to be worse at night, and the child may cause sores as he scratches himself in his sleep.

Your doctor will prescribe a suitable ointment. Apply it after the child is bathed, while the skin is still moist. Bed clothes should be sterilized if scabies is present.

Other Respiratory Infections and Complications

Diphtheria, a serious disease, can be avoided. A child who has received 3 injections in infancy, and booster shots on schedule, has practically no chance of catching it. It begins with sore throat and fever; hoarseness and sharp cough may develop. The throat and tonsils may become whitish in appearance. If a child who has not been immunized is exposed to diphtheria, the doctor will give him antitoxin immediately in an effort to prevent the disease.

Pneumonia is a general name for inflammation of the lungs and can be caused by a virus, bacteria, or foreign object. Each type has a different treatment. As a rule, there is fever, cough, and difficult, rapid breathing. Modern drugs bring about prompt recovery in most cases when the treatment is started early. A child with pneumonia may not seem to be very sick, but the disease may last a long time and needs medical supervision throughout.

Rheumatic fever is believed to be caused by a streptococcal throat infection. It is a serious disease because it can affect the heart. School-aged children are apt to be affected.

Rheumatic fever takes on different forms. It may be deceptively mild—simply a low recurrent fever—or acute with pain and swelling in the joints. It tends to recur again and again, so take seriously the first attack, however mild. Furthermore, the mildness of the symptoms bears no relation to the damage it can cause. The doctor can guide you in ways to ward off further attacks, and may prescribe regular preventive doses of medicine.

A doctor needs to check any child who complains of aching legs or mild joint pains, who is pale and tired, or who has slight fever for more than a few days without obvious cause.

St. Vitus Dance, or **Chorea,** may be a symptom of rheumatic fever. The child has jerky movements of face, arms, trunk, or legs which may vary each time. Don't confuse chorea with the restlessness of a child who's tired of sitting, or with nervous twitches such as eye blinks, head jerks, or other mannerisms which the child repeats. A child with chorea should be under a doctor's care. He needs sympathetic handling at home, too, for he's apt to cry easily and be frustrated by the jerkiness that appears when he wishes to dress or feed himself, pick up small objects, or use a pencil.

Tonsils and **adenoids** are small, spongy masses of tissue at the back of the throat which are similar in their function to other lymphatic glands in the body, particularly those at the side of the neck, in the armpit, and in the groin. Like these other glands, tonsils and adenoids combat germs; they become involved whenever a child has a cold or throat infection. After repeated respiratory troubles, they may remain so swollen they can interfere with breathing or swallowing. If the situation becomes urgent, the doctor may feel that obstructive tonsils or adenoids should be removed. Nowadays, the operation is never done routinely, in a general attempt to improve the child's health in some vague way. Don't urge your doctor to remove tonsils or adenoids; he'll do it if he's convinced it is necessary.

Stomach, Intestinal, and Genitourinary Disorders.

Nausea, vomiting, diarrhea, constipation, and abdominal pain are all symptoms of a great number of illnesses which range widely in degree of severity. Eating too much, or eating the wrong foods, may cause vomiting. On the other hand, it may be the first sign of a common childhood disease or an internal disorder. Stomachache or loose or hard bowel movements may mean anything from an emotional upset to having worms.

Check with the doctor when anything unusual appears. Treatment will vary according to the cause, not the symptoms.

Nephritis is an inflammation of the kidneys. With nephritis, the urine is scanty, dark colored, or bloody. Tell your doctor at once of any change in the amount or color of a child's urine. (See Diabetes, Vaginitis, Pyelitis.)

Pyelitis is more common in girls than in boys. The child may seem perfectly well except for cloudy or smoky urine, which may contain pus, the result of a kidney infection. In other cases, the child may seem sick, but is without fever or pain, or there may be a headache and low fever. In any case, get a doctor's diagnosis. Take a sample of urine along with you in a clean, small bottle.

Stomachache is the most common pain complained of by young children. It is often associated with eating. Before a meal it may indicate hunger, and after a meal it may mean overeating or may indicate the child's need to have a bowel movement. Most often the complaint is half-hearted and doesn't last long. When the pain is not both severe and prolonged it is not likely to require more than reassurance from the parents. Sometimes, however, the pain may be more severe over a longer period of time and in these cases it may require more careful attention.

The complaint of pain may be the first sign of an illness in which vomiting and/or diarrhea are the main symptoms. These illnesses are discussed under those headings. Stomachache may also accompany almost any of the ordinary children's diseases. And sometimes the pain may indicate a problem inside the abdomen for which surgery may be required—appendicitis is the best known of these. It is seldom easy for parents to decide how serious the problem may be or what treatment it needs. Therefore, if the problem of pain is severe or persists beyond 2 or 3 hours or in milder but more chronic form and interferes with daily activities like eating or sleeping, then you should seek advice from your doctor or clinic.

Parents should know, however, that far and away the most common cause of persistent stomachaches is tension and anxiety rather than any of the above. In children stomachaches are the equivalent of headaches in adults. This is particularly true of those stomachaches which appear at times when they help prevent the child from doing things the child doesn't want to do anyhow—going to school, eating dinner, visiting the doctor, and many more. This does not mean that the stomachaches are any less real. They are just as real as your headaches when you are tired and irritable. What it does mean is that the stomachache in these cases does not need medicine, or surgery, but rather an attempt to understand what is bothering the child. You can help him deal with the problem directly by talking about it rather than by the roundabout route of having stomachaches.

Vaginitis, a discharge from the vagina (the opening into the female reproductive system), may vary from mild and brief to mild yet persistent, or to thick and profuse. The urine may appear clouded or bloody if it becomes merged with the discharge. The doctor should be consulted to clear up what may be a mild or more serious infection. Occasionally, a girl has pushed some object into her vagina.

Worms can cause either constipation or diarrhea. Neither may be present, however. Actually seeing worms in the child's bowel movement, or noticing that he seems itchy and irritated around the rectum, may be the first signs of their presence. The common worms of children are *pinworms,* which appear to be active, white threads about half an inch long, and *round worms,* which are pale and smooth and about the size of an earthworm. *Tapeworms* are less common, and *hookworms* are confined to some regions of the South.

The eggs of worms can be picked up anywhere, so try to keep your child's hands and nails clean.

The doctor will want to see a portion of his bowel movement if he suspects worms. He needs to know exactly which type he is treating. In order to kill worms, the medicine must be strong.

Therefore, it must be given in exact dosage and under certain conditions in order that the child himself not be injured.

Vomiting

Another common symptom of illness in children, vomiting becomes important only when it continues and the child cannot hold fluids down over a period of time. One or two throwups with a sickness are not likely to cause any serious trouble. But the body needs adequate fluids circulating in the system in order to work properly. When children vomit a lot they lose fluids from the body. If they cannot keep fluids down they cannot replace what they have lost. Children in this condition become dried out inside—doctors call this *dehydration*—and you can see outward signs of this in a number of ways. Their eyes may look dry and sunken in. Their mouths become dry inside. Their skin becomes papery and dry. At the same time they urinate less often and in smaller amounts and they cry without tears.

All this is much more likely to happen in the first few years of life than later. It is a serious problem and you should get medical help immediately, before, in fact, things get as bad as listed above.

To prevent dehydration in the child who is vomiting or unwilling to drink, offer small amounts of fluid frequently, rather than larger amounts less often. When the child vomits, don't give him anything to eat or drink for one hour. Then give him ½ oz. of cold sweet juice, weak tea, or soft drink. Repeat this half-ounce feeding every 10 or 15 minutes for an hour. Give 1-ounce feedings every 10 or 15 minutes for the next hour, and 2-ounce feedings as often as he wants them for the following hour. If there is no more vomiting it is now safe to give small amounts of cereal, formula, crackers, or toast. But don't give more than 2 ounces to drink at one time until there has been no vomiting for 6 hours.

If he vomits after you start this routine, wait an hour and start again at the beginning with half-ounce feedings.

Just the opposite of what you might think, cold liquids are better than warm ones for upset stomachs. In fact, the ideal thing is to let the child suck on an ice cube or a popsicle. That way the liquid will come slowly and cold. Another very good liquid to use is cola. This is best given so that it is ice cold and flat with all the bubbles gone.

Used in small amounts in that way it will actually help settle an upset stomach. Jello water or Jello are also good liquids for this purpose.

By now you must have realized that the best fluids in this situation are those which are clear and light. Milk is not good for children whose stomachs are upset. It is one of the hardest things to keep down and even though it may be the child's favorite it is best avoided at such times.

If the child stops vomiting reasonably soon and still seems alert and active it is probably all right just to watch and see how things go. If the vomiting persists heavily for a while—or less heavily but over a longer period—then get in touch with the doctor. Other signs which should cause you to call the doctor are the presence of blood in the vomitus or increasing swelling and hardness of the child's stomach area.

Common Communicable Diseases

disease	first signs	incubation period*	prevention	how long contagious	what you can do
Chickenpox	Mild fever followed in 36 hours by small raised pimples which become filled with clear fluid. Scabs form later. Successive crops of pox appear.	2–3 weeks, usually 13–17 days.	None. Immune after one attack.	6 days after appearance of rash.	Not a serious disease; trim fingernails to prevent scratching; a paste of baking soda and water, or alcohol, may ease itching.
German measles (3-day measles)	Mild fever, sore throat or cold symptoms may precede tiny, rose-colored rash. Enlarged glands at back of neck and behind ears.	2–3 weeks, usually 18 days.	Vaccine may be given at 1 year of age as measles-rubella, rubella-mumps or measles, mumps, rubella combined vaccines; priority immunization should be given to children in kindergarten and elementary school; all children should receive vaccine.	Until rash fades. About 5 days.	Generally not a serious disease in childhood, complications rare; give general good care and rest.
Measles	Mounting fever; hard, dry cough; runny nose and red eyes for 3 or 4 days before rash which starts at hairline and spreads down in blotches. Small red spots with white centers in mouth (Koplik's spots) appear before the rash.	1–2 weeks, usually 10 or 11 days.	All children should receive measles vaccine at 12 months of age. If an unvaccinated child is exposed to measles, gamma globulin given shortly after exposure may lighten or prevent the disease.	Usually 5 to 9 days, from 4 days before to 5 days after rash appears.	May be mild or severe with complications of a serious nature; follow doctor's advice in caring for a child with measles, as it is a most treacherous disease.
Mumps	Fever, headache, vomiting: salivary glands near ear and toward chin at jaw line develop painful swelling. Other parts of body may be affected also.	11–26 days, usually around 18 days.	Live mumps vaccine may be used at any age after 1 year. Combination measles-mumps-rubella, rubella-mumps vaccines may be used.	Until all swelling disappears.	Keep child in bed until fever subsides, indoors unless weather is warm.

disease	first signs	incubation period	prevention	how long contagious	what you can do
Strep throat (septic sore throat) and scarlet fever (scarlatina).	Sometimes vomiting, headaches and fever before sudden and severe sore throat. If followed by fine rash on body and limbs, it is called scarlet fever.	4-7 days, usually 2-5.	Antibiotics may prevent or lighten an attack if doctor feels it wise.	7-10 days. When all abnormal discharge from nose, eyes, throat has ceased.	Responds to antibiotics, which should be continued for full course to prevent serious complications.
Whooping cough.........	At first seems like a cold with low fever and cough which changes at end of second week to spells of coughing accompanied by a noisy gasp for air which creates the "whoop."	5-21 days, usually around 10 days.	Injections of vaccine are usually given to all children in infancy. If an unvaccinated child has been exposed, the doctor may want to give a protective serum promptly.	Usually no longer after 4th week.	Child needs careful supervision by doctor throughout this taxing illness.

*Incubation period is the usual amount of time which elapses between exposure to the disease and onset of the first symptoms. For example, if a child is exposed to chickenpox, he can safely play with other children until 12 or 13 days afterwards. The following week, he should be kept way from other children since he may be in the early stages of the disease and it will be contagious before you note any symptoms.

Less Common Infectious Diseases

disease	first signs	incubation period	prevention	how long contagious	what you can do
Infectious hepatitis (catarrhal jaundice).	May be mild with few symptoms or accompanied by fever, headache, abdominal pain, nausea, diarrhea, general weariness. Later, yellow skin and white of eyes (jaundice), urine dark, and bowel movements chalklike.	2-6 weeks, commonly 25 days.	Injection of gamma globulin gives temporary immunity if child is exposed.	May last 2 months or more.	May be mild or may require hospital care.

disease	first signs	incubation period	prevention	how long contagious	what you can do
Infectious mononucleosis (glandular fever).	Sore throat, swollen glands of neck and elsewhere, sometimes a rash over whole body and jaundiced appearance, low persistent fever.	Probably 4-14 days or longer.	None.	Probably 2-4 weeks but mode of transmission is not clear.	Keep in bed while feverish; restrict activity thereafter.
Meningitis..........	May be preceded by a cold and/or earache, headache, vomiting, high temperature with convulsions or drowsy stupor; fine rash with tiny hemorrhages into the skin in certain types (meningococcemia).	2-10 days.	Prompt treatment of bacterial infections of the nasopharynx and ear may prevent development.	Until recovery.	Immediate treatment is necessary. Take child to hospital if doctor unavailable. Continue treatment with antibiotics as long as doctor advises.
Polio (infantile paralysis or poliomyelitis).	Slight fever, general discomfort, headache, stiff neck, stiff back.	1-4 weeks, commonly 1-2 weeks.	Be sure to complete the series of the Sabin vaccine.	1 week from onset or as long as fever persists.	Hospital care is usually advised.
Rocky Mountain spotted fever.	Muscle pains, nosebleed occasionally, headache, rash on 3d or 4th day.	About a week after bite of infected tick.	Vaccinations can be given to a child who lives in heavily infested area. Protect from tick bite by the use of proper wearing apparel or tick repellent.	Spread only by infected ticks.	New drugs have improved treatment.
Smallpox..........	Sudden fever, chills, head and back ache. Rash which becomes raised and hard, later blisters and scabs.	6-18 days, commonly 12.	Routine smallpox vaccination is no longer recommended.	Until all scabs disappear.	Doctor's care necessary.

14
Emergencies and First Aid

The following are some common household emergencies and what you should do about them. Always keep in mind, however, that for all but the most minor accidents, you should have your child checked by a doctor immediately.

Bites and Stings

Animal bites (cat, dog, squirrel, bat, or other): Even if the animal is a pet, your child should be seen at once by a doctor. Often a booster shot for tetanus is called for even if treatment for prevention of rabies is not.

Try to capture the animal so he can be kept under observation until it is determined whether or not he is rabid.

Insect bites (bee, wasp, hornet, yellow jacket, ant, mosquito, or gnat): Remove the stinger, if any, with tweezers. Apply vinegar, calomine lotion, or a thick paste of baking soda and water. Get medical help if your child shows an unusual reaction (paleness, nausea, vomiting, loss of consciousness, drowsiness, convulsions). These serious reactions generally happen quite rapidly. If complications have not occurred within 10–20 minutes they are far less likely to do so.

Snake bite: Try to kill the snake so it can be identified. There are four poisonous types in the United States—rattlesnakes, copperheads, moccasins, and coral snakes.

Go to a doctor or hospital as quickly as possible if you suspect your child has been bitten by a poisonous snake. Unless you have had instruction in the use of a snake bite or venom kit, you may do more damage than good by attempting to inject an antidote or use suction.

While waiting for the doctor or en route to the hospital, apply a constricting band just above the bite to slow the flow of venom into the body. Watch it carefully, though, as swelling from the bite may cause it to become too tight. Keep the child quiet and soothe him. Let the bitten limb hang down.

Tick bite: Most ticks are harmless, but some carry Colorado tick fever or the more serious Rocky Mountain spotted fever.

If you live in a tick infested area, check your children twice daily. Look for ticks especially in hair and folds of skin. Remove ticks (from humans or animals) with tweezers. Be sure to get the head as well as the body. If it clings, loosen its hold by smearing it with grease, oil, or turpentine. Crush the tick (but not with your bare finger), flush it down the toilet, burn it, or drop it into turpentine or kerosene. Clean the wound with soap and water or mild antiseptic.

Bleeding, Cuts, and Scrapes (See also Puncture Wounds)

Severe Bleeding: Apply pressure to an area on the side of the wound toward the center of the body. Blood flowing to the hand, for instance, can be slowed down by gradually and firmly pressing on the inner surface of the upper arm. If you have taken a first aid course, or have a first aid handbook, you will know where such pressure points are located.

If you don't know where the pressure points are, you can stop the bleeding by pressing with your hand directly on the bleeding spot. Get a clean cloth or piece of clothing under your hand and press firmly. Continue to press. If bleeding continues, add more cloth and continue to press, but don't remove the first cloth.

DO NOT use a tourniquet. Direct pressure from your hand will stop almost any bleeding. Even if an arm or leg is nearly cut off, you can stop the bleeding with pressure.

Cuts: Stop the bleeding by holding firmly with a clean cloth.

Wash thoroughly with soap and water. Pat dry. Cover with sterile gauze pad or adhesive bandage. *Don't* use iodine, mercurochrome, or first aid ointment. Soap and water will take care of germs. If the skin does not fall back into place neatly, or if the wound is as much as ¼" deep, stitches or a special bandage may have to be applied to speed healing and prevent scarring. If a child is cut in a part of the body where the scar will show and may make a permanent difference in the child's appearance—the face, for example—then careful treatment by a doctor may make a real difference in how little the final scar shows.

Scrapes: These are superficial breaks in the skin surface without any deep cuts. They may bleed or ooze slightly but seldom cause serious bleeding. Often scrapes are caused by falls which grind dirt into the broken skin area. It's a good idea to clean the area with soap and water or with hydrogen peroxide if you have some. Most of the medicines people used to use like iodine, alcohol, mercurochrome, and so forth are not worth using. If the scrape can be cleaned, and if bleeding has stopped, cover it with a clean bandage and leave it alone. If it seems worse than this, then a doctor should see it.

Broken Bones (Fractures)

If you suspect a break or fracture, don't let your child use the limb or part and don't move it yourself. Leave him where he is, if possible. Keep him warm and call a doctor. If a bone fragment protrudes through the skin, cover the wound lightly with sterile dressing.

If you must move him, apply a splint to the injured limb.

Arm: A sling may be the easiest way to keep the arm immobile. Or use a pillow as suggested below.

Leg: Slide a pillow under the leg. Be sure to include the joint at each end of the broken bone. Tie strips of cloth or bandage around the pillow at 3- or 4-inch intervals. A long board can be used if no pillow is available. Or tie the injured leg to the other leg, spacing the ties every 6 inches or so. Make sure they are not too tight.

Back or neck: If absolutely necessary, slide him on a board or door, but leave him where he is if you can. Get a doctor immediately.

Bruises

Bruises are black and blue areas or lumps which are caused by bleeding under the skin without the skin having to be broken in any way. Bruises may be painful but unless they keep getting bigger they are seldom dangerous. If you see a bruise starting to develop on your child after an injury, holding ice or other cold compresses on the area may help keep it from enlarging. If the bruise seems to keep growing in size, or if pain gets worse, then you should have a doctor see it.

Burns

The best immediate treatment for a burned area is rapid cooling—pouring on ice cold water and continuing to do so until the area is no longer hot. The faster this can be done, the better. Cover with sterile dressing or clean cloth. *Don't* use ointments or greases. A cold pack made by putting ice cubes in a plastic bag and covering it with several layers of cloth may relieve the pain of a fresh burn. If the burned area is small, then this may be the only treatment required. If the area is large, then medical help should be reached as fast as possible.

If a blister forms on the area it is best to leave the blister alone because it protects the raw area underneath. Eventually the blister will collapse or break by itself, but the longer this takes the more chance there will have been for new skin to begin developing underneath.

Sometimes burns are caused by hot liquids spilling on the child. When the liquid spills on the child's clothes you should immediately strip or cut the clothes off. The longer the clothes with the hot liquid in them stay in contact with the skin, the worse the burn will be. Handled properly minor burns can heal with little or no difficulty. Larger or deeper burns, though, can be very serious and should always be treated under a doctor's supervision.

Burns from Chemicals: If lye, oven cleaner, pesticides or other strong chemicals come in contact with his skin or eyes, wash it off with large amounts of water for a long time. Remove any contaminated clothing. Place the affected area directly under a faucet, garden hose, or shower and keep rinsing for 5 minutes. Use a bottle, cup, or gentle faucet to wash out eyes. Keep the eyelids open as much as possible.

Choking

Pick up the child by his feet and slap his back sharply. If a child is too heavy to pick up by his feet, place him in jack-knife position over your shoulder, knees, or a chair back. If the object does not come out, go to a doctor or hospital *at once*.

If a child swallows something small and smooth, such as a fruit seed, button or small coin, check his bowel movements for a few days to be sure he has passed it. If he swallows a sharp object, such as a pin or a needle, call a doctor immediately.

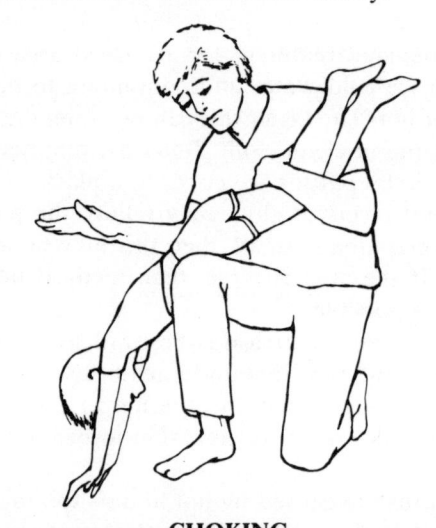

CHOKING
Hold child upside down and slap back sharply.

Convulsions

There are many kinds of convulsions (seizures or fits) that children may have, but this discussion will be limited to the kind that some children have with fever. Convulsions repeated at intervals and *without* fever may indicate epilepsy. The child with epilepsy will need medical supervision to keep him from having seizures.

Although many parents worry about convulsions, only 2 or 3 out of every 100 children have convulsions with fever. Half of those have a family history of convulsions, that is, someone else in the family has already been known to have had convulsions. The convulsion consists of a loss of consciousness and a stiffening out, with or without shaking. Usually the eyes roll upward and the child's breathing sounds noisy. Most often this problem is caused by a sudden rise in temperature rather than by a fever which is already high. Many children have a shaking chill—like a bigger and longer lasting shiver—when their temperatures are rising. This is not the same and does not have any of the other features which mark the convulsion.

Convulsions are frightening, particularly because the child loses consciousness, but they are seldom as dangerous as they look. Many times the convulsion will last only a few minutes and the child will come out of it spontaneously. Your main effort should be to keep the child from hurting himself. Place him on a bed or rug, away from sharp objects and furniture. Watch him closely. Do not put a child having convulsions into the bathtub. If possible turn the child's head to one side to allow saliva and mucus to run out of the mouth instead of down into the windpipe. *Don't worry about the tongue—children do not swallow their tongues in convulsions.* It is not necessary or even safe for you to put your hand or anything else into the child's mouth to try to pull the tongue forward. Many parents get badly bitten, and many children get badly cut inside their mouths or get broken teeth, because parents try to do this.

Call the doctor as soon as you can.

After the seizure is over, put the child to bed—he will usually want to sleep for a while. If the seizure does not end promptly by itself you should move rapidly, but not in panic, to get the child to the doctor.

Of all the children who have convulsions with fever at some time in the first few years of their lives only one out of three is likely to have a second one under the same conditions. No one can tell you for sure whether your child is in that group. But you should know that all children who have this problem tend to outgrow it as they get older. Most of them stop having febrile seizures by 4 or 5. Sometimes, if your child has had more than one seizure, your doctor may give you some medicine to keep the child on or to give the child at the first sign of illness. This medicine is intended to cut down the chances that your child will have another seizure with fever. So it is worth your while to follow the directions and to remember to give the medicine.

The kind of convulsion discussed here does not have any permanent effect on children's growth, development, intelligence or anything else. If you understand this you will worry less and be better able to help your child through one of these attacks.

Drowning or Electric Shock

Use mouth-to-mouth resuscitation until he breathes on his own or you reach a doctor. DON'T *use mouth-to-mouth resuscitation on a child who is breathing.*

If the child has *drowned,* first lay him over your knees with his head down for about 10 seconds in order to drain water from his lungs, then proceed *immediately* to Mouth-to-Mouth Resuscitation, Step 1, below.

MOUTH-TO-MOUTH RESUSCITATION:

1. Clear the mouth with your finger, quickly removing any mucus, vomit, food, or object.
2. Place him on his back on the floor, table or other firm surface.
3. Tilt his head way back with his chin up.
4. Cover his mouth and nose with your mouth and blow gently until you see his chest rise. Be sure not to blow as forcefully as you would for an adult.
5. Remove your mouth and let his lungs empty.
6. Take a quick breath yourself.
7. Repeat at a rate of about 20 times a minute.

If air is not moving, quickly check to make sure his head is tilted way back and try again. If still no movement, hold him upside down, slap him firmly between his shoulders, check his mouth for blocking, and try again. **DON'T STOP!**

Ear troubles

If an insect has crawled in, stop the buzzing, which frightens the child, by dropping in a little lukewarm olive oil or mineral oil. The oil will still the insect and may wash it out. Don't attempt to dislodge any other object yourself (candy, pebble, bean). Get a doctor.

MOUTH-TO-MOUTH RESUSCITATION (See instructions, p. 238)

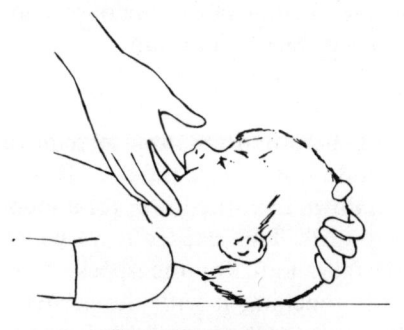

Clear the mouth.

Tilt head way back to open air passages.

Cover mouth and nose with your mouth.

If a child complains of earache, call the doctor. Apply either heat or cold for temporary relief. Use a partially filled ice bag or hot water bottle with warm, not hot, water. Or let the child lie on a heating pad with temperature control set at a moderate degree. You can warm a small bag of salt in the oven and place it over the ear. Warmed salt keeps heat a long time.

Particle in Eye

Wash your hands before attempting to remove a particle from the eye. Tell the child not to rub his eye. To dislodge the speck, bring the upper lid down over the lower for a moment or two while the child looks upward. This causes tears which may wash the speck out. If this fails, look for the speck. If you see it, try to remove it by gently touching it with the corner of a clean handkerchief or small bit of sterile gauze folded over to make a point.

Washing the eye may help. Drop fluid into the eye with a medicine dropper or use an eyecup. Use only boiled water, cooled to room temperature, to which a quarter teaspoon of salt is added per cup. If irritation continues, cover the closed eye with several gauze pads, tape them in place, and take the child to medical care.

Head Injuries

Injuries to the head worry both parents and doctors because of the possibility that some damage may have been done to the brain. Because a great many children seem to bump their heads almost every day it is important for parents to have some guidelines for knowing when they should worry.

If the child acts perfectly fine and seems alert and active after a bump on the head the chances are that everything is all right. This is particularly true if the child was not noticed to have had any loss of consciousness. One way to tell this is to notice if the child seems to cry immediately after the accident occurs. If there were no witnesses to the accident, it may be helpful to see if the child can remember the accident, how it happened, and what happened immediately afterwards.

Some injuries to the head, particularly around the forehead, can produce very large lumps and bruises. Almost nowhere else on the body do small bumps cause such large lumps. These don't necessarily mean that anything serious has happened or that there is any damage inside the head at all. Sometimes these may take weeks to go away, but if the child continues to act fine there is nothing to worry about.

But some signs *should* cause you to worry. One of these is *loss of consciousness* any time after the accident. Another is *increasing drowsiness,* with the child continuing to try to fall asleep and becoming harder to wake up. Another is *repeated vomiting*—especially if it occurs some time after the accident, rather than right away, and if it continues. These are all signs that there may have been some internal damage in the head which needs more expert attention. They should certainly cause you to get in touch with your doctor right away or to take the child to the emergency room. Even if those signs don't appear, the rule of "better safe than sorry" is a very good one here. If there is any question in your mind at all you should at least make contact with the doctor for an expert opinion.

Nosebleeds

These are among the most common problems children get. Almost every child gets one from time to time but some children seem more susceptible to them than others. Most nosebleeds are caused by the child's picking the nose or by rubbing it or poking at it some way or other. This happens more often when the air is dry or when the child has a cold or an allergy. In adults nosebleeds may be a sign of other diseases but they rarely are in children.

The most important thing to remember about nosebleeds is that no one ever bleeds to death from them. As terrible as they look, and it is amazing how far a little bit of blood can seem to spread, they will almost always stop by themselves if you and the child don't panic. Pressure, with or without ice, over the side of the nose which is bleeding should be kept up steadily for about 5 minutes *by the clock.* The child should lean forward rather than lie down—this will let the blood run out of the nose instead of back down the throat. Swallowing a lot of blood will often make the child vomit and this will start the whole process up again. If the steady pressure and the ice don't seem to stop the bleeding after 5 or 10 minutes, then it is time to call your doctor for further suggestions.

Poisoning

In accidental poisoning, no time should be lost in contacting your physician, a poison control center, or the nearest hospital emergency room. While such contacts are being made, and pending further instructions from the physician, a few simple steps may be taken.

External poisoning: When poisoning involves the external surface of the body, or the nasal or oral cavity, flushing or rinsing with water is useful in removing the poison.

Poisoning from Swallowed Medicines or Products:
1. Immediately have him drink as much milk or water as he will take, keep him drinking;
2. Call a physician, hospital emergency room, poison control center, or rescue squad. Tell them the name and brand of the substance that was swallowed. Keep the container, the label, and anything left in the container;
3. IF a DOCTOR advises it, make him vomit. **Make him vomit if you can't reach a doctor, but NOT if:**

- He is very drowsy, unconscious, or having a convulsion
- The substance swallowed was a strong alkali or acid (lye, ammonia, drain cleaner, oven cleaner, bleach)
- The substance swallowed was a petroleum product such as kerosene, gasoline, turpentine, lighter fluid, insecticide, or furniture polish. If any of these are swallowed, go directly to a hospital emergency room, clinic, or doctor's office.

4. Make him vomit by giving him 2 teaspoons of Ipecac syrup (1 tablespoon if he is over 1 year old). Always save the material vomited *and* the poison container to show to the physician. If Ipecac isn't available you may try warm water with a raw egg in it. Do *not* try to make the child vomit by sticking your finger down the back of the throat. You are more likely to scratch the throat and cause bleeding which only confuses the picture, and you may well get your hand or finger badly bitten in the process.

Poisoning from smoke or fumes: Remove him to a place where there is fresh air. Use mouth-to-mouth resuscitation (see Drowning) if he is not breathing.

Puncture Wounds (a deep prick from a pin, tack, or nail)

Gently press near the hole to encourage bleeding, which will wash out the wound. Cover lightly until the doctor can see it, but don't try to close it with bandage or adhesive. Be sure to check with the doctor on the advisability of a tetanus shot or, if your child's shots are up to date, a booster dose.

Shock

After any severe injury, burn, or bleeding, the child may become pale, clammy, and cold. Keep him lying down with his feet elevated slightly, and keep him warm with blankets. Get him to medical care immediately.

Splinters

Wash the area thoroughly. Soapsuds will help to soften the skin around the splinter and ease its removal. Use a sterilized tweezer, needle, or knife point to pluck out the splinter. The tweezer may be less upsetting to the child, but sometimes it won't catch hold unless the splinter is eased up with a sharper instrument. To sterilize, pass the instrument through a flame or wipe with alcohol. Your child may be able to remove the splinter himself. He'll be much less upset if you let him try.

After the splinter is removed, press the area gently to make it bleed a bit, then wash carefully or apply a mild antiseptic. A sterile bandage may be needed to protect the area. A splinter deeply imbedded in the flesh should always be removed by a doctor.

RECORD OF HEALTH SUPERVISION

BIRTH	Name of Hospital	Address	Telephone
	Name of Obstetrician	Address	Telephone

Date of Birth	Date Baby Was Due	

						IMMUNIZATIONS		
DATE	AGE	WEIGHT	LENGTH	HEAD SIZE	ANY PROBLEMS?	DPT	POLIO	OTHER
	Birth							

Index

Achievement tests, 171
Activities, family, 143-149; at home, 144-145; rituals and celebrations, 147-148; television, radio, movies, and comics, 145-147; time alone, 148-149
Acute (or chronic) poisoning, 109
Adenoids, 224
Allergies, 210-211
Allowance system, 150-151
Ambitions and abilities, 124
Anemia, 220
Anger, 72-73
Animal bites, 232
Antibiotics, 219
Arithmetic, 176
Asthma, 211
Athlete's foot, 222

Baby sitters, 29-30
"Baby tote" (or back pack), 33
Bare feet, running around in, 70
Bathing, first weeks, 12-13
Bedtime battles, dealing with, 191-192
Bedtime ritual, 62-63
Bites and stings, 232-243
Blanket bag, 9
Bleeding, 233-234
Boils, 222
Bottle feeding, 6-7, 10-12; special instructions, 11; what not to do, 11-12
Bowel movements; baby's, 16; disorders, 211-213
Breast feeding, 4-6
Broken bones (fractures), 234
Brothers and sisters: job of parenting and, 134-135; new babies and, 16; and 1 to 6 year olds, 80-82
Bruises, 235
Burns: first aid for, 235-236
Burping the baby, 8
Buttons, buttoning and unbuttoning, 55

Cephalohematoma, 43
Chemical burns, 235-236
Child care services, 30-31
Choking, 236
Clothing: first weeks, 9-10, 20-21; laundering, 21; for 1 to 6 year olds, 68-70
Colds, 42, 213-215
Cold sores, 222
Colic, 15
Community playgrounds, 163-164
Conjunctivitis, 216-217
Constipation, 80, 211-212
Convulsions, 236-238
Cradle cap (or seborrhea), 44
Cribs, 8-9: after first weeks, 28-29; safety, 47; taking child away from, 64
Crying, baby's, 14; waking up at night and, 64-65; when you leave, 30
Curiosity, channeling, 123
Cuts, 233-234
Cystic fibrosis, 220-221

Day care centers, 152; checklist for judging, 31-32
Death of a parent, 100-101
Development and health, 34-49; chart, 35; common problems and worries, 41-46; health supervision, 40-41; one to six years, 53-60; physical growth, 38; safety, 46-49; *See also* Health care
Diabetes (diabetes mellitus), 221
Diaper rash, 44-45
Diapers, 9-10; laundering, 21, 32
Diarrhea, 212-213
"Difficult" babies, 25
Diphtheria, 223
Discipline, 70-77, 137-138; and punishment, 76-77; teaching (after first weeks), 25-27
Divorce, 99-100
Doctors: choosing, 40; using, 40-41; disagreement among, 41
Drowning, 238

Ear infections, 215-216
Ear troubles, 238, 240
Eczema, 211, 222
Electric shock, 238
Emergencies and first aid, 232-243; bites and stings, 232-233; bleeding, cuts, and scrapes, 233-234; broken bones, 234; bruises, 235; burns, 235-236;

245

choking, 236; convulsions, 236-238; drowning or electric shock, 238; ear troubles, 238-240; head injuries, 240-241; nosebleeds, 241; particle in the eye, 240; poisoning, 241-242; puncture wounds, 242-243; shock, 243; splinters, 243
Emotional problems, help for, 201-206; severely shy children, 203-204; troublemakers, 204-205
Energy, lack of, 219-220
Eye infections, 216-217, 240
Eyes, yellow discharge, baby's, 42; crossed, 42

Family discussions, 142-143
Family life (in the 6-12 age group), 132-153; activities, 143-149; brothers and sisters, 134-135; discipline, 137-138; favoritism, 135-136; making rules, 138-139; parenting as a partnership, 141-143; parents as family leaders, 136-137; personalities, 133-134; personal relationships, 133; punishment, 139-141; work and money, 149-153
Favoritism, 135-136
Fears, 93-98, 129; conquering, 120
Feet, baby's, 43-44
Fever, 217-218
Fighting, 102-103, 154-156; self-control and, 160-161
Fingers, sucking, 45
Firearms, 194
Fire safety, 194
First weeks, 3-17; asking questions, 3-4; bathing, 12-13; bottle feeding, 6-7; bowel movements, 16; breast feeding, 4-6; clothing, 9-10; colic, 15; crying, 14-15; equipment and supplies, 8-13; feeding, 4-8; feeding equipment (using formula), 10-12; feeding schedule, 7; food intake, 7-8; getting advice, 16-17; place to sleep, 8-9; self-care, 4; siblings and, 16; sleeping, 13-14; spitting up food, 8
First weeks (up to 6 months), 18-33; clothing, 20; discipline and teaching, 25-27; feeding, 18-20; leaving the baby, 29-32; penny pinching, 32-33; play and exercise, 27-29; temperament, 21-25
Flannelette sheeting, 9
Food and feeding, 184-191; by the age of two, 55; amount of food (first weeks), 7-8; Daily Food Guide, 185-187; equipment (using formula), 10; family meals, 188-189; first weeks (up to 6 months), 18-20; new baby, 4-8; for one to six year olds, 65-68; penny pinching, 32; puréed foods, 67; schedule (first weeks), 7; school lunch, 190-191; snacks and treats, 189-190
Formula, 10, 11-12, 32
Friends, 82-84, 154-157; *See also* Group membership

Genitals, baby's, 42-43
Genitourinary disorders, 225-227
Group membership, 157-166; clubs, 157; organizations, 161-162; parental guidance and, 157-158; popularity, 158-159; religious organizations, 165-166; self-control and, 160-161; shy children, 159-160; summer camps and community playgrounds, 163-164; using the library, 162-163
Growth rate (6 to 12 year olds), 128-130, charts (first year), 38-39

Handicaps, help for, 206-209; mental retardation, 206-207; parents and, 208-209
Hay fever, 211
Head injuries, 240-241
Head shape, baby's, 43
Health care, 180-197; basic facts, 181-184; eating right, 184-191; emotions and, 182-183; getting help for, 107; immunizations, 105-106; one to six year age group, 104-111; outside (6 to 12 age group), 180-197; rest and sleep, 191-192; and safety, 107-111, 192-197; school, 168, 177-178; well-child care, 104-105
Healthy child: help and, 201-243; infancy, 3-49; introduction to, vii-viii; one to six years, 53-111; six to twelve years, 115-197
Help, 201-243; emergencies and first aid, 232-243; for handicaps and emotional problems, 201-209; for illnesses and disorders, 210-231
Hernia, 46
Hives, 211, 222
Home appliances, safety and, 193-194
Hospitalization, 99, 101-102
Household duties, 149-150

Illnesses and disorders, 210-288; allergies, 210-211; bowel movements, 211-213; colds, 213-215; ear and throat, 215-216; eye, 216-217; fever, 217-218; infections, 218-219; lack of energy, 219-220; metabolic, 220-221; overweight, 221; preventing, 184; res-

piratory, 223-224; skin, 221-223; stomach, intestinal, and genitourinary, 225-227; vomiting, 227-228
Immunizations, 105-106
Impetigo, 222
Independence, learning, 119
Individual style, child's (from age 6 to 12), 116-119; abilities and limitations, 117-118; physical makeup, 117; self-image, 118-119
Infancy, 3-49; after first weeks, 18-33; development and health, 34-49; first weeks, 3-17
Infant formula, see Formula
Infantile paralysis, 105
Infections (treating), 218-219
Injuries, 111
Insect bites, 232
Intelligence tests, 170-171
Intestinal disorders, 225-227

Kindergarten, 169

Language development, 56-58
Languages, 176
Lead poisoning, 109-110
Learning: growth rate and, 168-170; at school, 166-168; through class projects, 176-177
Leaving the baby, 29-32
Legs, baby's, 43-44
Libraries, using, 162-163
Lice (prediculosis), 222-223
Lisping, 58
Lying, 60

Make-believe, 59-60
Masturbation, 85-86
Mealtime, 68; *See also* Food and feeding
Medicines and poisons, 194-195
Mental retardation, help for, 206-207
Metabolic disorders, 220-221
Milk, 66-67
Mongolian spots, 44
Mouth-to-mouth resuscitation, 238, 239
Moving to a new home, 98

Navel (or belly button), 45-46
Nephritis, 216, 225
New baby, *see* First weeks
Nightfall, safety after, 197
Night light, 64
Nightmares, 64
Nipples, 10
Nosebleeds, 241
Nursing bottles with caps, 10

One to six years, 53-111; everyday life, 61-92; health care, 104-111; physical growth and development, 53-60; special problems, 93-103
Outside world (6 to 12 year age group), 154-179; friends, 154-157; group membership, 157-166; school, 166-179
Overweight children, 187-188, 221

Parental guidance, 157-158
Parents: going out, 29; handicapped children and, 208-209; hospitalization of, 99; and leadership, 136-137; as a partnership, 141-143; and teachers, 173-174; when both work, 151-153
Penicillin, 219
Persistence, baby's, 24-25
Personalities, differences in, 133-134
Personality and physical development (from age 6 to 12), 115-131; child's individual style, 116-119; growth rate, 128-130; importance of play, 120-122; learning to be independent, 119-120; preadolescence, 130-131; rules, 122; self-control, 124-125; self-expression, 122-124; sex, 125-128
Personality traits, 133-134
Pets, 123-124
Physical growth and development, 38-39; one to six years, 53-60; personality and (from age 6 to 12), 115-131
Physical illness, signs of, 183-184
Plastic pants, 10
Play equipment safety, 193
Play and exercise: after the first weeks, 27-29; health care and, 181-182; importance of, 120-122
Playpen safety, 47
Pneumonia, 223-224
Poisonings, 108-110; first aid for, 241-242
Poliomyelitis, 105-106
Poor nourishment, 220
Popularity, 158-159
Preadolescence, 130-131
Preschool programs, 91-92
Privacy, need for, 123
Psychologist (school), 178
Puberty, 130-131
Puncture wounds, 242-243
Punishment, 26-27, 60, 76-77, 139-41; *See also* Discipline
Pyelitis, 225

Quarreling, brother-sister, 134-135

Reading, 176
"Receiving blankets," 9
Records (health), keeping your own, 41
Relatives, 84-85
Religious holidays, 148
Religious organizations, 165-166
Respiratory infections and complications, 223-224
Rest and sleep, 191-192
Rheumatic fever, 216, 224
Ringworm, 223

Safety, 107-111, 192-197; accident prevention, 107-108; automobile, 47, 110-111, 197; caution and, 193; Checklist, 46-49; fire, 194; firearms, 194; from strangers, 196-197; home appliances, 193-194; medicines and poisons, 194-195; at nightfall, 197; outside the home, 195-197; poisonings and, 108-110; toys and play equipment, 193; water, 197
St. Vitus Dance (or chorea), 224
Scabies, 223
Scarlet fever, 216
School, 166-179; achievement tests, 171; extra lessons, 175; getting used to, 171-172; growth rate and learning process, 166-167, 168-170; health care, 168, 177-178; homework, 174-175; intelligence tests, 170-171; lunch, 190-191; new teaching ways, 175-177; special services, 177-179; teachers and, 172-177; time out, 168
School readiness, 88-92
Scrapes, 233-234
Seborrhea, 44
Self-control, 124-125; fighting and, 160-161
Self-expression, 122-124
Self-image (age 6 to 12), 118-119
Seminal emissions (wet dreams), 131
Separation anxiety, 94
Separation situations, 97, 98-102; death of a parent, 100-101; divorce, 99-100; hospitalization, 99, 101-102; moving, 98-99; vacation, 99
Sex and sex play, 125-128; concerns about, 127-128; one to six year age group, 85-88
Sexual stereotypes, de-emphasizing, 87-88
Shock, 243
Shoes, 20-21, 69-70
Shy children, 159-160, 203-204
Sick child, care of, 41-42
Six to twelve years, 115-197; family life, 132-153; health care, 180-197; outside world, 154-179; personality and physical development, 115-131
Skin, baby's, 43
Skin infections, 221-223
Sleep, 13-14, 61-65, 191-192
Sleeping bag, 9
Snacks and treats, 189-190
Snake bite, 233
Social development, 58-60
Sore nipples (when breast feeding), 1, 6
Speech, (development) 56-58; (problems, help for) 207
Spitting up food, 8
Splinters, 243
Stammering, 58
Stomach disorders, 225-227
"Stork bites," 44
Strangers, safety from, 196-197
"Strawberry marks," 44
Strep throat, 216
Styes on the eye, 217
Sucking, baby's, 43
Sugar in milk, 66-67
Sweet foods, 67-68

Teeth: baby's, 45; care of, 183
Television, radio, movies, and comics, 145-147
Temperament, first weeks (up to 6 months), 21-25
Temper tantrums, 75-76
Tetanus (or lockjaw), 105
Throat infections, 215-216
Thumb sucking, 45
Tick bite, 233
Toilet training, 77-80
Tonsillitis, 216
Tonsils, 224
Toys, 28, 55; safety, 193
Troublemakers, help for, 204-205

Umbilical cord, 45-46
Underweight children, 188
Urination, frequent, 46

Vaginitis, 226
Virus infections, 217
Vision problems, help for, 208
Vitamin A, 186
Vitamin C, 186, 189
Vomiting, 227-228

Work and money, 149-153; allowance system, 150-151; household duties, 149-150; when both parents work, 151-153
Worms, 226-227